UCD W

A Simple Matter of

Theorizing Lesbian and Gay Politics

*The Cassell Lesbian and Gay Studies list
offers a broad-based platform to lesbian, gay
and bisexual writers for the discussion of
contemporary issues and for the promotion
of new ideas and research.*

COMMISSIONING:
**Steve Cook
Roz Hopkins**

CONSULTANTS:
**Liz Gibbs
Christina Ruse
Peter Tatchell**

A Simple Matter of Justice?

Theorizing Lesbian and Gay Politics

Edited by Angelia R. Wilson

CASSELL

Cassell
Wellington House
125 Strand
London
WC2R 0BB

387 Park Avenue South
New York
NY 10016–8810

First published 1995

British Library Cataloguing-in-Publication Data
A catalogue record for this book is available from the British Library.

ISBN 0–304–32957–6 (hardback)
     0–304–32955–X (paperback)

Typeset by York House Typographic Ltd
Printed and bound in Great Britain by Mackays of Chatham, plc

Cover photographs by Robert Taylor

Contents

Notes on contributors

Jean Carabine lectures in social policy at the University of Loughborough. Her research interests are in the areas of women, sexuality and social policy, and sexual risk and social policy. She is currently working on a book, *Women, Sexuality and Social Policy*, to be published by Macmillan.

Paisley Currah is an assistant professor of political science at Brooklyn College, City University of New York. She works in the areas of feminist theory, political theory, and lesbian, bisexual and gay studies.

David T. Evans lectures in sociology at the University of Glasgow, specializing in social stratification and the sociology of sexuality. His publications include 'Section 28: law, myth and paradox', *Critical Social Policy* (1989/90), *Sexual Citizenship: The Material Construction of Sexualities* (Routledge, 1993), and 'Falling angels: the material construction of children as sexual citizens', *International Journal of Children's Rights* (1994). In addition to his continuing research into sexualities he is currently researching and writing a sociology of opera.

Didi Herman is a law lecturer at Keele University. She has written extensively on the relationship between law, sexuality and social change. Her books include: *Rights of Passage: Struggles for Lesbian and Gay Legal Equality* (University of Toronto Press, 1994) and *Legal Inversions* (co-edited with Carl Stychin) (Temple University Press, forthcoming 1995).

Anya Palmer is the Deputy Director of Stonewall and has recently published a survey concerning job discrimination experienced by gay men and lesbians entitled *Less Equal than Others*.

Shane Phelan is associate professor of political science at the University of New Mexico. She is the author of *Getting Specific: Postmodern Lesbian Politics* (University of Minnesota Press, 1994) and *Identity Politics: Lesbian Feminism and the Limits of Community* (Temple University Press, 1989) and has written articles on feminism, lesbian theory, Foucault, Adorno, and other topics.

David Smith is the editor and formerly the news editor of the London-based monthly magazine *Gay Times*.

Angelia R. Wilson is a political theorist currently writing a critical analysis of liberalism and the language of gay and lesbian activism entitled *The Gay & Lesbian Agenda: Justice, Equality & Freedom*. She and Joseph Bristow have co-edited *Activating Theory: Lesbian, Gay, and Bisexual Politics* (Lawrence & Wishart, 1993). She is a lecturer in social policy at the University of Central Lancashire.

Acknowledgements

I would like to note my appreciation to all contributors for their co-operation and diligence in meeting the publication timetable. In addition, I would like to thank Roz Hopkins, Steve Cook and Liz Gibbs at Cassell for their expert advice during the editorial process and their confidence in this collection.

The root of the word 'oppression' is the element 'press'. The press of the crowd; pressed into military service; to press a pair of pants; printing press; press the button. Presses are used to mould things or flatten them or reduce them in bulk, sometimes to reduce them by squeezing out the gases or liquids in them. Something pressed is something caught between or among forces and barriers which are so related to each other that jointly they restrain, restrict or prevent the thing's motion or mobility. Mould. Immobilise. Reduce.[1]

Vicky: *You lived in a cocoon because you couldn't tell anybody. I mean nobody knew at work, when I was going out to work. You had to live a sort of fictional life because you couldn't talk about it.*

George: *I had friends who didn't even know my real name. I can only speak for me, I can't say that everyone else was like me, I think a lot of us were. But certainly you never discussed where you worked, you never gave your real name . . . And if they've (careless gay friends) got your telephone number . . . I lived in terror. But, as I say, that's the way I felt, I can't say how others felt, I never really discussed it with any of them but I was terrified of the law, terrified of them.*

James: *You had to be careful about taking and keeping photographs. The whole thing was so illegal. The police could take your family album, your photograph album and ask, 'Who is this? Who is that? What is going on here?' It was too risky.*

Vicky: *It was a very insular position really because you became part of a very close-knit family, if you like. And the outside world didn't really encroach on it. And if you didn't go looking for trouble, trouble didn't find you. I mean, you didn't go out blazoning the fact. If you went anywhere, you went by taxi. You didn't walk on the streets dressed like we used to dress for instance. If you couldn't get in a car or get a taxi, then you didn't go.*[2]

'. . . reduce them in bulk . . . reduce them by squeezing out . . . restrain, restrict or prevent . . . motion or mobility. Mould. Immobilise. Reduce.'

Notes

1. M. Frye, quoted in A. Brittan and M. Maynard, *Sexism, Racism and Oppression* (Oxford: Blackwell, 1984), p. 1.
2. These quotations are from Brighton Ourstory, *Daring Hearts: Lesbian and Gay Lives of 50s and 60s Brighton* (Brighton: QueenSpark Books, 1992), pp. 33–8.

Introduction

IN April 1993 three hundred thousand supporters of the 'gay and lesbian movement' converged on Washington DC to protest against oppression based on sexual identity. The focal point of the rally, the banner at centre stage, proclaimed that the fight to end this oppression was *A Simple Matter of Justice*. The march on Washington was significant for a number of reasons. It testified to the large number of people who believe that now is the time for laws discriminating on the basis of sexuality, enforcing heterosexuality, and criminalizing homosexuality to be repealed and replaced with new laws protecting the human rights of gay men and lesbians. And as the day's events were broadcast live on American television, it showed the increasing acceptability of these sentiments in 'middle America'. But perhaps most importantly the march on Washington signified the progress of the social movement sparked by the Stonewall riots in 1969. The gay and lesbian movement, or sexual politics more generally, has become in the 1990s a formidable actor on the mainstream political stage. The unprecedented support for Clinton's campaign from gay and lesbian constituents, the invitation to discuss policy and legal changes with the President in the White House and the Prime Minister in No. 10, gave gay and lesbian activists a heady feeling of excitement like a debutante at her 'coming out' ball. After twenty-five years of struggle, finally our protest, our case for change, was going to be heard by those in power.

The events following Clinton's inauguration in 1993 were, to say the least, a dose of reality for American activists who had placed their hopes in his sympathies with difficulties facing gay men and lesbians. We may no longer be on the margins of the political agenda, but we are not, by any means, serious contenders against elected officials whose power lies in the hands of those who see heterosexuality threatened by granting human rights to gay men and lesbians. The compromise over the 'gays in the military' issue should have been foreseen, since the same November election that put Clinton in power also passed legislation in some states legalizing discrimination based on sexual orientation. And since then similar state and local legislative proposals have become the focus for gay and lesbian activism in the USA. With our new positioning in the political mainstream, gay men and lesbians have become the primary target for the financial and religious powerhouses of the New Right. In America, where Church and State are theoretically separated, gay and lesbian activists seeking justice are becoming increasingly aware that first they must 'Fight the Right'.

In Britain, the wrath of the moral right was felt most severely during the premiership of Margaret Thatcher and her 'campaign for family values'. In 1988, Conservatives succeeded in passing Section 28 of the Local Government Act (1988) which prohibited local governments from 'promoting homosexuality' or promoting 'pretended family relationships' (for text see p. 129 below). After the heady days of 1970s sexual liberation, and the frightening reality of the AIDS crisis, the proposed Section 28 caught gay and lesbian activists ill prepared for a 'fight with the Right'. The result was a mass revival of gay and lesbian politics with the emergence of the direct action group OutRage! and the lobbying organization Stonewall. So that when John Major launched his 'Back to Basics' campaign, hoping to befriend Tory moral conservatives, the political landscape had significantly altered. While gay and lesbian activists may be less responsible for the failure of this initiative than Tory MPs caught, often quite literally, with their trousers down, the readiness of activists does ensure that the campaign against discrimination will continue to grow. Today in Britain, gay and lesbian activists are networked across the country and provide a strong challenge to the dated policies of discrimination and injustice.

This struggle for justice recently reached a high point as Parliament considered lowering the age of consent for gay male sex from twenty-one to sixteen. After an impressive lobbying campaign, activists were more than a little disappointed, indeed many stormed the doors of Parliament, as MPs voted for a 'compromise' of eighteen. However, since this was the first time in twenty-seven years that legislators had reformed the laws regulating gay male sex, the debate was a milestone in British activism. Stonewall Deputy Director Anya Palmer notes in her contribution that getting gay and lesbian concerns on the political agenda is the first task for activists. And one lesson that has proved to be central is that, in order for change to take place, activists must communicate those concerns to the general public, either 'middle America' or 'middle Britain'.

Our new positioning in mainstream politics has been accompanied by the need to articulate the changes we propose to the majority of the population, and to those in whom that majority places its power. It is perhaps unsurprising then that the language we have chosen is one which is familiar, is acceptable, to that majority. Like the slogan of the Washington march, gay and lesbian lobbying groups speak of justice, equality and human rights. It is a language embedded in the western political tradition, and one which appeals to our intuitive sentiments about the role of the state and the protection of individual freedoms. Communicating our experiences of oppression, and the need for protection against injustices and discrimination, to the 'public' has taken on this familiar language as if to say 'no, we are not a threat to social stability, we simply want justice done'.

This familiar language has been adopted by activists in America, Britain and Europe. In position briefs and publicity, Stonewall, the British gay and lesbian lobbying group, often describes various acts of injustice perpetrated by police, employers and homophobic individuals and then connects this injustice with their mandate to work for 'social justice'. Similarly, campaigners in Europe have sought protection against discrimination based on sexual orientation by appealing to the European Convention on Human Rights. For example, P. Dijk argues that:

> The human-rights aspect of homosexuality in reality comes down to the issue of the recognition of the right to self-determination of homosexuals: the right to express and practice their sexual orientation and have homosexuality legally and socially recognized as a way of life of equal legitimacy and value as heterosexuality.[1]

He concludes that a 'dynamic' interpretation of the Convention, one that reflects the developments of society, could be an adequate basis for the rights of homosexuals. And the recent recognition of the International Lesbian and Gay Association (ILGA) by the United Nations testifies that, even on the world political stage, the injustices suffered by gay men and lesbians are beginning to be considered breaches of fundamental human rights.

Now while this new positioning may require, or be a result of, employing the familiar language of the political mainstream, it may also sit rather uncomfortably with the language that has historically been linked to the Stonewall riots. In particular, the rise of the Gay Liberation Front was fuelled not by mainstream, liberal, political language but by the imagery and ideology of a socialist revolution. Shortly after the riots, the American *Village Voice* newspaper captured the spirit of the birth of this new movement:

> The forces of faggotry, spurred by a Friday night raid on one of the city's largest, most popular, and longest lived gay bars, the Stonewall Inn, rallied Saturday night in an unprecedented protest against the raid and continued Sunday night to assert presence, possibility, and pride until the early hours of Monday morning. 'I'm a faggot, and I'm proud of it!' 'Gay Power!' 'I like boys!' – these and many other slogans were heard all three nights as the show of force by the city's finery met the force of the city's finest. The result was a kind of liberation, as the gay brigade emerged from the bars, back rooms, and bedrooms of the Village and became street people.[2]

The manifesto adopted by the GLF movement in Britain was a clear rejection of the heterosexual dominated culture: 'The long-term goal . . . is to rid society of the gender role system which is at the root of our oppression. This can only be achieved by the abolition of the family unit in which children are brought up . . .'[3] The revolutionary motivation behind political demands could be encapsulated in one word: Liberation!

The cry for liberation was indicative of the feeling of potential power. Jeffrey Weeks summarizes the political role the GLF played in the history of the gay and lesbian movement:

> GLF did not cause the changes that have taken place, but it
> suggested that they might be possible. That was its historic
> function . . . GLF helped make homosexuality a political
> issue in the broadest sense. In terms of legislative change, the
> effect so far has been nugatory; but in terms of homosexuals'
> ability to conceptualize their social position, the change has
> been immense – and it is this which portends most for the
> future.[4]

And while GLF's revolution, and its utopia, have faded into
the annals of gay and lesbian history, their language has been quietly
avoided by contemporary activism. This is not to say that radical
politics does not have a visible place in current activism. Groups like
ACT UP and OutRage! continue to challenge heterosexism and
homophobia with radical methods of 'in-your-face' activism. But
even these large groups no longer cry 'liberation!'. Instead, they, like
their more traditional counterparts, employ the language of equality, rights and justice. So while liberation may have been our first
public word as a new social movement, we have quickly learned to
speak the language of the empowered.

It is this shift in language that is the overall motivation for
this collection of essays. Taking its title directly from the words of
activists, and reformulating the demand for justice as a question, the
writers here implicitly ask, *Is it A Simple Matter of Justice?* And if
so, is it really that 'simple', or is more detailed inquiry required? For
example, 'What policy changes are needed to reflect this justice?'
'What strategies within different systems of justice will enable us to
ensure justice is done?' 'What, or whose, conception of justice will
best serve the diverse needs of gay men and lesbians?' The
contributions here by activists, journalists, social policy experts,
legal theorists and political theorists, address these questions,
offering reflections upon recent campaigns in the USA and Britain,
strategies for securing legal justice and questions for current
theoretical frameworks for justice that legitimate much of western
political discourse.

This book opens with a journalist's account of the recent age
of consent campaign in Britain. The age of consent campaign
testified to the extent of grassroots political activism across the

country, and to the level of professionalism in lobbying and campaigning around gay and lesbian concerns. David Smith, editor of *Gay Times*, provides a detailed account of the 'anatomy' of this campaign and, in doing so, highlights the potential, the determination and the power of the gay and lesbian movement in the 1990s. In this contemporary history he documents the words of the new leader of the Labour Party, Tony Blair, during the heated Parliamentary debate, 'It is wrong to treat a man as inferior because his sexuality is different' (p. 28 below). And this intensity of commitment was reflected in the activists outside, who, upon hearing of the 'compromise', hammered the doors of Parliament and marched up Whitehall to Downing Street shouting, 'sixteen now! sixteen now!' (p. 30 below). Following this informative account of that campaign is a reflection on current and future campaigns by Anya Palmer, Deputy Director of Stonewall. Her insight 'From the Coalface' offers both a personal perspective on the day-to-day tasks of a professional lobby group and a knowledge of the difficulties that lie ahead for the struggle to secure equality, or justice. 'We are now witnessing', Palmer declares, 'a profound shift in social attitudes, the beginning of a time when sexual apartheid will be seen for what it is' (p. 33 below). Combined, these two chapters present British activists with the realities of legislative challenges within a parliamentary system, as well as providing a source of strategic information for activists in other countries.

The next two essays in this book move in a somewhat different direction as they report on the state of the gay and lesbian struggle within judicial and legislative systems. Paisley Currah takes stock of the various arguments used by gay men and lesbian activists trying to secure rights in the American legal system. Her article asks significant questions about the kinds of comparisons and arguments activists are forced to make when the Constitution is interpreted to protect the rights of those oppressed because of immutable characteristics, and when homosexuality is interpreted as a 'choice'.

The assertion that homosexuality is not a chosen but an assigned identity constitutes an attempt to correspond not only to popular fictions about rights and immutability but also to the prevailing legal standards in US constitutional law.

These standards require, among other things, that a group should exhibit 'immutable characteristics' before the judiciary will intervene to shield a 'discrete and insular minority' from state-sponsored discrimination. But this emphasis on immutability is more than an attempt to conform to the legal doctrine; the quest for equality on the basis of an authentic, fixed orientation moves the mainstream of the gay, lesbian and bisexual movement firmly into the domain of 'identity politics' (p. 58 below).

From inside a different system of justice, or legislative regulation, Jean Carabine considers the effects of Section 28 of the Local Government Act (1988). Many feared that the impact of this blatant discrimination, which prohibited local governments in Britain from 'promoting' homosexuality or 'pretended' families, would cause local governments to discontinue providing services for lesbians and gay men. Jean Carabine reports that within Sheffield City Council these fears were indeed well grounded. Remarking on the small amount of 'liberal' opposition to Section 28, she states that 'the liberalism of many of the campaigns opposing Section 28 pronounced an equality in the freedom of expressions of sexuality, whilst upholding the heterosexual system which enshrines the values of family and notions of morality. In doing so, the power and influence of heterosexuality remained unchallenged' (pp. 93–4 below).

Securing rights under systems of justice which do not take into account oppression under the heterosexual hegemony is a difficult, long road for activism and it raises important questions about the kinds of compromises, and sacrifices, we may make in the process. Indeed, it may be impossible. It may be that the systems of justice themselves are inherently heterosexist and that what is needed is a more critical analysis of the theories of justice that underpin, and legitimate, those systems. And in chapters 5 and 6 David T. Evans and I offer very different critiques of the one theory of justice which has informed western political thought for the last twenty years, John Rawls's *A Theory of Justice*. In '(Homo)sexual Citizenship: A Queer Kind of Justice', Evans argues that if we continue to be silent and accept a heterosexual justice, the 'unfairness' of existing homosexual citizenship will continue (p. 134

below). He proposes that an appeal to a just society based on Rawlsian principles of fairness might illuminate the injustice, the 'lesser entitlements', suffered by gay men and lesbians. In contrast, my understanding of Rawlsian justice is offered in chapter 6. It seems to me that, because this 'theory of justice' is ultimately based on a 'family', or 'heterosexual', justice, the resulting society is remarkably similar to that found in Britain and America where heterosexism permeates public policy. What is needed is a re-imagining of justice that is inclusive of lesbian and gay, or all sexual, citizens.

The final section of this book considers the interesting new directions for such a re-imagined justice. Both essays are written by lesbian political theorists but, unlike radical lesbian feminists, both argue against a separatist 'lesbian' justice. Didi Herman directly challenges such a lesbian system of justice recently outlined by Ruthann Robson. In her book *Lesbian (Out)Law*, Robson proposes a lesbian legal jurisprudence:

> If a lesbian legal theory is a theory of law that has as its purpose lesbian survival; if it is relentlessly lesbian and puts lesbians rather than law at its centre; if it distinguishes between intralesbian situations and nonlesbian situations; if it is not feminist legal theory and not queer legal theory; if it does not seek to explain the entire enterprise of law, then some of the preliminary work toward developing a lesbian legal theory has begun.[5]

Taking issue with this essentialist notion of lesbian sisterhood and justice, Herman argues that the 'very category of "lesbian" is a far more contested one than Robson's approach seems to allow for'. Continuing she notes that 'but to say that imagining is difficult is not to say that it is pointless; my argument is simply that lesbian life is perhaps more complicated than Robson's framework suggests' (p. 182 below). The final chapter, by Shane Phelan, builds upon a similar discomfort with Robson's lesbian justice and re-imagines what justice might come to mean to those in the 'house of difference'. If identity politics is not a 'sufficient ground for trust or political agreement . . . then we need to get specific with one another about what we value and what we will do to realize that value'. By building coalitions we can begin to understand our multiple identities and 'forge links between ourselves and other marginal citizens of the world' (p. 218 below).

The language of justice, probably because it is so prominent in western political discourse, often imports assumptions about what kinds of justice are appropriate, and for whom. If we are to take advantage of our new positioning in the mainstream, we must be careful that the language we employ articulates the fundamental changes we would wish to make to the construction of sexuality in western society. And in each system of justice we may be forced to make initial compromises, to re-articulate, to build coalitions if a different kind of justice is to be realized. The question of justice for lesbians and gay men is not, as this book will testify, and as we have experienced, a simple matter.

Notes

1   P. V. Dijk, 'The treatment of homosexuals under the European Convention on Human Rights', in K. Waaldijk and A. Clapham, eds, *Homosexuality: A European Community Issue* (London: Matinus Nijhoff, 1993), p. 183.

2   *Village Voice*, IV (3 July 1969), quoted in S. Jeffrey-Poulter, *Peers, Queers & Commons: The Struggle for Gay Law Reform from 1950 to the Present* (London: Routledge, 1991), p. 99.

3   GLF manifesto published in October 1971, cited in *Peers, Queers & Commons*, p. 102.

4   J. Weeks, *Coming Out: Homosexual Politics in Britain from the Nineteenth Century to the Present* (London: Quartet, 1977), p. 206.

5   R. Robson, *Lesbian (Out)Law: Survival Under the Rule of Law* (Ithaca: Firebrand, 1992), p. 23.

Chapter one

The Anatomy of a Campaign

David Smith

THE age of consent for sex between men in England and Wales was set at twenty-one by the Sexual Offences Act of 1967. This was the first time since the introduction of the offence of so-called 'gross indecency' in 1885 that any sex between men anywhere in Britain had been decriminalized in any way. The age of consent was set at what was then the age of majority, but other parts of the United Kingdom had to wait more than a decade for the same liberalizing reform to filter down. Gay sex was not decriminalized in Scotland until 1980, and Northern Ireland did not follow until 1982 after the law had been successfully challenged in the European Court of Human Rights and Fundamental Freedoms by the gay rights activist Jeffrey Dudgeon.

Equality with heterosexuals, with a common age of consent of sixteen for all, was a central aim of gay campaigning organizations throughout the 1970s and 1980s, though it moved up and down the political agenda depending on the political climate. But it was not until after the 1992 general election that the first real chance of having the issue seriously debated in Parliament presented itself.

In the 1970s and early 1980s, achieving even the minimum demand of decriminalization in Scotland and Northern Ireland had required a high level of campaigning and a favourable political wind, but following those successes, throughout the 1980s with what the British press gleefully described as 'the gay plague' and the continuing domination of the political scene by Prime Minister Margaret Thatcher with her right-wing moralist base and her invocation of 'Victorian values', any progress on the age of consent issue had been practically impossible.

As late as February 1990, in her last year of office, Mrs Thatcher told a Conservative backbench Member of Parliament at Prime Minister's Question Time that she was very much opposed to reducing the gay age of consent. She had been asked to condemn just such a proposal from the opposition Labour Party. 'Any such proposal would give totally the wrong signal,' she said. 'It would give offence to many people and worry many more and would give us great problems in the future.' In April of the same year, a survey of MPs carried out for the *Guardian* newspaper and the Channel Four lesbian and gay television series *Out* had found that only 11 per cent of MPs would support a gay age of consent of sixteen; 31 per cent supported eighteen and 50 per cent supported no change.

Also throughout the 1980s, the 'metropolitan socialist' politics of the left of the Labour Party, with their emphasis on rainbow coalitions of oppressed sectors of society, had the effect of lowering the priority of reform of the age of consent. It was dismissed as an issue which concerned only men, and in any case attempting reform through a hostile Parliament seemed a lost cause when access to power and the prospects of social change were most obviously available in the local councils which were controlled by the left of the Labour Party.

The response of the Thatcherite moralists to this latter tactic by lesbians and gay men was the passing of Section 28 of the Local Government Act (1988) which banned the 'intentional promotion of homosexuality' by those same local councils (for text see p. 129 below). But, as it turned out, the huge upsurge in campaigning on specifically lesbian and gay issues which Section 28 provoked would be the starting point for a sea-change in lesbian and gay politics. Within a year, in May 1989, Britain's first professional and properly funded lesbian and gay rights lobbying organization, the Stonewall Group, was formally launched, citing as one of its early priorities the implementation in some form of recent recommendations by the Law Commission on reform of sexual offences and the age of consent.

12: *A Simple Matter of Justice?*

A year later, just as the ultimate lesbian and gay 'rainbow politics' group the Organization for Lesbian and Gay Action (OLGA) folded, the new ACT UP-style civil disobedience and direct action group OutRage! emerged with a mandate to break with the politics of the 1980s and focus exclusively on identifiable lesbian and gay concerns. It chose as the focus for its first street action in June 1990 the issue of the recent police use of agents provocateurs to arrest men for 'gross indecency' in a public toilet at Hyde Park in London.

The issue of gay male sexual offences was firmly back on the gay and lesbian political agenda, and the age of consent was top of the list. Writing in the April 1990 issue of *Gay Times*, the then editor John Marshall had bemoaned the notion which had grown up in the 1980s that sexual offences law reform was a 'stale . . . old-fashioned and irrelevant' issue:

> It is time to recognise that the gay male age of consent is the central issue at the present time for our movement – with enormous implications not only for the general principle of legal equality, but also for the whole philosophical basis of lesbian and gay liberation . . . The law assumes that homosexuality is immoral and undesirable, and it therefore assumes that every young person must be 'protected' from the dangerous temptation to drift into such lifestyles . . . By altering the age of consent for gay men, we not only break this legal framework, but we also challenge the underlying philosophy: we challenge the notion that homosexuality is a second-rate lifestyle and we question the idea that barriers should be placed in the way of people who might choose to adopt such a lifestyle. By reducing the age of consent we go a long way towards legitimising homosexuality in our culture as morally equivalent to heterosexuality.

A key turning point for the prospect of reform was to come, however, with the replacement of Mrs Thatcher with John Major, an event which signalled to some a shift in power in the Conservative Party, away from the moralist right towards the more liberal left.

One of Mr Major's key early comments, which set the tone for his leadership, and was picked up by the gay press, was that he viewed Conservatism not as 'a creed' but as 'essentially the common-sense view of life from a tolerant perspective'.

And it quickly emerged, through the efforts of the gay campaigning journalist Neil McKenna working for the *Independent* newspaper and the London weekly *Capital Gay*, that within days of his elevation to Prime Minister, Mr Major had told a gay Conservative MP that he would 'willingly' give consideration to pressure for reform of the age of consent. Unlike others in the party, he had voted in the early 1980s in favour of decriminalization of gay sex in Scotland and Northern Ireland, and as early as 1980 when he was a newly elected MP he had told gay activists in his Huntingdon constituency that he favoured lowering the age of consent from twenty-one to eighteen, though not to sixteen.

Even before Mr Major came to power, there had been signs that pressure for change in a number of legal and social spheres was beginning to mount. Throughout 1990 the Home Office, fearing adverse criticism from the European Commission on Human Rights, had been putting pressure on independent British territories like the Isle of Man, Jersey and Guernsey, Gibraltar and Hong Kong to finally decriminalize homosexual sex. Pressure from OutRage!, the Gay London Policing organization (GALOP) and other London gay organizations had borne fruit at Scotland Yard, the headquarters of the Metropolitan Police, which had announced new policies for dealing sympathetically with victims of anti-gay violence and had begun to adopt a softer line on the policing of 'gross indecency' in public places.

And in the first few months of the Major premiership, the Criminal Justice Bill provided an ideal vehicle for comprehensive debate about gay sexual offences. Writing in the June 1991 issue of *Gay Times*, journalist and activist Peter Tatchell spoke for many when he confidently predicted that the debate had 'helped put gay law reform back on the political agenda and created a strong foundation for renewed campaigns for lesbian and gay equality'.

The prediction seemed to begin to come true with almost startling speed. In April, it became known that the Lord Advocate of Scotland, Lord Fraser of Carmyllie, the head of the Scottish legal system and a confidant of John Major, had plans to issue a directive to his public prosecutors not to bring criminal proceedings for any consenting sex involving gay and bisexual men over the age of sixteen.

In May, a committee of MPs reviewing the Armed Forces Bill, the five-yearly review of military regulations, recommended that male members of the forces should no longer be prosecuted or court-martialled for gay sex which would be legal in civilian life, thus addressing one of the restrictive measures included in the 1967 Sexual Offences Act.

By the summer, the so-called 'new mood' in the Conservative Party was encouraging a significant number of Conservative MPs to become involved in lobbying for reform on a number of fronts. Their efforts were co-ordinated by the new dynamic Tory Campaign for Homosexual Equality (TORCHE). And in response to a planted parliamentary question from the veteran liberal Conservative MP, Sir John Wheeler, Mr Major revealed that he was scrapping the rules which automatically barred lesbians and gay men from top government jobs, including the Security Service and the Foreign Office. In a remarkable statement of the shift in approach by the Conservative Government, Mr Major stated that he had done so 'in the light of changing social attitudes towards homosexuality in this country and abroad, and the correspondingly greater willingness on the part of homosexuals to be open about their sexuality, their lifestyle and their relationships'.

Privately, even in advance of his historic meeting in the Prime Minister's residence, 10 Downing Street, in September 1991 with Sir Ian McKellen, founder member of the Stonewall Group, Mr Major had also made it plain to Sir John Wheeler that he was prepared to offer a free vote on the age of consent after the general election. With the Labour Party and Liberal Democrats also offering reform after the election, it was now just a matter of time. In a Liberal Democrat policy document, published that month, the party's home affairs spokesman, Robert Maclennan, said: 'The boundaries of law and morals have not been properly reviewed since the Report of the Wolfenden Committee in 1957, and we believe it is time for a fresh look at the question of where the boundaries of the criminal law should be drawn in this area.'

15: *The Anatomy of a Campaign*

Even *The Times* newspaper had picked up on the new mood. Commenting on the Major–McKellen meeting, it said in an editorial:

> No society functions happily if a minority feels excluded from a hearing. To be sure, gay activists sometimes ask too much. But such demands should only be turned down with stated reasons after discussion, or the dangerous language of persecution will work its poison on the minds of those denied. Mr Major need only listen patiently to revive a tradition that wore threadbare under Mrs Thatcher: the tradition of One Nation Conservatism.

Both before and after the Conservative victory in the general election of April 1992, there were to be false dawns and apparent setbacks, mixed up with signs of progress. While the Lord Advocate of Scotland was forced to withdraw his proposed new liberal prosecution policy, lobbying by Conservative MPs resulted in government acceptance of a proposal (which it had initially rejected) to allow lesbian and gay council tenants to inherit their partners' council property. After much delay and hesitation, the government eventually also accepted the decriminalization of gay sex in the armed forces and merchant navy but continued to insist that homosexuality would be grounds for dismissal.

In the post-election reconstruction of parliamentary committees, however, pro-gay Conservatives lost what had seemed to be a key power base. Sir John Wheeler was removed from his position as chairman of the influential backbench Select Committee on Home Affairs, which he and others had planned as a forum for an up-to-date review of the age of consent. The new chairman, right-winger Sir Ivan Lawrence, was on record as saying that sixteen was 'a very vulnerable age'. 'Adults should be free to make their own decision. But to make it [the age of consent] so low it brings in school children is going too far.'

Gay lobbyists were forced to be sanguine and rethink their tactics, but the loss of Sir John Wheeler and his proposed investigation proved to be a serious setback. When the House of Commons debate on the age of consent finally happened in February 1994, the

16: *A Simple Matter of Justice?*

Home Secretary Michael Howard based his rejection of equality at sixteen on a selective reading of the findings of previous reports on the issue – the 1957 Wolfenden Report and a report from the Home Office Policy Advisory Committee in the early 1980s. At that key moment in the debate, a fresh report on the matter was sorely missed.

Throughout the latter half of 1992 and the whole of 1993, campaigning, lobbying and preparations for what still seemed to be the inevitability of a debate and vote continued apace. OutRage! made a big show of marking the twenty-fifth anniversary of the 1967 Act on 25 July 1992. In October, Stonewall began its search for articulate young gay men who were prepared to challenge the age of consent laws in the European Court, eventually choosing Ralph Wilde, Hugo Greenhalgh and Will Parry who all caught the imagination of the media during the campaign and proved an enormous asset.

By early 1993, pro-gay Conservative MPs were using the threat of an adverse European Court judgement as a lever in their meetings about the prospects of reform with Home Office ministers.

In June the government of the Republic of Ireland finally bowed to pressure from the European Court to equalize its ages of consent at seventeen, leaving Britain and Germany alone among the twelve European Community countries with discriminatory laws. Germany was already planning reform which it implemented in March 1994.

By the end of the summer, it was clear that the government would announce a new Criminal Justice Bill in the Queen's Speech outlining the Government's legislative programme for 1993–4. Several of the leading pro-gay Conservative MPs had by this time been promoted into the Government and it fell to Edwina Currie MP, the most senior of TORCHE's backbench supporters, to be the MP most likely to propose an age of consent amendment to the Bill. And, with suggestions that the Bill might be rushed through Parliament before the end of November, campaigning went into overdrive.

There were fears, however, that Michael Howard's aggressive 'law and order' speech to the Conservative Party conference, alongside some reportedly anti-gay remarks made by John Major to party agents and the new 'Back to Basics' theme for the Conservative agenda, would spell the end to prospects for reform, and Conservatives were obliged to renew their appeals to the government for a chance of an amendment to the Criminal Justice Bill. And as Parliament reconvened, Stonewall launched its Equality Week campaign, beginning with a packed public meeting in the House of Commons which heard MPs and Lords and a wide range of representatives of legal, AIDS, police, counselling and campaigning organizations all voice their support for equality.

The House of Commons meeting was followed by others in towns and cities around the country. Stonewall published fifty thousand copies of its persuasive pamphlet, *The Case for Change: Arguments for an Equal Age of Consent*, advising and encouraging gay men and lesbians throughout Britain to lobby their MP. And the week concluded with a star-studded gala at the London Palladium.

'The important thing is to win the debate in the country, to win the debate for change,' said Angela Mason, Stonewall's Executive Director. 'We have to take the argument to the country, to every town and village and public bar. Once the Government knows that debate is really happening, once they know that the overwhelming majority of people in the country support the case for change then the change will come about.'

It was not until mid-November, however, that Home Office minister David Maclean finally let it be known that the government would not stand in the way of amendments to its Bill, and finally on 16 December (a moment memorably caught on film by Will Parry for his video diary film for Channel Four) the news came through to the Stonewall offices that possibly in early January there would be a full debate on floor of the Commons followed by a free vote.

The quiet announcement was followed by five weeks of the most intense lobbying on a gay issue since 1988.

The news leaked out in a front-page lead story in *The Times* on 21 December announcing that the House of Commons debate would take place 'within weeks'. The Stonewall Group's offices had already gone into overdrive. They would be closed on Christmas Day, but on every other day in the lead up to the vote at least twenty volunteers were turning up to help with the campaign. Work had already begun on putting the finishing touches to letters and leaflets which Stonewall would send out to all thirteen thousand contacts it had on its database, urging them one last time to lobby their MPs for equality. 'It is these people', said executive director Angela Mason, 'who have really created the groundswell of opinion that has reached MPs. They are the bedrock of the campaign.'

In the first few days of the New Year, meetings involving Stonewall's core 'members' and workers, activists in TORCHE and supportive MPs were putting the final touches to the age of consent amendment, while, in one of many examples of specialist target lobbying, the Jewish Lesbian and Gay Helpline offered to write to all Jewish MPs urging their support for equality. And another main plank of the arguments for change – the need to remove obstacles in the way of HIV and AIDS education for young gay men – came into play when Nick Partridge, Chief Executive of the Terrence Higgins Trust, wrote to the Health Secretary Virginia Bottomley asking her to explain how her view that there should be no change in the law would actively help improve health education and reduce the number of suicides among young gay men. Mrs Bottomley would later change her view and support eighteen, but not sixteen.

On 4 January Stonewall hosted a meeting of lesbian and gay campaigning groups to agree on strategies and to plan a mass lobby of Parliament for Monday 17 January. The organizations also helping to arrange the campaign included OutRage!, the Pride Trust, the Labour Campaign for Lesbian and Gay Rights, Democrats for Lesbian and Gay Action, London Lesbian and Gay Switchboard, the lesbian and gay groups from the trade unions MSF and Unison, Rank Outsiders, the Jewish Lesbian and Gay Helpline and TORCHE. There would be an effective show of unity which lasted right up to the day of the debate on 21 February. But there would later be private complaints that Stonewall used the notion of a broad front to its own advantage without really consulting with the other groups. And there was some resentment that on the night of the debate OutRage! was left to carry the can for the charge on the doors of the Commons by participants in the candlelit vigil outside.

As the campaign proceeded, there seemed to be a new intervention from a specialist organization every day for several weeks. For example, in one of many such lobbying efforts by medical and specialist organizations, Maureen Moore, Chief

Executive of Scottish AIDS Monitor, wrote early in January to all Scottish MPs urging them to support sixteen. 'The importance of the vote can be measured in lives,' she said. And in what proved to be one of the most significant of such interventions, senior members of the Royal College of Psychiatrists, whose patron it was pointed out is the Prince of Wales, said in an open letter to actor Michael Cashman, one of the founder 'members' of Stonewall, that 'there are no psychiatric or developmental reasons that the minimum age for homosexual practices should be other than sixteen years'.

The *Daily Telegraph* meanwhile, on Monday 10 January, revealed a split among the bishops of the Church of England over how they should react to the age of consent debate. The Archbishop of York, the Bishop of Bath and Wells and the Bishop of Oxford had said they were in favour of eighteen, the compromise strongly advocated in an article by the Archbishop of York in the *Independent*. Evangelicals such as the Bishop of St Albans supported the status quo, and only the Bishop of Edinburgh and the Bishop of Monmouth, later joined by the retiring Bishop of Durham, were in favour of sixteen. The Archbishop of Canterbury was refusing to comment until the issue was debated in the House of Lords.

The following day Sir Ian McKellen made a significant intervention when he had lunch with the *Daily Mirror*'s veteran agony aunt Marjorie Proops. In the *Sunday Mirror* two days earlier she had said: 'At sixteen, boys are often still at an experimental stage. They could go either way . . . Making the legal age of consent for boys eighteen gives them the extra couple of years to make more mature judgements about their sexuality.' But after lunch with Sir Ian, 'Marje' went back to the office to write a full-page article headlined 'How Sir Ian won my vote on gay sex at 16'. Looking very frail, she would later join a delegation of agony aunts and uncles handing in a letter from twenty of their advice column colleagues to John Major at 10 Downing Street. Agony aunt Claire Rayner, a long-term supporter of gay equality, meanwhile added her voice to the campaign. 'How terrible to tell a young man that the feelings he has are criminal,' she said. And on another front, long years of campaigning for equal opportunities through the trades unions bore more fruit when Campbell Christie, general secretary of the Scottish Trades Union Congress, told the press that he believed the case for equality was 'absolutely clear'. He announced that the STUC had written to all Scottish MPs urging them to support sixteen.

On the same day, the Criminal Justice Bill began its second reading in the House of Commons. At 3.35 p.m. the text of the age of consent amendment was pressed into the hands of Edwina Currie who was asked to present it to the House of Commons authorities for approval as soon as the second reading was over. At 6.30 p.m. she stood up to speak in favour of her proposed amendment:

> In a free society, in which individual liberty and freedom of action and thought count for a great deal, the burden of proof and argument is not on those of us who seek equality before the law. The onus is on those who would argue in favour of discrimination to explain how that is in the public interest and how it is in the interests of any of our fellow citizens that the law should intervene to make their activities illegal . . .
> The law as it stands is not helpful to vulnerable young men. In fact, it works in exactly the opposite way. If a boy wished to make a complaint about an unwanted homosexual approach today, he would think twice about going to the police. He would immediately be the one who was questioned – the one who was the criminal . . . I do not feel that that can be right . . . The law as it stands is not a shield for the young, but an enforcer of their silence.

During her speech, Mrs Currie was barracked by Tory MP Tony Marlow asking: 'What about Back to Basics?' in a reference to the moralistic tone of many recent ministerial statements and of a spate of newspaper condemnations of the private lives of a number of MPs. Those who spoke against the proposed amendment included, significantly, Sir Ivan Lawrence, the new chairman of the Home Affairs Select Committee.

At 9 a.m. the following day, 12 January, the Stonewall Group held a press conference to announce the names of MPs who would be sponsoring the amendment. Along with Edwina Currie and Neil Kinnock, the former leader of the Labour Party, these included the Liberal Democrats' home affairs spokesman Robert Maclennan,

Labour's shadow heritage secretary Marjorie Mowlam, and Conservative MPs Harold Elletson and Jerry Hayes. The amendment restricted itself to the age of consent, and decisions about whether to table other amendments on 'gross indecency', 'buggery', the privacy restrictions on gay sex, and the formal implementation of the decriminalization of gay sex in the armed forces and the merchant navy would be made at a later date.

The Council of the British Medical Association meanwhile voted overwhelmingly in favour of sixteen. Unsafe sex was on the increase, the Council said in a statement, and young gay men were disproportionately affected. The criminalization of gay sex was inhibiting effective health education and health care.

Later that evening, a public meeting at the House of Commons for young gay men and lesbians and their parents, expected to attract around forty people, in fact attracted over 250 people. Ralph Wilde, one of the 'Stonewall Three' challenging the age of consent law in the European Court, said the age of consent was robbing young gay men of their adolescence. His mother told the meeting she was 'angry' that Ralph, who had always been a very open and talkative child, had felt he had to keep his sexuality secret from her until he was nineteen and bear the burden of rejection alone.

At the end of the meeting it emerged that government business managers had decided to delay the vote which had been expected on 20 January. While Stonewall was relieved to be given extra lobbying time, the delay which continued for another month fuelled speculation that, because of newspapers' obsession with the 'Back to Basics' theme, the government might get cold feet.

The next most significant development came on Sunday 16 January. Interviewed by David Frost on *Frost on Sunday*, on BBC television, the Labour Party leader, the late John Smith, said: 'I will vote to change the law to allow it at sixteen. I think it is a matter of equality and freedom. I think the boundaries of the criminal law should be very carefully drawn indeed. I think the case for this reform has been made.' The following morning the *Daily Mail* newspaper published the first mainstream press story which suggested that those in favour of sixteen could win, while further support for the campaign came from organizations including the

National Association of Probation Officers (NAPO), the mental health charity, MIND, the constitutional reform organization, Charter 88, Liberty (formerly the National Council for Civil Liberties), and Project Sigma, the AIDS research project funded by the Medical Research Council. In a letter to the *Independent*, former Conservative MP Humphry Berkeley, who had made the very first attempt to decriminalize homosexual sex – with a Private Member's Bill in December 1965 – voiced his support for sixteen.

In the evening a mass lobby of Parliament saw as many as three thousand gay men and lesbians turning up at the House of Commons to personally urge their MP to vote in favour of sixteen. At a meeting in the Grand Committee Room, a succession of MPs made appearances to express their support for Edwina Currie's amendment, and a message of support was read out from the Bishop of Monmouth. At eight o'clock, three hours after the start of the lobby, several hundred people were still queuing outside the House of Commons in sub-zero temperatures. While Sir Ian McKellen went off to a meeting with Virginia Bottomley, Edwina Currie, swathed in a big black coat, was still working the crowd offering words of encouragement. It was after this meeting that Mrs Bottomley revealed that she was now prepared to vote for eighteen.

Two days later, with consummate timing, Stonewall revealed that the European Commission on Human Rights had ruled that the challenge to the British age of consent law by the 'Stonewall Three' would be heard by the European Court, thus adding strength to one of the main arguments for reform. And the following day another piece of information was released which would be often repeated throughout the following days and weeks. The findings of Stonewall's survey of the first sexual experiences of 2,088 gay men found that the majority who started having sex in their teens were having sex with contemporaries rather than the mythical older seducer and proselytizer. And the case for change was bolstered again that week when the respected medical journal the *Lancet* published an editorial in support of sixteen.

With the debate likely to happen at any time, Stonewall was busy urging individual lesbians and gay men around the country to use the weekends as an ideal opportunity to visit their MP's surgeries. Once the campaign was over, Stonewall's Deputy Director, Anya Palmer, was able to boast that the group's network was so effective that, if a wavering MP showed any sign of changing his or her mind, the group could organize visits to the MP's constituency office within hours. And as the campaign progressed, Stonewall had to issue a plea to people to stop writing letters to MPs as their postbags were becoming unmanageable. Personal visits would become the key to successful lobbying, and much of this work was undertaken by local lesbian and gay organizations.

A notable group lobbying effort came in the form of a petition which was sent to every Member of Parliament signed by 150 of Britain's most prominent entertainers and opinion formers. They included eight trade union leaders, two bishops and three rabbis, six leading novelists and playwrights, the president of the Law Society, campaigning barristers Helena Kennedy and Michael Mansfield, and from the arts Emma Thompson and Kenneth Branagh, Dame Judi Dench and Lord Attenborough.

On 1 February, the long-expected counter-amendment calling for the age of consent to be reduced not to sixteen but to the so-called compromise of eighteen was finally tabled in the House of Commons. It was sponsored by several Conservative MPs, chief among whom was the archetypal 'knight of the shires' Sir Anthony Durant. And two days later Cardinal Basil Hume, leader of the Roman Catholic Church in England and Wales, made his expected intervention. He released a statement in which he urged MPs to be 'cautious' in the way they voted. He repeated the standard Vatican position that 'homosexual genital acts' are 'always wrong', adding that 'the law should always seek to protect young people and to promote moral values that society recognises as wholesome'. Significantly he refused, however, to dictate how MPs should vote. 'The Church,' he said, 'does not expect that acts that are morally wrong should, by that fact alone, be made criminal offences.'

On Saturday 5 February, several thousand lesbians and gay men attended the Equality Rally, organized in London's Trafalgar Square by a coalition of groups, and heard speeches of support from prominent figures in politics, the theatre, radio, television, AIDS campaigning and gay activism. It was a humorous and colourful event, with rainbow balloons, intended to keep up enthusiasm among the campaign's activists who might be in danger of losing steam as the delay in the vote grew longer and the pace of the campaign seemed to slacken.

Over the next two weeks, the interventions continued but at a slower pace. Britain's discriminatory laws were criticized during a debate on lesbian and gay rights at the European Parliament. And twelve leading organizations working with young people released a statement via Stonewall speaking in favour of sixteen. They included the National Children's Bureau, Save The Children, the British Youth Council and Youth Clubs UK. Months and even years of lobbying, campaigning and networking by gay and lesbian organizations and key gay and pro-gay individuals seemed to be paying handsome dividends. The National Association of Citizens Advice Bureaux released copies of a briefing it had sent to all MPs in support of equality. Labour MP Jack Straw wrote a moving article in *The Times* about a fellow school pupil back in 1963 who had committed suicide because he was homosexual. The Bow Group of Conservative MPs released a briefing to MPs urging them to vote for sixteen. And two senior police officers, Chief Superintendent Tony Buchanan and Chief Superintendent Bill Wilson, the chief officers in Hampstead and Brixton, two of the gayest areas of London, backed the campaign for sixteen.

But the newsworthiness of the campaign had been utterly undermined by what seemed to be the biggest political sex scandal of the year. The MP Stephen Milligan was found dead wearing women's stockings, bound and gagged with a plastic bag over his head – a case of masturbatory auto-asphyxiation. For more than a week, the public debate about gay sex subsided in favour of ever more lurid revelations and speculation, and campaigners suffered renewed fears that 'Back to Basics' could still blow the campaign off course.

Parliamentary business managers finally bit the bullet, however, by naming the evening of Monday 21 February as the day. On the day of the debate, the campaign was once again front-page in almost every newspaper in the country. And from 7 p.m. that evening several thousand lesbians and gay men began gathering outside Parliament for a candle-lit vigil, the mood for which was set by the news of the death two days earlier of the queer activist and film-maker Derek Jarman, for whom a one-minute silence was held.

Inside the Commons chamber two hundred MPs were present as Edwina Currie opened what she called 'a historic debate'. It was, she said, 'the first time in a quarter of a century that the age of consent for homosexuals has been discussed by the House of Commons. The taboo of silence that has denied the sexuality of young gay men has been decisively broken.'

Mrs Currie, who compared Britain unfavourably to the rest of Europe, was barracked and jeered by her own side during her speech. When she suggested that an equal age of consent was the mark of a civilized society, some Tories cried out, 'Rubbish!'. She seemed nervous at first, struggling at times to be heard against a background of noise from the Tory benches. Significantly, all of the hostile interventions during her speech came from Conservatives.

It was left to the former Labour leader, Neil Kinnock, and the shadow Home Secretary, Tony Blair, to make the most forceful and passionate speeches in favour of equality. Mr Kinnock said an equal age of consent would be 'equitable, rational and wise'. He said that he himself had undergone a conversion from being a supporter of the compromise position of eighteen to favouring equality at sixteen. Eighteen seemed 'sensible, liberal and realistic,' he said.

> Then, just as I was comfortable with that, the facts started to intervene. I had made the assumption that young men and young women were somehow more able to determine their sexuality if they were heterosexual . . . On reflection, however, it became difficult for me to convince myself . . . If I and the majority of other heterosexual men knew our sexual orientation by the age of sixteen, why should not homosexuals be equally sure of their sexual orientation? . . . In other countries, a common age of consent at sixteen has not damaged those societies or corrupted their youth.

Mr Kinnock's powerful speech and the arguments in favour of equality were undermined, however, when he admitted that he 'gave thanks' that his own son and daughter were not gay.

However, by the end, Mr Kinnock rallied, regaining his stride in the face of a Tory intervention. John Gorst, of Hendon North, a self-confessed waverer, asked how far ahead of public opinion MPs should go. Mr Kinnock replied:

> In some cases we follow public opinion, but in other cases, it is our duty to step slightly ahead. If, in 1967, our pre-decessors in this House had waited for a consensus of the public opinion before supporting a change in the law, we would still have total criminalization of homosexual beha-viour. The change that came about twenty-seven years ago was an advantage for our society. In the quarter of a century that has passed, we have come to realize, as the Wolfenden Report did a long time before 1967, that people determine their sexual orientation before reaching the age of sixteen. Join me and take the further step of admitting that it is wrong that the behaviour of people following the orientation that is natural to them should be criminalized. I ask the House to do no more in 1994 than it was wise enough to do in 1967.

Mr Kinnock concluded:

> The new clause will help to protect young men. It would provide them with a basic legal framework for making vital decisions about themselves without the danger of criminality . . . The new clause is . . . also about encouraging respect for those who are different – one of the basic tests of our democracy. It is about tolerance, equality before the law and the free secure and pluralistic society we want to build, whatever else divides us in the House.

In contrast to Mr Kinnock's eloquent and passionate speech – which was received in respectful silence by the House – the next speech, which would eventually win the day for eighteen, was delivered in a fumbling and hesitant manner by Sir Anthony Durant. His contribution had many of his colleagues squirming with embarrassment and shifting uneasily in their seats.

Sir Anthony relied heavily on a thirteen-year-old document from the Home Office Policy Advisory Committee which had concluded that young men do not mature until they are approaching the age of eighteen. He quoted approvingly the opposition to equality expressed by the director of Relate (the marriage guidance agency), and prayed in aid the Archbishop of York's article in the *Independent*. Dr Habgood had written that a compromise of eighteen would signal 'that homosexuality in young men is neither to be treated as uncontroversial nor to be penalised beyond the age of maturity. A reduction of three years will provide an opportunity to assess the social consequences.'

Sir Anthony's line of argument was picked up by Home Secretary, Michael Howard, who quoted the 'Wilfenden Report' (*sic*) to argue that 'a boy is incapable at the age of sixteen of forming a mature judgement about actions of a kind that might have the effect of setting him apart from the rest of society'. 'There are likely to be, not all, but a number of young men between the ages of sixteen and eighteen who do not have a settled orientation and who may benefit from the extra time. . . . That is the essential point.'

Despite cogent interruptions from MPs on both sides of the House who challenged Mr Howard's logic, the Home Secretary insisted that:

> the majority of parents would surely wish their children to grow up with the desire and possibility of marriage and children. It is a fact that the way of life we are currently discussing involves an abandonment of that possibility which sets those people who choose it apart and which requires the criminal law to give all the protection that it can to the young and vulnerable before they are confirmed in that orientation and before they take that decision.

Mr Howard's shadow, Tony Blair, raised the debate to an altogether higher plateau. Insisting that the issue was one of discrimination and equality, he set out an uplifting case for change. However, before he got fully into his stride, he was ambushed by the eccentric and unsteady figure of Sir Nicholas Fairbairn, Tory MP for Perth and Kinross, on this occasion sparing us his tartan trews.

For him, the matter at hand was a simple one. Heterosexuality, he averred, is normal; whereas homosexuality is about 'putting your penis into another man's arsehole'. The rest of his comments were drowned by the ensuing uproar. Though the

Speaker reprimanded him – 'we can well do without language like that' – Sir Nicholas had raised a subject which was clearly on the minds of most MPs but which has received scant attention throughout the entire campaign for reform.

Bill Walker, Tory MP for Tayside North and one of the arch-opponents of change, was moved at this stage to ask the chairman whether it was indeed 'in order to describe what it is that we are debating – the actual act?'. But Tony Blair told Sir Nicholas, to the amusement of many, 'I do not think that I will answer that intervention.'

Rejecting Michael Howard's arguments, Mr Blair continued his speech by contending that:

> being homosexual is not something that people catch, are taught or persuaded into, but something that they are. It is not against the nature of gay people to be gay; it is in fact their nature. . . . At sixteen, boys and girls, particularly nowadays, are aware of their sexuality and that sexuality is normally developed with those of their own age, not with predatory elders. However, let us assume for the purposes of argument that there is a small minority that fits into the category that has been described. How would use of the criminal law assist such a situation? . . . How does the criminal law help to resolve that confusion? Indeed it merely complicates it. It deters many from seeking the information, advice and help that they need.

Mr Blair brought his peroration to a climax with an emotional plea for 'the courage to change'. 'It is wrong to treat a man as inferior because his sexuality is different. A society that has learned, over time, racial and sexual equality can surely come to terms with equality of sexuality. That is the moral case for change tonight.'

A number of speeches followed of which only two, one from each side, contributed significantly to the debate. Tristan Garel-Jones, Tory MP for Watford, a former junior Foreign Office minister, distrusted by the right for his suspected role in Mrs Thatcher's downfall and for his Euro-enthusiasm, spoke strongly for sixteen. 'The age of eighteen is not a happy compromise,' he said. 'Compromises only work when all parties agree with them. In this

case, the homosexual community will be gravely disappointed. . . .
It will bring the matter back to the House of Commons again and
again and again. The vote for eighteen will not make the issue go
away, but a vote for sixteen will.'

Mr Garel-Jones addressed many of his remarks to his own
side, scorning 'Back to Basics' with its 'homilies to single mothers'.
He pointed to the missing elements of Michael Howard's speech.

> He has made no mention of his intention rigorously to
> enforce the law if the committee votes for the age of consent
> to be lowered to eighteen. . . . He did not mention the
> guidance that he would give to police officers about enforcing
> that law. . . . or how much of the public resources he intended
> to devote to enforcing the law. . . . We are not in the business
> of voting for guidelines; we want laws that are rigorously
> enforced and applied. . . . I fear that if we vote for eighteen,
> we shall end up with the worst of all possible worlds.

Speaking in the closing minutes of the debate, Chris Smith,
MP for Islington South and Finsbury, the only openly gay member
of the Commons, began his remarks with a warm tribute to the late
MP, Jo Richardson, who had been a long-standing supporter of
lesbian and gay equality:

> She deeply wished to be present to vote for this clause.
> Perhaps we shall do something to pay tribute to her memory.
> . . . The kernel of tonight's debate is the argument about
> equality. . . . I believe in the fundamental principle that we
> are all equal before the law. At present the law does not
> permit that for young gay men. This country has laws that
> say that one may not discriminate on the grounds of race or
> gender. Perhaps those laws are not always implemented as
> Parliament wished when it passed them, but they say that one
> shall not discriminate. But the law discriminates in respect of
> the relationships of young gay men. To my mind that means
> that it should be changed.

He challenged the Home Secretary's assertion that young gay
men could be converted into being gay. 'That is not so. We are who

we are. No amount of attempts by anyone to convert us into something else would pose a threat or a danger. . . . Yes, we are different, we have a different sexuality but that does not make us less valid or less worthy citizens of this country, yet the law at present says that we are.' He ended by quoting the poet A. E. Housman:

> Oh who is that young sinner with the handcuffs on his
>   wrists?
> And what has he been after that they groan and shake
>   their fists?
> And wherefore is he wearing such a conscience-stricken
>   air?
> Oh they're taking him to prison for the colour of his hair.

As the vote approached, the House filled up rapidly, almost to capacity, and there was a palpable sense of excitement. The vote had to be taken twice as the first attempt was declared invalid. And the tension mounted as MPs filed into the lobbies for the second time to reject sixteen by 307 votes to 280, a majority of just twenty-seven. The announcement was greeted with jubilation by the Tory Right.

In a third division, MPs accepted eighteen by the huge majority of 265 votes. Activist Lisa Power cried from the public gallery, 'Thanks for nothing!'. Came the smug reply from a Tory MP, 'Don't mention it!'.

When the news of the vote reached the candle-lit vigil outside the Palace of Westminster, the crowd attempted to storm the Parliament buildings, hammering on the doors and climbing statues to wave banners. The police were badly rattled by the ferocity of the assault. After more than an hour, the demonstrators marched up Whitehall to stage a sit-down protest at the gates of Downing Street, shouting 'sixteen now! sixteen now!'. There were eight arrests in an atmosphere charged with anger and emotion. The rage of the demonstrators was almost universally condemned even by ostensibly liberal commentators, but it was considered by the gay press to be entirely understandable.

Rather than embracing a concept of equality which befits a modern democracy, a truly British coalition of fundamentalist Christians, uptight traditionalists and working-class homophobes had chosen, in the face of heart-rendingly powerful argument, to reaffirm the notion of homosexuals as 'the other'. The set-piece debate which defines our place in British society for much time to come was over in just three hours, after a campaign which had matured over a quarter of a century. The vote was lost though the argument appeared to have been won.

In the following weeks and months, the Bill completed its passage through Parliament. The lowering of the age of consent to eighteen gained approval in the House of Lords. Gay male sex in the armed forces was decriminalized, but the ban on lesbians and gay men serving in the forces was written into the Bill – enshrined in the criminal law for the first time. And in one remarkable success for gay campaigners, the House of Lords agreed to create a new statutory offence of 'male rape'.

Along the way the government dropped hints that it might indeed be high time for a full Sexual Offences Bill to accommodate pressure from many quarters for a full-scale review of all sex offences legislation. Suggestions by the Stonewall Group that they would attempt to use the Criminal Justice Bill to have the offence of 'gross indecency' repealed had come to nothing. And while the age of consent could, according to the optimists, be equalized at sixteen in another Criminal Justice Bill, only a Sexual Offences Bill could even hope to address more technical questions such as the everyday problem of arrests of gay men for 'gross indecency' in 'public' places or in the darker reaches of gay clubs – arrests which were proceeding apace before, during and after the age of consent debate.

Achieving symbolic justice and equality for gay men with an equalization of the homosexual and heterosexual ages of consent seemed perhaps not too far away, but achieving freedom of sexual expression appeared a far more complicated affair.

Chapter two

Lesbian and Gay Rights Campaigning: A Report from the Coalface

Anya Palmer

FOR the citizens of the new South Africa, 1994 will be remembered as the year apartheid died. We can all take inspiration from the success of their long struggle for a democracy open to all, and indeed from their new constitution which guarantees equal rights to all, including lesbians and gay men.

But there is more to democracy than the right to vote. For lesbians and gay men in Britain, 1994 could go down in history as the year Parliament reaffirmed our status as second-class citizens by refusing to enact an equal age of consent; the year Parliament reaffirmed a system of sexual apartheid.

It may seem far-fetched to compare the situation facing lesbians and gay men with the terrible oppression of apartheid. After all, lesbians and gay men in Britain are not denied the vote, are not forced to live in overcrowded townships and do not live in shacks without electricity or running water. Yet to my mind the comparison stands. What apartheid denied to black people was full citizenship, and what British law and policy denies us is full citizenship. Consider the facts:

- Gay men are not entitled to equality under the law. There is an unequal age of consent for gay sex (a law which criminalizes the very young men it claims to protect) and there is a law against 'gross indecency' which applies only to gay male sex.

- Lesbians and gay men pay taxes to maintain a defence force in which they are not allowed to serve. This policy is maintained on the hypothetical grounds that if they were allowed to serve they would be a disruptive influence and would force themselves on others.
- Lesbians and gay men are not entitled to equal treatment and non-discrimination on the grounds of sexuality; they are not entitled even to claim equal pay and benefits with their heterosexual colleagues.
- Same-sex relationships are officially deemed not to exist. Same-sex couples are denied immigration rights, pension rights, inheritance rights, tax perks for married couples, and next of kin visiting rights.
- The law says lesbians and gay men do not have families, they have only pretend families. Society tells young lesbians and gay men that they are second best, that heterosexuality is a better way of life, and it also tells the children of lesbian mothers or gay fathers that they do not come from real families.

This is the sexual equivalent of apartheid. Lesbians and gay men are set apart from society, and society then blames them for setting themselves apart. And there is no legal redress under the unwritten constitution. Nearly every example of discrimination outlined above has been upheld by the European Commission of Human Rights.

Unfortunately the difference between this form of apartheid and the racist variety is that, while the latter is now completely discredited, the sexual apartheid outlined above can still be found, give or take some variation, in nearly every country in the world.

Nevertheless we are now witnessing a profound shift in social attitudes, the beginning of a time when sexual apartheid will be seen for what it is. There is a growing movement for change, and, especially in the last few years, a growing recognition by heterosexuals of the injustices lesbians and gay men face. To look back now to ten years ago, when I came out, is to know we have come a very long way in that time. Looking forward and speculating about ten years hence, I feel very confident that the position of lesbians and gay men in society will have changed beyond recognition.

This chapter is less of a theoretical analysis, more of a report from the coalface. I work as a campaigner for the lobby group Stonewall. I propose to look at where lesbians and gay men as a movement are coming from and where we are now, to examine in some detail the recent age of consent campaign, and to try and suggest ways in which we can take our cause forward.

The background

There has been a lesbian and gay rights movement in Britain since the 1960s. And there has been a flourishing community and business sector which has grown steadily since gay male sex was decriminalized in 1967. Yet for a number of reasons the political movement was in decline for most of the 1970s and 1980s and did not keep step with the growing community.[1]

During the 1980s, in particular, political campaigning involved a fairly small number of people, and lesbian and gay rights issues came to be associated very strongly with the Left. At a time when the Right held power in the House of Commons by a large majority, the result was a community wide open to attack, especially when there was a backlash of anti-gay prejudice as the AIDS epidemic took hold.

The attack came in 1987 with Section 28 of the Local Government Bill, which aimed to ban local authorities from 'promoting' homosexuality (for text see p. 129 below). The measure was highly controversial and was met with protest on a huge scale, but still passed into law in June 1988. The campaign against the clause had been very creative, extremely high-profile and had won support from a substantial part of the population, but party political polarization was enough to guarantee its passage – only three Conservative MPs voted against it.

Section 28 has been described as the British equivalent of the Stonewall riot.[2] Without denying the impact of the Stonewall riot itself through the importing of Gay Liberation Front from America, I would have to agree that Section 28 was a defining moment. It helped to politicize a new generation of lesbians and gay men, people like myself who had come out in the early 1980s and were not activists in any sense of the word, who perceived only hazily, if at all, that we were lacking basic civil rights. The marches against Section 28 were much larger than the Pride march was at the time, and on a day-to-day level just out in the street it was exciting to see so many people wearing 'Stop the Clause' badges. This was before the days of red ribbons, and the badges gave us a new visibility. I had never realized there were so many of us. Or were some of those people just supportive heterosexuals? It hardly mattered.

But marching was not enough. Some of those who afterwards analysed the campaign against the clause drew the lesson that not only were lesbians and gay men ill equipped to fight the clause because of their wide-scale disaffection from the political process, but that, if they had been better organized, the clause would never have taken them by surprise in the first place. It was not as if there had been no warning signs. In 1986 a well-researched booklet purporting to show how public money was being used to promote homosexuality to children had been paid for, printed and used by the moral Right to lobby MPs,[3] and in December 1986 a backbench bill forbidding local authorities from promoting homosexuality had been tabled by Lord Halsbury; this bill had passed several stages before falling at third reading in May 1987, and the Prime Minister herself had said it was a great pity it did not complete its passage.[4] Yet in December 1987 the lesbian and gay community was still caught by surprise when the clause that was to become Section 28 was tabled. It was introduced late at night and passed its second reading immediately; this meant the principle had been approved, which made it practically impossible to delete the clause itself from the bill, and no amount of lobbying efforts could do more than try to water down the clause and lessen its impact.

Some activists concluded that we as a community would have to learn to lobby, we would have to access the political process and we would have to organize across the political spectrum if we were ever to repeal Section 28 or indeed to campaign proactively for equal rights in other areas.

The result of this analysis was that the Stonewall Group was born. Initially consisting of no more than a small group of activists, mainly drawn from three groups which had campaigned against Section 28 (the arts lobby, the media lobby and the Organization for Lesbian and Gay Action, OLGA), Stonewall's aims were quickly agreed to include fundraising for an office and full-time staff for a new lobbying organization, to be independent of government or local government funding, and to be run, somewhat controversially, on a management committee basis, like many of the new AIDS charities, rather than on a democratic membership basis. The organization would work towards legal equality and social justice for lesbians and gay men, using a combination of lobbying, campaigning, research and education. The first paid worker was appointed in 1989 and since then Stonewall has grown to a point where it now employs five staff and involves hundreds of people as volunteers and thousands as paid-up supporters. Since 1992 the number of supporters has grown to the point where they also constitute a powerful lobbying force. At the same time there has been a shift in the emphasis of Stonewall's work from being largely behind-the-scenes lobbying to placing much more emphasis on grassroots campaigning.

Stonewall's increased grassroots work has become possible only as the support base has grown, but the difference it makes to our lobbying is enormous. Although we are using very traditional lobbying techniques such as letter-writing, which is clearly less colourful than direct action, the simplicity of letter-writing allows us to mobilize people on a wider scale than ever before. Thus Stonewall in its work both draws on and in itself further contributes to the increased visibility of the lesbian and gay community in the 1990s.

The birth and growth of Stonewall is of course only one outcome of the new wave of activism in the wake of Section 28. Others include the birth of OutRage!, a creative direct action group in 1991; the expansion of the lesbian and gay publishing sector; the growth of lesbian and gay groups in trades unions and in political parties; and the enormous growth in the scale of the annual Pride march and festival, and other festivals such as It's Queer Up North and Glasgay. All these and more have contributed to the visibility which now gives lesbians and gay men a political force we have never known before.

Where we are now

It was never guaranteed that there would be a vote on the age of consent in 1994. How did it happen? For some years now an equal age of consent has been widely viewed as top priority among lesbian and gay activists, and in the gay press – but that in itself didn't make it happen. It moved up the agenda in 1992 when Tory MPs like Edwina Currie and Sir John Wheeler spoke out in favour of equality, but slipped back down when Sir John lost his chairmanship of the Home Affairs Select Committee, which we had hoped would review the issue and recommend equality. Under the new chairman, Sir Ivan Lawrence, such a review was neither likely to happen nor likely to make favourable recommendations if it did.

From then on lobbyists gave up on the idea of a review and set their sights on a backbench amendment to the Criminal Justice Bill (1993–4). Stonewall and TORCHE (the Tory Campaign for Homosexual Equality), began lobbying for a free vote on the age of consent as part of that bill as early as 1991. What really made the difference, though, was personal letters from individuals. Edwina Currie always told people that the single most important thing for them to do was to write to their own MP, rather than to her – she was in some danger of being seen as the MP for lesbians and gay men. TORCHE said the same thing, and Stonewall took up the refrain. In the summer of 1993 Stonewall distributed fifty thousand copies of a survey on the age of consent. This was a piece of action-research – the last question was 'Are you prepared to write three letters for an equal age of consent?' Hundreds of people who said yes were sent briefings and asked to write to their own MP and to John Major and the Home Office.

As the success of this tactic became apparent we realized that there were thousands more people out there willing to write. In the autumn we distributed fifty thousand copies of *The Case for Change*, with briefings on the issues and tips on how to lobby your MP. Most of the people who were writing would have never written to their MP before, so we had to start by educating people on the way to go about it. We also began to use the community networks to mobilize people. With the help and support of *Gay Times* and lesbian and gay groups up and down the country, we were able to distribute tens of thousands of the briefings through their mailing lists. Those who did write as requested may have been disappointed to receive standard letters from Downing Street and the Home Office saying that there were 'no plans' for further legislation in this area, but only two months later a vote was announced. From discussions with Home Office officials we later discovered that for months the Home Office had been getting more letters on the age of consent than on any other issue.

Once it was announced that there was going to be a vote, there was a third surge of letter-writing, this time on a massive scale. Stonewall moved into full gear, contacting everyone on our database personally asking them to write to their MP, calling people in key constituencies at home. And people did write, in their thousands. There can be little doubt that it was these letters that made the difference. One Conservative MP told us a few weeks before the vote that he had had fifty letters in favour of equality and only one letter against. The letters were all individual, personal and clearly genuine. This had helped make up his mind to vote for equality.

From the copies of letters which were sent to us we know that people from all walks of life wrote letters, including heterosexuals, people of all parties, and in particular gay men and lesbians young and old. Many of the most moving letters came from older gays, telling of the torments they had faced in their youth, and expressing the hope that the younger generation would no longer have to go through the same thing. There were also letters from young gay men, some of whom didn't dare give their name and address. But an extraordinary number did state their sexuality in their letters, making the whole campaign a sort of grand-scale coming out exercise. Until this debate MPs had often expressed doubts whether they had many gay constituents, or whether, if they did have gay constituents, the age of consent was something they really cared about. Most MPs need no longer be in any doubt on this point.

Stonewall was not the only organization by a long shot to encourage the lobbying of MPs. TORCHE helped to lobby Tory MPs, Democrats for Lesbian and Gay Action (DELGA) lobbied the

Liberal Democrats, OutRight Scotland lobbied the Scottish MPs, other local and regional groups targeted their MPs, trade union groups lobbied their sponsored MPs, a Jewish group lobbied Jewish MPs, a Catholic group lobbied Catholic MPs, and so on. Information technology helped here in the form of Stonewall's database of MPs, which we used to pool the latest information with all these groups, producing a gradually diminishing list of those who still needed lobbying and those who had now committed themselves to vote for equality. It also helped us to identify which MPs were responding to lobbying, and to target further lobbying where there were most gains to be made. People in these constituencies were sent extra mailings asking them to visit their MP in person.

There were lessons to be learnt, of course. For example we learnt not to take anyone for granted. For some reason Stonewall had assumed that Ann Taylor, the shadow education secretary, would vote for equality along with most of her colleagues in the shadow Cabinet, and we were shocked when she did not. Again, many of those who had still not committed themselves even on the day of the vote did in the end vote for equality, having been lobbied up to the last possible moment, whereas one or two who had said, under pressure, that they would vote for sixteen, and had been taken off our lobby lists, turned out to have reneged by the time their votes were cast. (Stonewall will be publishing a booklet of MPs' voting records before the next general election, and where we have evidence of broken promises this information will be included.)

Although in the end the motion for an equal age of consent failed, in my view the movement for equality made massive progress in 1994. Forget, for a moment, the twenty-seven votes we lost by and the thirty-nine Labour MPs who voted against equality. Think of our achievements:

- We got this issue on the agenda, and we did so at a time when no one wanted to think about it – this was probably the hardest thing of all to do.
- We mounted the biggest ever proactive campaign for equal rights for lesbians and gay men, and we began to realize our own strength from it. We learnt on the hoof that we could put aside our differences, work together, and use the vast

network of social, political and business groupings among us to work for change.

- We finally broke the party political barrier so that it became respectable for Conservative MPs to vote for equality: forty-four Conservatives voted for sixteen, more than the thirty-nine Labour MPs who voted against, opening the way to further support in the Conservative Party – which we will need if we are to win any lasting change.

- We finally forced MPs to say where they stood. For twenty-seven years MPs have not had to make a stand on lesbian and gay issues. If nothing else we now know who our friends are. In future elections we can and will hold our elected representatives to account for the way they voted.

- We forced the opposition to justify themselves, and in doing so they turned out to be divided and confused. For a long time during the run-up to the debate, no one seemed prepared to put forward an amendment for eighteen. One of those who eventually did so, Tim Devlin, was later persuaded to vote for sixteen himself.

The MPs can be divided into several distinct groups depending on how they voted and the reason given for their vote:

1 Those who think homosexuality, which they equate largely with 'buggery', is disgusting and unnatural; these people voted against any reduction and are probably not worth talking to.

2 Those who believe, with impeccable logic, that it is OK for young gay men to have sex at eighteen because that is the age at which they can vote. Some of these explicitly reject the equality argument because they say homosexuality and heterosexuality are not equal. Others are simply concerned to follow rather than lead public opinion and therefore their opinions may change in time.

3 Those who say the age of consent should be eighteen for everyone – these people accept the equality argument, even if they did not vote for it this time.

4 Those who prefer incremental change: they know the age of consent should be equal and they know it will go down to

sixteen eventually, but twenty-one to sixteen would just be too much too soon – especially for their constituents.

5 Those who voted for sixteen. *This is the largest single group.* It includes many who were converted during the campaign from groups 2, 3 and 4.

We very nearly made it this time. Next time I believe we will convince most of groups 3 and 4, and some of group 2, and we will win.

Of course an equal age of consent is only one part of the reforms we are seeking. The amendment which lost so narrowly on 21 February would only have made the age itself equal, not the penalties, which are harsher for under-age gay sex, nor would it have addressed the fact that young men under the age of consent are themselves criminalized whereas young girls are not, nor would it have ensured that the law was applied even-handedly. And that is only the age of consent. We also need other reforms to the criminal law as well as civil law and family law as outlined above.

But it will not be this difficult to get every little change, because the vote on the age of consent vote was not just about the age of consent. We fought the campaign on the principle of equality, and most of the MPs who voted for an equal age of consent accept this principle and they will vote for equality in other areas as well. The hardest part – and this is the lesson we must learn – will not be winning the vote but getting a vote to happen in the first place. So where do we go from here?

Getting our issues on the agenda

It is unlikely that there will be another vote on the age of consent until after the next general election. This is probably a good time therefore to take stock of where we now stand on other issues and – I believe – recognize just how far down the political agenda they are.

We need also to recognize that in some areas a simple demand for equality does not translate easily into an achievable, or desirable, political goal. Demands for an equal age of consent were relatively easy to formulate, but do we want, for example, the right to get married? Or do we want to reject marriage altogether? And if so, is that a realistic or achievable objective?

We must keep in mind the need for practical achievable goals which can be clearly understood and fought for. The achievement of reformist goals such as recognition (in some form) of lesbian and gay relationships will go beyond reform, transforming society's understanding of sexual relations and indeed of family relationships. In my view this is true even if we do end up with TV ads featuring happy gay couples talking about how they bought their furniture at IKEA.

We also need to identify and build alliances with other interest groups who stand to gain from such a transformation. For example there is the women's movement, and by that I don't mean just those who identify as feminists. A great deal of Edwina Currie's mailbag of support during the campaign came from middle-aged housewives who simply found it offensive that boys should be protected from predatory older males but girls of the same age should not.

The following list will I hope give some indication of just how much work there is still to do.

The criminal law

The age of consent is now on the agenda but most people still do not realize that this is only one problem in the criminal law, that there is an offence called 'gross indecency' which applies only to consenting gay sex between men, or that hundreds of men are charged with this offence every year.[5] As a gay-only offence, gross indecency carries all the stigma of homosexuality itself. Men charged with gross indecency often have their names printed in the local paper and they can lose their job as a result.

We need to establish the principle that sexual offences law should be gender-neutral, and that the only valid distinctions are whether there are victims of any kind and whether there is informed consent. In doing this we will have to tackle such questions as when and where sex in public or semi-public places is acceptable, and what, if any, consenting sexual activities the law should rightly prohibit. For example, some of the most homophobic MPs were quick to point out that 'buggery' between heterosexuals is completely illegal, so in the interests of equality 'homosexual buggery' should also be completely illegal! Another example is raised by the judgement in the Operation Spanner case where eight adult males were convicted for participating in consensual SM sex in private. Can it be right that the law should prohibit all SM sex, even with consent? And do we really want equality with heterosexuals on prostitution laws when the law gives female prostitutes even fewer legal rights than male prostitutes, and when the whole framework of laws dealing with prostitution clearly needs revising?

Where the existing law is plainly absurd, unnecessary or unfair we will have to address ourselves to wider questions than equalization. But we have first to raise the issues and point out what a mess our sexual offences law is in.

We also have to think carefully about how we would want the law to be reviewed. We should not forget the way in which the age of consent fell off the agenda in the 1970s. It had been an issue for activists ever since 1967, but in 1975 the Labour Government, in response to growing calls for an equal age of consent, set up a wholesale review of sexual offences law. The recommendations were not ready until 1984, so for nine long years it was difficult to lobby on that whole area since it was under review. And when the recommendations came they were less than adequate, recommending for example an age of consent of eighteen for gay sex. Even then they were not acted on, because by then the Labour Government that had set up the review had long since lost power. So we do need to be very wary of allowing any future campaign to lose momentum while a committee of the great and good goes off on a long-term project to review the law.

Discrimination

The disability lobby has been bringing civil rights bills before Parliament year after year for several years now. Because it has been doing so we now know what the government's objection is: cost. This is interesting, because traditionally the Conservative position on discrimination has been to oppose legislation altogether and encourage voluntary initiatives instead. There now seems to be a tacit recognition in the case of disability discrimination that voluntary initiatives are not enough. Objections on grounds of cost could not be made in relation to sexuality discrimination. It costs no more to employ a lesbian or a gay man than it does to employ a heterosexual. But we won't even know what the government's objections are unless we start raising the issue. If we are going to have to bring presentation bills for ten years in a row before we get somewhere, we may as well start now.

We also need to unite behind demands for an end to the ban on lesbians and gay men serving in the armed forces. We cannot afford to ignore the witch-hunts – the fact that lesbians and gay men can automatically lose their jobs as a matter of government policy diminishes every one of us. The position will be reviewed in 1995–6 and we should perhaps be planning now for a mass campaign in 1995 to lift the ban.

We should also start raising the issue of equal pay. At present there is no requirement on an employer to pay lesbians and gay men the same in terms of pensions and other partner-related benefits as they do to married or even cohabiting heterosexual employees. Historically it is worth noting that the women's movement succeeded in winning the right to equal pay before it won the right to equal treatment. We should perhaps learn from this. It is often difficult to prove discrimination, but it is very easy to prove unequal pay. And it probably affects more of us than we realize. According to a survey Stonewall carried out,[6] 90 per cent of lesbians and gay men who are in full-time employment do not receive equal pay and benefits in relation to their partners, so we should be able to mobilize a very broad campaign on that basis.

The demands for equal pay and equal treatment provide ideal objectives for us to campaign for now, because there is already very broad agreement on what our demands are in this area. They are easily formulated and they provide us with local goals as well as national goals. As well as campaigning for new laws binding on all employers, we can campaign for the same objectives in each and every workplace, and we can work to build support for these objectives in trades unions and political parties.

Recognition for same-sex relationships

Government policy on lesbian and gay relationships is never under any circumstances to acknowledge that they exist. This affects most same-sex couples in one way or another. They have no immigration rights if one partner comes from outside the European Community. Lesbian and gay workers have no right to a lifetime pension for their partners, although our contributions help to subsidize pensions for colleagues' partners, and our national insurance helps to pay for the widow's pension.

A question was recently asked in the Commons about whether same-sex partners of prisoners could benefit from the assisted visiting scheme if they were hard up. The scheme is designed to help keep families on a low income together while prisoners serve their sentences. Relatives eligible for assistance include spouses, children, siblings, and partners – defined as persons of the opposite sex with whom the prisoner has a child or with whom they have lived for four months before being imprisoned. The question was asked by Barry Jones MP on behalf of a lesbian constituent who was looking after her partner's children while her partner was in jail, but could not afford to travel hundreds of miles to see her. The Home Secretary, Michael Howard, clarified that the scheme would not be extended to cover such cases because, as he put it: 'I do not believe taxpayers' money should be used for this purpose.'[7]

This is the contempt in which we are held by the people who rule Britain. Even those who think monogamy is a hardwood used to make furniture should sit up and take notice, because the view is that our money is good enough to help pay for these schemes, but our relationships are not good enough to benefit from them.

Similarly, in response to a motion for debate tabled by Lynne Jones MP, the immigration minister Charles Wardle explained why Home Office policies on common law couples could not be applied in the case of same-sex couples: 'Discretion will not normally be exercised in [a homosexual] applicant's favour unless compelling compassionate circumstances are present.' From other statements by the Home Office we know that the sort of 'compassionate circumstances' referred to mean 'the grave illness of the British partner'. In other words a non-UK partner might be admitted if his or her partner was dying of AIDS but not if they were merely healthy and planning to spend the rest of their lives together. The only reason Mr Wardle could give for this policy was that 'English law does not afford any legal status to homosexual relationships. Immigration practice in relation to homosexuals reflects this general position. It would be illogical to try to construct an immigration policy which did not accord with the general position.'[8]

Heaven forbid that any government policy should ever be illogical. Yet if one were to argue that policies should always be well-founded in logic one might well ask why the Home Office can recognize the same-sex partners of its own staff where the couple has been together for six months or more, but cannot recognize the same-sex partners of UK citizens or prisoners.

What remedy should we be asking for? It is tempting to argue for a partnership law on the Danish and Norwegian model. But a partnership law might raise more problems than it would solve. Some people would argue we should take special privileges away from married couples rather than extend them to registered same-sex couples. Others rightly point out the risk that a partnership law would confine the new rights acquired to those who felt able to lodge their names publicly in a partnership register. Certainly in Denmark there has been a very low take-up rate, particularly among women.

However, at the moment the question is academic, because as far as the government is concerned the issue is not up for discussion, and most of the rest of the country does not even know that the problem exists.

The Danish partnership law was not passed until the whole issue of same-sex relationships was reviewed by a special commission. Perhaps we need to push for a similar review. We certainly need to push to get the issue further on to political agendas. This issue has not been pushed, as the case for an anti-discrimination law has, by the trade union movement, and it is not clear at the time of writing whether even the Labour Party or Liberal Democrats would do anything about it.

On a grassroots level, we can help raise the issue by lobbying for partnership recognition in the workplace (see the discussion on equal pay above). The whole area of pensions, for example, provides a clearly defined goal for us to work towards. We can also push partnership issues by consumer activist methods, such as campaigning for equal treatment on special deals for couples. It is clearly true that there is much less discrimination in the provision of services than there is in the employment field. We need to make the point that discrimination is bad for business if the consumers start to complain about it or take their business elsewhere. For example airlines, whose marketing strategies are based very much on wooing and retaining frequent fliers, should be an easy target for pressure to make couples deals available to same-sex couples. Once one airline agrees to this, the others will be forced to follow suit.

One of the theoretical attractions of a partnership law is that there is a whole range of laws where same-sex couples are treated differently. A partnership law would, at least for those who felt able to register, reform all of these areas overnight. Yet given that in practice a partnership law is so far down the agenda as to be off the page, a fight for partnership recognition on a whole range of fronts from immigration to airline tickets seems a good way to proceed.

Parenting

Childcare law in Britain is actually less discriminatory than most. Even in Denmark and Norway it is still not possible for lesbians and gay men to adopt. Childcare law and policy is based on the principle that the interests of the child come first. This principle, which had been gradually established in the courts, was formally expressed in statute law by the Children Act (1989). The result is that in making decisions about who should look after a child, the law no longer looks at the formal legal relationship between the parties – mother, father, stepmother etc. – but rather looks at the de facto relationships in order to decide where a child would be best off. Thus a child can be placed in the primary care of its de facto parent rather than with its birth parent if in practice it has always been looked after by the de facto parent. This principle could apply even if the de facto parent was, for example, the lesbian partner of the child's mother, and such an interpretation has recently been applied in one case in Manchester.

Nevertheless it is still difficult for lesbians and gay men to foster children and extremely difficult to adopt. But it is hard to formulate our demands on this issue. They cannot be framed in terms of our right to look after children – they must be framed in terms of the child's right to the best possible home. From our point of view this means that all we can argue for is the right not to be discriminated against in childcare law and policy. But until we have gained broad acceptance of the principle that we are entitled to equal citizenship, we don't stand a chance in this debate.

Education

Education as a whole is a battleground, and sex education is particularly contested. It is one of the thorniest issues we face. Yet we have to face up to it. A Stonewall survey of over two thousand lesbians, gay men and bisexuals[9] found that 82 per cent had learnt nothing about homosexuality in school, and 89 per cent had learnt nothing about lesbianism. Even worse, only 2.5 per cent of young gay men who had received sex education since 1987 had been told anything about safer sex for gay men. We face a situation in which sex education is framed in terms of parents' rights rather than children's rights, in which all children, and all parents, are assumed to be heterosexual, and the popular view on whether sex education should address homosexuality is much the same as the House of Lords' view of lesbianism in the 1920s: don't talk about it or you might give them ideas.

That education, and not just sex education, should address homosexuality is important for three reasons:

- to validate the young lesbians and gay men who currently find themselves ignored in the classroom and bullied in the playground;
- to ensure that young people know what they need to know about safer sex before they have unsafe sex; and
- to educate young heterosexuals about their fellow citizens and hopefully prevent them growing up into bigots and queerbashers (this affects all of us, not just those of us who are still in school).

Obviously we will need the repeal of Section 28 but we also need to campaign for sex education guidelines which recognize the points made above.

Conclusion

By now it should be clear that we have our work cut out for us to get our issues on to the political agenda. But we also have a wealth of means by which to do so.

Although we face perhaps the most oppressive legislation in Europe, we also have one of the most open and thriving communities of any country in Europe. We can use this to help build a movement for change. As Angela Mason has observed, the age of consent campaign settled for us the long-running question whether or not there is a lesbian and gay community. We have an extensive network of lesbian and gay businesses, social and community groups. We have more clubs, social groups, helplines, newspapers, magazines, radio programmes, TV programmes, than most of our European friends could dream of. We have the largest Pride march in Europe, and the only twenty-four-hour Switchboard. As communities go, we are more out than most. Every year there are more of us on the Pride march. Every year we become more visible. It was this visibility which made the age of consent campaign possible.

We are beginning to establish the infrastructure of networks and organizations that are increasingly successful and individuals who are articulate and willing to be engaged in the broader political culture. The experiences of the 1980s when lesbians and gay men were alienated from the wider political culture and scapegoated are behind us. We are, perhaps for the first time, becoming a real political force, a voting block that all political parties will need to recognize and respond to. As the politics of the 1990s unfolds, single-issue and pressure-group politics are increasingly the basis of politics for individuals who are unable to feel an involvement in traditional party politics. Our role as activists will be to develop this re-involvement in politics – to inform and educate individual lesbians and gay men about the legal issues and social policies that affect all our lives. In part this will be achieved by simply encouraging greater visibility: coming out, after twenty-five years of modern lesbian and gay politics, remains the central key to our liberation. Coming out, telling the truth about our lives, is still the most important contribution any of us can make. We have our work cut out for us, certainly. But we are beginning to form ourselves into a political constituency, one which will not be denied. As surely as the people of South Africa have overturned apartheid, our time will come.

Notes

1   T. Barnett and L. Power, 'Gathering strength and gaining power: how lesbians and gay men began to change their fortunes in Britain in the nineties', in A. Hendricks, R. Tielman and E. van der Veen, eds, *The Third ILGA Pink Book* (New York: Prometheus Books, 1993).

2   S. Jeffrey-Poulter, *Peers, Queers & Commons: The Struggle for Gay Law Reform from 1950 to the Present* (London: Routledge, 1991).

3   R. Tingle, *Gay Lessons: How Public Funds are used to promote Homosexuality among Children and Young People* (Pickwick Books, 1986).

4   Jeffrey-Poulter, *Peers, Queers & Commons*, p. 211.

5   'Gross indecency' in law refers to any consenting sex between two men other than anal intercourse which is an offence because one or both parties is under age, and/or because the act does not take place in private. Gross indecency is *always* consensual; where one party does not consent another charge would apply such as indecency assault. In 1992 there were 774 prosecutions, 577 convictions and eight sentences of immediate custody for this offence.

6   A. Palmer, *Less Equal than Others* (London: Stonewall, 1993).

7   Michael Howard, quoted in the *Daily Mail* (26 January 1994).

8   *Hansard* (4 May 1994).

9   *Arrested Development? A Survey on the Age of Consent and Sex Education* (London: Stonewall, 1994).

10   A. Mason, 'New departures', *Rouge*, vol. 16, 1994.

Chapter three

Searching for Immutability: Homosexuality, Race and Rights Discourse

Paisley Currah

If the Court [in *Bowers* v. *Hardwick*] was unwilling to object to state laws that criminalize behavior that defines the class [sodomy], it is hardly open to a lower court to conclude that state-sponsored discrimination against the class is invidious. After all, there can hardly be more palpable discrimination against a class than making the behavior that defines the class criminal.[1]

Sexual orientation will not be a bar to [military] service unless manifested by homosexual conduct. The military will discharge members who engage in homosexual conduct, which is defined as a homosexual act, a statement that a member is homosexual or bisexual, or a marriage or attempted marriage to someone of the same gender.[2]

IN 1986, in its now infamous *Bowers* v. *Hardwick* decision, the highest court in the United States concluded that there is no 'fundamental right' to engage in homosexual sodomy. A few years earlier, Michael Hardwick had been charged with violating Georgia's sodomy law when a police officer discovered him engaging in 'sodomy' with another adult male in the privacy of his own bedroom.[3] Hardwick had decided to use the occasion to challenge the constitutionality of Georgia's sodomy law, all the way up to the Supreme Court of the United States.[4] Many lesbian and gay rights advocates considered Hardwick's lawsuit an ideal test case for challenging Georgia's sodomy laws, since Hardwick had been engaging in that activity in the privacy of his own home. In the tradition of constitutional interpretation in the USA, there is a practice of identifying rights that are not explicitly mentioned in the Bill of Rights as no less fundamental than those that are.[5] Hence the Supreme Court has ruled that a right to privacy, though not explicitly enunciated in the Bill of Rights, is implied by other explicit rights, such as the right of free association and 'the right of the people to be secure in their persons, houses, papers, and effects, against unreasonable searches and seizures'.[6] It is this right to privacy that provides the justifications for Supreme Court decisions upholding rights of reproductive freedom, including *Roe* v. *Wade* (abortion), and *Griswold* v. *Connecticut* (contraception).[7] Hardwick challenged the constitutionality of the Georgia sodomy law on this basis, claiming that the law violated his constitutional right to privacy, since its enforcement would – and did – bring the state (the police) quite literally into his bedroom.

The Supreme Court decided in *Bowers*, however, that the unenumerated rights that are 'implicit in the concept of ordered liberty' did not include the right to commit homosexual sodomy. In fact, the Court found Hardwick's claim to a right to engage in homosexual sodomy as 'at best, facetious'. *Bowers*, then, put a definitive end to using the courts to make the claim that the 'Constitution confers a fundamental right upon homosexuals to engage in sodomy'.[8] The Court implicitly upheld any law that criminalizes any of the sexual practices of gay, lesbian, and bisexual people.[9] At the same time the Court refused to rule on the constitutionality of laws that apply to *heterosexual* sodomy; presumably, however, heterosexual conduct would have been protected from state sanction because of the earlier reproductive rights decisions that had found and upheld a fundamental right to engage in non-procreative heterosexual sex.[10]

Bowers constituted a serious defeat for gay and lesbian rights advocates in the United States. Although sodomy laws are rarely enforced, they are most effective in their indirect effects on gays and lesbians: for example, sodomy laws justify solicitation and loitering laws that are used to entrap men soliciting sex from other men in public places. (In a few states, sodomy laws apply only to male–male sex.) Sodomy laws can also make lesbians, bisexuals and gay men ineligible for public employment in many states, because of the presumption that those who apparently regularly engage in illegal sexual acts are ineligible for public employment.[11] The outcome in *Bowers*, however, did not put an end to the pursuit of rights in the United States for gay, bisexual and lesbian people;[12] it simply precipitated a shift in strategy, from challenging the criminalization of homosexual 'conduct', specifically homosexual 'sodomy', to challenging discrimination against people on the basis of a homosexual 'identity'. The new legal approach entailed arguing that the 'suspect' or 'quasi-suspect' class status in the law that has been applied to the categories of race and gender, among others, should be applied to sexual orientation.[13] If gays, lesbians and bisexuals were designated a suspect or quasi-suspect class, then laws that discriminated on the basis of sexual orientation would be much easier to challenge successfully. However, because the *Bowers* decision effectively allows states to criminalize homosexual sex (whatever it may be), advocates for gay, lesbian and bisexual rights are forced to argue that the sodomy decision has no bearing on our designation as a suspect class. The epigraphs above, however, allude to the difficulties that ensue in pursuing an emancipatory strategy that distinguishes 'conduct' from 'identity', a strategy that is premised on the notion that conduct and identity *can* be completely split: the author of the *Padula* decision (quoted in the first epigraph) decided that sodomy as a behaviour defines homosexuality; the military regulations (quoted in the second epigraph) summarily define 'homosexual conduct' as, among other things, identifying oneself as a homosexual.

For the purposes of queer activism, then, the identity-based approach to what used to be called 'gay liberation' must undergo a thorough interrogation. What works? Why? If identity-based claims to freedom from discrimination are successful, what practices/ identities are construed as outside the bounds of these rights claims? If identity-based rights claims are unsuccessful, how and why does the identity/conduct opposition collapse? What remains a legitimate target of discrimination? Are identity-based rights claims necessarily based on the affirmation that homosexuality results from an innate, immutable characteristic, similar to the way that race is believed to be an immutable characteristic in legal discourse? In which spheres do identity-based rights claims have legitimacy and in which spheres are they subject to regulatory norms?

For political and legal theorists, the phenomena of gay, lesbian and bisexual identity-based rights claims maps on to current controversies about the relation between identity politics and rights discourse. The appearance of the idea of 'homosexual rights' in the popular imagination may be recent, but the political and theoretical issues raised by the rights claims of gay, lesbian, bisexual people are not. Indeed, the debate about bestowing the right of equal protection of the laws to people on the basis of sexual orientation only exacerbates dilemmas already present in the western rights tradition. The 'death of man' brought on by the nineteenth-century historicism of Marx, Darwin and Nietzsche has forced the 'rights of man' – a doctrine announced with such certainty during the Enlightenment but only partially realized by that period's revolutionary offspring[14] – to founder on the twin shoals of relativism and constructionism.[15] Both the postmodern and the communitarian critique of the idea of rights have questioned whether an atomistic, transcendental subject exists to exercise those rights.[16] These critiques of the notions of the self associated with the rights tradition are especially pertinent to gays, lesbians and bisexuals since the outcome of equal protection claims in the courts usually hinges precisely on the question of how homosexual identity is produced. First, if subjectivity is constructed in and through social practices, as communitarian critiques of rights discourse have suggested, or if identity is as radically indeterminate, contingent and fragmented as postmodern critiques of modernity's ontology have suggested, can rights be conferred on such indeterminate subjects? Second, if rights themselves are merely the contingent products of history, can the pursuit of rights be meaningful? Third, how do we conceptualize, for both analytic and strategic purposes, the relation between the law and the culture that produces it? Finally, if identity is neither 'pre-political' nor constituted outside a narrowly construed public sphere, what is in store for the future of identity-based rights claims?

My analysis centres on US case law because gay, lesbian and bisexual people in the United States have often turned to the judiciary for redress. That is not to say that queer emancipatory political struggles are articulated only in the courts; one can argue, however, that the ubiquity of rights claims in the courts and of 'rights talk' in general in the popular discourse demonstrates the centrality of rights discourse in the political national imagination in the USA.[17] Moreover, the particular institutional practices of the courts – a certain interpretive anarchy between competing herme-neutic strategies, a capricious willingness on the part of the judges and justices to address every conceivable issue related to the question at hand (including questions of identity formation, agency and immutability) and the privilege assumed by practitioners to repeat cultural myths, anxieties and stereotypes around issues of sexuality as authoritative fact – make the courts especially sympto-matic of the larger cultural constructions of citizenship, sexuality and rights.

More importantly, the judiciary's pronouncements have real effects on the lives of those challenging the law. As the late legal historian Robert Cover writes, the interpretive acts of judges 'take . . . place in a field of pain and death'. The Supreme Court's decision in *Bowers* v. *Hardwick*, for example, upheld the right of the state of Georgia, and, implicitly, any state that desires to do so, to send individuals convicted of engaging in sodomy with someone of the same gender to jail for up to twenty years; examining *Bowers* and other cases, then, is more than a matter of performing a close reading in order to make a formal argument about, for example, the play of *différance* inscribed on the text. But one might take issue with the radical dichotomy that Cover insists exists between 'the social organization of law as power and the organization of law as meaning'.[18] The former has to be produced, reproduced and legitimated through the cultural organization of meaning, of which the law is a part – whether one sees the cultural organization of

meaning as totalizing, hegemonic or always and inevitably fragmented. When Justice Burger writes in his concurring opinion in
Bowers that '[d]ecisions of individuals relating to homosexual
conduct have been subject to state intervention throughout the
history of Western civilization' and '[c]ondemnation of those
practices is firmly rooted in Judeo-Christian moral and ethical
standards', he is not only exposing the state's monopoly over the
legitimate use of violence, he is also participating in the cultural
production and reproduction of discourses, of 'meaning', around
sexuality. Rather than signifying a radical dichotomy, those two
aspects of Justice Burger's pronouncements have 'meaning' only in
so far as they are articulated together, within a larger discursive field
that makes them both intelligible. And just as Justice Burger's
pronouncements cannot intelligibly be separated into the two
separate realms – one of power, the other of meaning – neither does
it make sense to separate the judiciary's pronouncements from the
cultural constructions that produced them.

Identity politics redux

A poll commissioned by the *New York Times*, headlined
'How the public views gay issues', found that 78 per cent of the
respondents agreed that homosexuals should have equal rights in
terms of job opportunities, but only 46 per cent agreed that
homosexual relations between consenting adults should be legal.[19]
Another poll found that individuals who believed that homosexuality was inborn were much more likely to support civil rights
for lesbians, gay and bisexuals than those individuals who believed
homosexuality was a matter of choice.[20] These results reflect the
axiomatic truths of both the popular and legal vernacular of
contemporary rights discourse: that discrimination on the basis of a
trait perceived as an unchangeable characteristic is unfair; it is also
axiomatic, however, that if the identity under which one prefers to
live is perceived as a choice, then the state has no business in
protecting that 'lifestyle' against discrimination. Taken together,
one might postulate that these polls reflect 'the public's' aversion to
behaviour and acts, such as sodomy, that it construes as an aberrant
choice of free will; this same 'public', however, is apparently more

willing to tolerate (within limits) an 'identity', an 'orientation', that it construes as fixed from birth, or at least unchosen.[21]

Because race has served as a foundational category of civil rights discourse in general, and of anti-discrimination law in particular,[22] both the popular and legal discourses on these issues are always mediated, either directly or indirectly, through an analogy with race – and in the popular and legal vernacular of rights discourse it is a truism that race is an immutable characteristic.[23] For example, the most common argument made in favour of completely lifting the US Department of Defense's ban on homosexuals serving in the military compares the military's resistance on that issue with its resistance to integrating African American soldiers and sailors into all-white units in the 1940s. Or consider this counter-example: when a civil rights bill that would have added sexual orientation to the other protected categories was proposed in the New York State legislature, one state senator succinctly enunciated the 'common-sense' notions of the popular discourse about rights, agency and immutability:

> I don't condone their life style. I think it's their choice and they have to live with it. I look at it different than an Italian person or blacks or Chinese, people who have genetic traits that they can't do anything about. Sexual orientation is their choice and I don't think it's our place to force people that might have a moral opposition to it to have to put up with it and condone it.[24]

It is no surprise, then, that many advocates for gay, lesbian and bi-sexual people now attempt to portray homosexuality as an identity in itself – defined primarily not by one's sexual practices but by one's sexual orientation, one that is not chosen but assigned. Indeed, a brief submitted to the Supreme Court by counsel to the Georgia man charged with practising 'sodomy' argued that homo-sexuality 'may well be a biological condition' and 'in any event [is] usually not a matter of choice and rarely subject to modification'.[25] And, more recently, the gay, lesbian and bisexual plaintiffs challenging the constitutionality of Colorado's anti-gay 'Amendment Two' (discussed later in the chapter) also argued that sexual orientation is not a matter of choice:

the origin of sexuality – whether homosexual or heterosexual – appears to involve multiple genetic and environmental factors. [The Coalition for Family Values, the sponsors of Amendment Two,] emphasized an environmental understanding of sexual orientation because it was then easier to argue that homosexual orientation can be changed. Even 'the most staunch environmental theorists,' however, posit that sexual orientation is set in place between ages 4 and 7, a view that is inconsistent with the notion that a child of that age chooses sexual orientation. . . . Sexual orientation is highly resistant to change by the time a person is an adult.[26]

The assertion that homosexuality is not a chosen but an assigned identity constitutes an attempt to correspond not only to popular fictions about rights and immutability but also to the prevailing legal standards in US constitutional law. These standards require, among other things, that a group should exhibit 'immutable characteristics' before the judiciary will intervene to shield a 'discrete and insular minority' from state-sponsored discrimination. But this emphasis on immutability is more than an attempt to conform to the legal doctrine; the quest for equality on the basis of an authentic, fixed orientation moves the mainstream of the gay, lesbian and bisexual movement firmly into the domain of 'identity politics'.[27]

As identity politics comes more and more under attack by postmodern critiques of the subject,[28] and by communitarian critiques of the partiality of 'interest group liberalism',[29] it is, ironically, the mainstream wave of the gay, lesbian and bisexual movement that now affirms, more than in the past, the concept of a 'gay identity': one that is fixed, unchangeable, immutable.[30] Yet it was only in the nineteenth century that the concept of the 'homosexual' – and soon after the 'heterosexual' – came into being. Foucault has identified the discursive construction of 'the homosexual' as 'a species' in the nineteenth century;[31] before that paradigm shift, the concept of sexuality in western discourse was more likely to be arranged into categories organized around sexual *practices*. John D'Emilio has argued that the emergence of a homosexual identity is tied to the social transformations brought on by the rise of capitalism, including the introduction of wage labour, the increased mobility of workers and the dissolution of the family as a unit of production.[32] Of course, the recognition that homosexuality is culturally produced, as is heterosexuality, does not mean that one's sexual orientation is necessarily a choice, the result of individual agency; neither, however, does it necessarily entail that there exists an ascriptive 'homosexual identity', fixed since birth. Unfortunately, however, the socially-constructed approach often becomes the oft-forgotten third term, quietly dropping out of the 'nature/nurture' debate.

Steven Epstein writes of a contradiction between the constructionist theories of sexuality and the actual practices of the lesbian and gay political movement:

> Gays in the 1970s increasingly came to conceptualize themselves as a legitimate minority group, having a certain quasi-'ethnic' status, and deserving the same protections against discrimination that are claimed by other groups in our society. To be gay, then, became something like being Italian, or black, or Jewish. The 'politics of identity' have crystallized around a notion of 'gayness' as a real, and not arbitrary difference. So while constructionist theorists have been preaching the gospel that the hetero/homosexual distinction is a social fiction, gays and lesbians, in everyday life and in political action, have been busy hardening the categories. Theory, it seems, has not been informing practice.[33]

But the recognition of the historically contingent, rather than a natural, or essential, basis for homosexual and heterosexual identity does not compel us to regard those identities as meaningless, hollow categories. Indeed, the very appeal to gay and lesbian people of the idea of homosexuality as an 'ethnic group' demonstrates the potency of identitarian categories in organizing our experiences into coherent, intelligible narratives. The error lies in assuming that identity is either essential, natural, or genetic, *or* that it is an entirely irrelevant derivative of structural arrangements, over which an individual agent has no control. An individual's invention of his or her self as, among other things, lesbian or gay does not require that an analysis of the social construction of identity be suspended. As Anthony Appiah contends, emphases on either agency or structure need not be contradictory. Instead, he argues, we might see the relation between structural explanation and the logic of the subject 'as a competition not for causal space but for narrative space: as different levels of theory, with different constitutive assumptions, whose relations make them neither mutually competitive nor mutually constitutive, but quite contingently complementary'.[34] Even in the postmodern schema, then, we might find space for political agency by distinguishing, according to Judith Butler, a socially-constituted subject from a determined one.[35]

But if homosexuality as an assigned, not chosen, orientation becomes the basis for legal challenges to state-sponsored discrimination, the legal explorations of those claims often steer us into the false nature/nurture binarism. The crux of these challenges routinely centres on determining whether homosexuality is a choice or is an immutable characteristic. Corresponding to this agency/immutability opposition is a distinction between 'homosexual identity' and 'homosexual conduct'. Any legal strategy that asserts a fixed, authentic homosexual orientation must also hold that homosexual conduct is not central to the construction of homosexual orientation – since homosexual orientation is already assigned at birth, or by early childhood. Following the same logic represented in the polls above, and the logic of the legal doctrine around rights discourse, the identity politics strategy asserts that it is homosexual orientation itself rather than homosexual conduct that should be the basis for the inclusion of gays, lesbians and bisexuals – *as* gays, lesbians and bisexuals – into the category of citizenship. (It is important to point out that, in the legal arena, this strategy was largely forced on advocates for gays, lesbians and bisexuals by the Supreme Court's decision in *Bowers* v. *Hardwick*, which held that states may criminalize homosexual sodomy.) But, if one agrees with the postmodern critique of modernity's ontological notions, that there is 'no doer behind the deed . . . that "the doer" is constructed in and through the deed',[36] the effect of arguing that only the 'doer', not his or her 'deeds', belongs inside the boundaries of rights discourse may only play into the same epistemological and ontological notions that have worked against gays, lesbians and bisexuals in the first place.

Separating orientation from conduct

Litigation around issues of sexual orientation has loosely followed three different strategies. First, before the court ruled definitively in *Bowers* that homosexual sodomy was not a fundamental right, much litigation on behalf of gay, lesbian and bisexual people centred on the issue of sexual freedom, following the line of argument that one of the rights implicitly guaranteed by the notion of substantive due process was the right of intimate association. The presence of sodomy laws in the majority of states in the United States in 1986 made an assault on the constitutionality of sodomy laws a priority. The decision in *Bowers*, however, forced lesbian, gay and bisexual advocates to shift their strategy from emphasizing sexual practices to stressing sexual orientation. This second strategy involved pursuing the same quest for suspect class status that those advocating against racial and gendered categorizations had sought. Finally, since the special status strategy has recently proved ineffective,[37] the latest tactics now emerging involve a shift to a different kind of equal protection analysis. The most recent tactics do not require gays, lesbians and bisexuals to be designated as a suspect or quasi-suspect class. Rather, one of the new strategies is to ask that the 'fundamental right' of gays, lesbians and bisexuals to participate equally in the political process should be protected;[38] the other recent tactic is to challenge the laws using only the minimum standards set forth in equal protection analysis, standards that do not require the designation of a suspect class status.

After the disastrous *Bowers* decision, litigation strategies for lesbian, bisexual and gay rights in the United States changed course radically from the privacy-oriented reasoning successful in the earlier *Griswold* and *Roe* reproductive rights decisions. Upholding the criminalization of homosexual conduct (typically 'sodomy') forced gay, lesbian and bisexual rights advocates to adopt a different strategy: using the equal protection components of the Fifth and Fourteenth Amendments, the revised strategy was to argue that discrimination against homosexuals as a group was unconstitutional. Certainly, after *Bowers*, litigating to protect classes of people on the basis of their status as gays, lesbians and bisexuals rather than on the basis of their sexual conduct – much of which had been deemed constitutional to criminalize – seemed perhaps the only viable avenue left to follow.

In the terms of art of legal doctrine, the goal became the successful classification of homosexuals as a 'suspect' or 'quasi-suspect' class; only groups that constitute a 'discrete and insular minority' may be deemed 'suspect' or 'quasi-suspect'.[39] The actual doctrine of 'suspect class' emerged, ironically, from the Supreme Court's decision in *Korematsu* v. *United States*, upholding the internment of Japanese Americans during the Second World War. In that case, Justice Black wrote that 'all legal restrictions which curtail the civil rights of a single racial group are immediately suspect. That is not to say that all such restrictions are unconstitutional. It is to say that courts must subject them to the most rigid scrutiny.'[40] Under standards set by the Supreme Court, to determine if the class is suspect, the plaintiff must prove: first, that the group in question has suffered a history of discrimination; second, that the group in question exhibits obvious, immutable or distinguishing characteristics; and third, that the group is politically powerless to address discrimination through legislative channels.[41] Thus far, race, national ancestry, alienage, and ethnic origin have been designated suspect classes; women, men, and illegitimate children have benefited from quasi-suspect classification.

When a group has received the suspect class designation, legislation or state constitutional amendments that discriminate against members of that group will be subject to 'strict scrutiny' by the courts. In these cases, the state must demonstrate a compelling state interest before the legislation will be upheld. Quasi-suspect class status means that the law in question will be subject to 'heightened' or 'intermediate' review. In these cases the state must show that the law in question is substantially related to a sufficiently important government interest. In other cases in which a plaintiff does not belong to a suspect class or quasi-suspect class, the legislation must merely be rationally related to a legitimate state interest. In these rational standard cases, the burden of proof lies with the plaintiff, rather than with the state as in cases involving suspect or quasi-suspect classes.[42] The purpose of these three tests is to limit the ability of the courts to intervene into the democratic process that gave rise to the legislation in the first place. As Justice

White stated, '[w]hen social or economic legislation is at issue, the Equal Protection Clause allows the States wide latitude and the Constitution presumes that even important decisions will eventually be rectified by the democratic process'.[43]

The shift in strategy after *Bowers* not only involved shifting the focus to homosexual orientation in itself from homosexual practices; *Bowers*, in fact, forced the advocates of gays, lesbians and bisexuals to prove that the judicial effect of the decision should be limited to sanctioning only the criminalization of homosexual sodomy – and not to sanctioning also state-sponsored discrimination against homosexuals as a class. Without such an interpretation, *Bowers* would apply to all cases involving homosexuality, rather than just cases specifically touching on the question of homosexual sex: the task was to prevent interpretations of *Bowers* like the one in *Padula* v. *Webster*, in which a federal appellate court upheld the Federal Bureau of Investigation's decision not to hire an otherwise qualified lesbian applicant. (See first epigraph.)

Proving that there is a viable distinction between homosexual conduct and homosexual orientation is no easy task. The orientation/conduct distinction has been upheld in other areas, most notably when the Supreme Court ruled that states cannot criminalize the status of being addicted to narcotics, rather than just the act of using them.[44] But many higher courts have not chosen to make a distinction between conduct and identity when faced with the prospect of applying it to homosexuals.[45] Especially in more regulated areas – the armed forces, elementary and high schools, and industries and agencies requiring security clearances – where much of the litigation has taken place, the notion that a distinct 'homosexual identity' exists, apart from the sexual practices that gays, lesbians and bisexuals might engage in, has not been accepted by the courts.

Much of the litigation around issues of sexual orientation involved the old Department of Defense regulations banning homosexuals and those who engage in homosexual conduct from serving in the military. It might seem that the new policy recently designed by the Clinton administration would be a significant improvement over the old one since homosexuality in itself is no longer a bar to military service;[46] but by including any speech that involves 'coming out' into the proscribed category of 'homosexual conduct', the new policy actually codifies much of the recent case law on the issue because in many cases it was the issue of 'coming out' as a homosexual that was contested as a violation of the First Amendment right to free speech, as in the case of Miriam Ben-Shalom, a US Army Reserve sergeant. Following the trends in the case law, most notably Ben-Shalom's case, the new policy takes the step of defining most types of 'coming out' speech as conduct: 'The military will discharge members who engage in homosexual conduct, which is defined as a homosexual act, a statement that the member is homosexual or bisexual, or a marriage or attempted marriage to someone of the same gender.'[47]

Ben-Shalom's status as a homosexual was determined solely by her own public acknowledgement that she was a lesbian; no proof that she had engaged in homosexual acts, including making 'homosexual advances', was brought forward by the Army. Ben-Shalom was involuntarily separated from the Army in December 1976 under Army regulations that allowed for discharge of any soldier who 'evidences homosexual tendencies, desire, or interest, but is without overt homosexual acts'. During the initial hearing, it was adduced that Ben-Shalom 'had publicly acknowledged her homosexuality during conversations with fellow reservists, in an interview with a reporter for her division newspaper, and in class, while teaching drill sergeant candidates'.[48]

After an initial defeat in a federal district court, the Army adopted a new regulation that defined a homosexual, in part, as 'an individual who is an admitted homosexual but as to whom there is no evidence that they have engaged in homosexual acts either before or during military service, or has committed homosexual acts'.[49] On the basis of this new regulation, after over a decade of litigation, during which not only the Army but all segments of the Armed Forces, and the Department of Defense itself, adopted new (now outdated) regulations regarding homosexuality (and *Bowers* was decided), a higher court eventually found the Army's failure to re-enlist Ben-Shalom constitutional.[50]

According to the Seventh Circuit panel, the new regulations were constitutional because the Supreme Court had determined that the government can limit First Amendment freedoms if it does so only incidentally in the course of pursuing other legitimate goals.[51] In this case, the legitimate goals were deemed to be the suppression of homosexual conduct; thus the suppression of performative statements such as 'I am a homosexual' is justified because it is only incidental to the legitimate goal of prohibiting homosexual sodomy. According to the opinion,

> Ben-Shalom is free under the regulation to say anything she pleases *about* homosexuality and about the Army's policy toward homosexuality. . . . What Ben-Shalom cannot do, and remain in the Army, is to declare herself to *be* a homosexual. Although that is, in some sense, speech, it is also an act of identification. And it is the identity that makes her ineligible for military service, not the speaking of it aloud. [emphasis in original.][52]

Any public construction of herself as a lesbian, any speech or deeds that might 'reveal' her status, is thus prohibited. The new regulations fit into this justification for limiting homosexual conduct only too well since 'coming out' speech is now formally included in the definition of homosexual conduct – and the suppression of homosexual conduct has been deemed a permissible state goal by the courts, and now by the Clinton administration and Congress.[53] These new regulations echo an earlier case involving a bisexual high school counsellor, in which a federal appellate court held that there was, in effect, no distinction between being bisexual and talking about being bisexual. Arguing that there was no way to discover if the plaintiff was dismissed for being bisexual, or for saying she was, the court in this case found the dismissal permissible.[54]

Generally, the distinctions made in First Amendment law have been between distinguishing the more protected category of pure speech from the less protected category of speech plus conduct.[55] But in the case of gays, lesbians and bisexuals, it is limiting speech *qua* speech that has been held constitutional. In the *Ben-Shalom* case, then, the court implicitly recognizes that the construction of a homosexual identity is always articulated through practices, including speech: following the logic of the opinion, then, there is no sphere in which Ben-Shalom's speech, her 'act of identification', would be protected – be it coming out in a newspaper, to a class or to a friend in private. Although it was Ben-Shalom's speech that occasioned her termination, the court reasoned that it was not the speech itself, but what the speech revealed about her sexual orientation that justified the Army's refusal to re-enlist her.[56] The new Department of Defense policy on homosexuals serving in the military apparently reverses the speech/conduct distinction: homosexual identity itself is no longer a bar to military service, but any speech or conduct that indicates that the service member in question is homosexual constitutes grounds for discharge. Speech, conduct and identity remain inextricably bound up together. Thus the new regulations actually codify the judicial interpretations, extending the domain of 'homosexual conduct' to circumscribe even further the public construction of a homosexual identity. The identity/conduct distinction that advocates for gay, lesbian and bisexual rights have been so eager to assert is collapsed, in this instance through the mediating category of speech: homosexuality is articulated through speech, and speech has been summarily defined, by the courts, and by the Clinton administration, as conduct.

Defining speech *as* conduct is not the only way in which the new guidelines and the legislation vastly expand the definition of 'homosexual conduct'. The old Department of Defense regulations, and the courts' justification for upholding them, are premised on the *Bowers* decision upholding the constitutionality of criminalizing homosexual sodomy; the new guidelines, however, extend the definition of homosexual conduct to include not just homosexual sodomy but 'any bodily contact which a reasonable person would understand to demonstrate a propensity or intent to engage in homosexual acts'.[57] The directive applies to conduct both on and off the base. Dancing with someone of the same gender, or holding hands, would thus constitute 'homosexual conduct'. Thus the effect of the new policy is to construct a bifurcation between private and public practices, leaving room only for a wholly private construction of a homosexual orientation. Homosexuals can serve if they 'pass': if they make no statements about their sexuality, if they refrain from any intimate contact with someone of their own gender. The concept of passing carries with it the assumption that one's acts, one's behaviour, even one's politics, can be split from one's definition of self, that the self is not constructed in and through social practices.

While the courts were busy upholding the Department of Defense's prohibition on homosexuals serving in the armed forces, basing their arguments on *Bowers*'s sanctioning of criminalization of homosexual sodomy, they found no problem with the Department of Defense directive that exempts heterosexuals who engage in homosexual conduct from dismissal.[58] Similarly, most of the laws prohibiting 'sodomy' do not address the genders of those engaging in it. Heterosexuals are not up in arms about these statutes, however, because they are almost never prosecuted on the basis of them. Instead, the statutes are used directly, though infrequently, to regulate homosexual behaviour; more importantly, and more frequently, they are used indirectly to justify discrimination against homosexuals as a group.

Foucault has identified the historical moment in which the medicalized and pathologized *identity* of 'the homosexual' displaced the juridical dominance of the *practice* of sodomy in producing and regulating sexuality.[59] Although many of the statutes were originally written when the juridical dominance of the sodomitical model prevailed,[60] the application of these statutes has now shifted, if we agree with Foucault's paradigm shift, to the 'homosexual' model. And the *Bowers* decision codifies that shift: as a decision on the constitutionality of Georgia's sodomy laws, its logic depends for its coherence on the equation of homosexual identity with sodomy, the equation of the sick 'invert' with the juridical sodomy-practising subject produced by the law. That equation is implicitly made when the Supreme Court refused to consider the question of whether laws criminalizing heterosexual sodomy are constitutional, and thus implicitly granted to heterosexuals the right to engage in sodomy. *Bowers*, one federal appellate judge concludes, is not about sodomy *per se* but about homosexuality, since 'sodomy is an act basic to homosexuality'.[61] In fact, in a petition for a rehearing of *Bowers*, after the Supreme Court had handed down its decision, Laurence Tribe, counsel for Michael Hardwick, noted that the plurality opinion in *Bowers* restricts itself to reviewing the constitutionality of the Georgia statute as applied to homosexual sodomy *even though the gender of Hardwick's partner was never stated in the original complaint*, the only official record of the incident.[62] It is the assumption of Hardwick's identity as a gay man and not as a 'sodomite' that becomes the focal point for *Bowers*. Similarly, both the old discriminatory regulations that governed the presence of homosexuals in the Armed Forces and the new compromise position recently put into law by Senator Nunn's bill ('Don't Ask, Don't Tell') also reflect the medicalized, pathologized 'homosexual' model: the Department of Defense regulations mandated the discharge only of those who adopt or are assigned the identity 'homosexuals'; they did not mandate the discharge of those who engage in 'homosexual sex' but, for one reason or another, are not 'homosexuals'.

The quest for immutability

The distinction between orientation and conduct that gay rights advocates have tried to assert addresses only one aspect of equal protection claims. Even if the courts can be convinced that a proper interpretation of *Bowers* does not preclude equal protection claims, they must agree that homosexuals constitute a suspect or quasi-suspect class: one of the tests, of course, is that homosexuality is defined by an immutable characteristic. Recent Supreme Court opinions have conceded that the trait in question need not be the result of nature but can be the product of social or even legal constructions.

Whereas the binarism set up in the legal discourse of suspect class analysis has previously set immutability in opposition to choice, it has recently shifted to set the effects of social practices in opposition to choice. So, for example, the Supreme Court ruled in *Plyer* v. *Doe* that illegal aliens do not constitute a suspect class because their own conscious actions determine their status as illegal aliens; the Court ruled, however, that the children of illegal aliens are in fact a quasi-suspect class because they did not choose their condition.[63]

Some have argued that the move in suspect class doctrine to recognize that the characteristics on the basis of which a class is discriminated against may in fact be socially constructed mandates the inclusion of gays, lesbians and bisexuals into equal protection analysis. For example, Janet Halley argues that the 'equal protection clause vigilantly protects not monolithic groups but rather the dialogue that generates group identity and suggests that gay rights advocates attend not to product but to process.'[64] While it is true that race, gender, sexual orientation, and ethnicity are all to some degree constructed in and through social practices, in pursuit of consistency we must also recognize that the identity of members of the judiciary is also generated discursively. Thus the problem with an analysis such as Halley's is that it assigns judges and justices to an Archimedean position outside of the discursive structures in which they themselves take part. It is unlikely that the courts will recognize that, since all identity is constructed in and through social processes, the 'fairness' of those processes must be protected: the federal appellate courts' willingness to limit the First Amendment rights of gays, lesbians and bisexuals – in the country with one of the most liberal traditions of freedom in the world – attests to that. In deciding claims of suspect class status for homosexuals, the courts, no less than other institutions, have availed themselves of the social constructions of homosexual (and implicitly heterosexual) identities that inform the culture at large to support their decisions. After all, Justice White's opinion in *Bowers* was explicitly based on the fact that he believed that the right to practise sodomy was not 'deeply rooted in this Nation's history and tradition'.[65] But the recognition that the courts reflect and participate in the cultural production of identity does not mean that those cultural constructions are static.[66]

The precedent-setting opinions may have moved from requiring 'natural' immutable characteristics in order for groups to receive the suspect class designation, to requiring only characteristics that they did not choose, but most courts have steadfastly clung to the presupposition that homosexuality is neither natural nor socially determined but is, to some degree at least, a conscious choice. For example, the Ninth Circuit found in *High Tech Gays* that 'Homosexuality is not an immutable characteristic; it is behavioral and fundamentally different from traits such as race, gender, or alienage'.[67] And the district judge presiding over *Steffan* v. *Cheney* argued that:

On the matter of suspect classifications, the Supreme Court seems to focus on the question of whether an individual *chooses* the characteristic that defines the class. . . . One's race is determined genetically, and one's gender is – unless there is new evidence worthy of a Nobel prize – commonly believed to be a random event. . . . One's national or ethnic origin and whether one was born out of wedlock are characteristics similarly not subject to choice by the person being so classified. . . . Homosexual orientation, plaintiff asserts, is not a matter of choice. . . . [The Department of Defense], on the other hand, agree[s] with the Federal Circuit in *Woodward* that the characteristic is primarily behavioral in nature, and that if man is a mammal in control of his own behavior, he therefore chooses his sexual orientation. As aforementioned, the scientific community is unclear and unsure about many of the causes and attributes of sexual orientation. It is not for the Court to say definitively whether sexual orientation is *always* chosen by the individual, but it is apparent that *sometimes* it is chosen [emphasis in original].[68]

Certainly, then, many social theorists have been unfairly denied the Nobel prizes they deserved because neither race nor gender is solely determined genetically: consider the 'one drop' rule that governed racial definition earlier in US history and transvestism, sex changes, transgender behaviour, and even the amount of daily labour that goes into the production of, for example, a feminine appearance.[69] What is interesting here, however, is not so much the assumption that gender and race are determined genetically – as I have shown above, those assumptions are axiomatic in the popular discourse about rights and immutability – but the way this common-sense 'truism' is inevitably invoked to renounce the rights claims of lesbians, bisexuals and gays. In *Woodward* v. *United States*, for example, the Federal Circuit Court held that homosexuality could not be the basis for a suspect class classification because, unlike blacks or women, who 'exhibit immutable characteristics . . . homosexuality is primarily behavioral in nature', adding that the conduct or behaviour of suspect classes 'has no relevance to the identification of those groups'.[70] Thus both arguments, that homosexuality is 'primarily behavioral' – in opposition to the popular ontological beliefs about race and gender – and that it is sometimes 'chosen', are invoked to justify the denial of suspect class status to gays, lesbians and bisexuals.[71]

According to the logic represented in the *Cheney* decision, the classification of race as genetic category, for example, ultimately provides the basis for its designation as a suspect class. However, it is the attribution of some sort of racial 'essence' to certain biological traits that gives rise to racism – and, eventually, to the need for equal protection challenges – in the first place. As Appiah writes,

> The truth is that there are no races: there is nothing in the world that can do all that we ask race to do for us. . . . The evil that is done is done by the concept, and by easy – yet impossible – assumptions as to its application. Talk of 'race' is particularly troubling for those of us who take culture seriously. For, where race works – in places where 'gross differences' of morphology are correlated with 'subtle differences' of temperament, belief, and intention – it works as an attempt at metonym for culture, and it does so only at the price of biologizing what *is* culture, ideology.[72]

In fact, one of the other criteria for suspect class status, as outlined by the Supreme Court, requires that the group in question should have suffered a history of discrimination. Indeed, if one had to attribute more weight to only one of the three criteria for suspect class status, it would seem more appropriate to put the 'history of discrimination' criteria at the centre of equal protection claims: the immutability criteria themselves tell us nothing about whether the equal protection claim is, in fact, warranted. There are innumerable characteristics assigned to each and every one of us that we do not choose, yet relatively few have any bearing on a history of discrimination. It is the cultural constructions produced around some of those apparently immutable, morphological characteristics that actually give rise to discriminatory practices. And thus the effects, the history, the frequency of those cultural constructions must necessarily be the focal point of equal protection analysis, rather than the characteristics themselves. The Supreme Court has often given more weight to the history of discrimination criteria in upholding affirmative action policies, though more recently, with a more conservative Court, the boundaries of the 'history' have been circumscribed in order to limit affirmative action policies.[73] Yet when it comes to adjudicating the equal protection claims of gays, lesbians and bisexuals, the immutability criteria become the justification for refusing to designate homosexuality a suspect or quasi-suspect class.

In short, then, the courts are having it both ways – justifying discriminatory policies on the basis of homosexuality both as a fixed identity and as a mutable behaviour. Obviously, it is inconsistent to construe homosexuality, sometimes, as a fixed identity, rather than merely conduct, and to construe it, at other times, as a choice. The overlap between the identity/conduct equation and the immutability/choice binarism creates a contradiction, one that both generates a certain 'panic' at the thought that homosexuality might be catching and simultaneously fixes homosexuality as stable enough to distinguish the homosexuals from the errant heterosexuals from among those who engage in homosexual conduct under the old Department of Defense regulations, for example.[74] In another case, for example, a federal appellate court upheld the dismissal of an out bisexual high school counsellor, expressing concern that she might somehow cause students to choose bisexuality, or homosexuality.[75] But if one can 'choose' an identity, or 'choose' to behave in a certain way, how can policies discriminating against such a mutable, fluid, identity be practical, or even intelligible? What if the next day the person discriminated against on the basis of their homosexuality chose to be heterosexual instead? And if the identity is indeed fixed, why worry about the effects homosexuals might have, for instance, on students or soldiers? These contradictions represent the epistemic gaps, the definitional crises that ensue when the courts try to come to grips with the fluidity of sexuality, with the myriad practices – discursive, historical, behavioural – that go into the construction of a 'sexual orientation'. Unfortunately, however, these inherent contradictions have not yet caused the courts to agree that gays, lesbians and bisexuals do indeed constitute a suspect class, or that anyone has a fundamental right to engage in same-sex sexual practices.

Rethinking rationality

The most recent strategies pursued by advocates for gay, lesbian and bisexual rights involve making equal protection claims without seeking the designation of suspect or quasi-suspect class status. There are two different approaches to the strategy.[76] The first approach is to convince the courts to safeguard the 'fundamental right' of gays, lesbians and bisexuals merely to enter the political arena, to participate in the political process, in order to fight for substantive rights – such as serving openly in the Armed Services, or engaging in 'sodomy' – within the majoritarian legislative process. As Justice Brennan has argued, '[b]ecause of the immediate and severe opprobrium often manifested against homosexuals once so identified publicly, members of this group are particularly powerless to pursue their rights openly in the political arena.'[77] These types of equal protection claims, then, are limited to seeking protection for the rights of members of 'identifiable' groups to take part in the political processes through which the society's substantive decisions are made.[78] The second approach is merely to invoke the minimal tier of equal protection analysis: to argue that the legislation or regulation in question is not *rationally* related to a legitimate government goal. Since suspect class status has rarely been granted, some legal advocates for gays, lesbians and bisexuals have recently been asking the courts to strike down discriminatory statutes and regulations simply because they serve no rational purpose.

The first approach is best illustrated in the legal challenges to Colorado's homophobic 'Amendment Two', a constitutional amendment initiated by Colorado's Christian Right wing and passed by the voters of Colorado on 3 November 1992 with 53.4 per cent of voters in favour of the amendment.

> *No Protected Status Based on Homosexual,*
> *Lesbian or Bisexual Orientation*
>
> Neither the State of Colorado, through any of its branches or departments, nor any of its agencies, political subdivisions, municipalities or school districts, shall enact, adopt or enforce any statute, regulation, ordinance or policy whereby

homosexual, lesbian, or bisexual orientation, conduct, practices or relationships shall constitute or otherwise be the basis
of or entitle any person or class of persons to have or claim
any minority status, quota preferences, protected status or
claim of discrimination. This Section of the Constitution
shall be in all respects self-executing.[79]

The constitutionality of the amendment has been challenged by nine
gay, lesbian and bisexual plaintiffs (including famed tennis player and
Aspen resident Martina Navratilova), one school board, and the
cities of Aspen, Boulder and Denver. These plaintiffs of *Evans* v.
Romer argued that Amendment Two deprives them of their First
Amendment right to free expression and their Fourteenth Amendment right to the equal protection of the laws. The plaintiffs' advocates did not argue that lesbians, gay men, bisexual people constituted a 'suspect class'; rather, they argued to the court that the
constitution guaranteed a fundamental right to participate *equally*
in the political process because Amendment Two singles out an
identifiable group – gays, lesbians and bisexuals – and puts burdens
on their political participation that it does not put on other
identifiable groups. In a decision that is not the final word on the
case, but that is predictive of the case's final outcome in the
Colorado courts, the highest court of Colorado agreed with this
argument: 'Amendment 2 alters the political process so that a
targeted class is prohibited from obtaining legislative, executive, and
judicial protection or redress from discrimination absent the consent
of a majority of the electorate through the adoption of a constitutional amendment.'[80]

Extending the analysis of a series of US Supreme Court cases
on voting rights issues,[81] the Colorado Supreme Court found that
'the Equal Protection Clause guarantees the fundamental right to
participate equally in the political process and any attempt to
infringe on an independently identifiable group's ability to exercise
that right is subject to strict judicial scrutiny'.[82] In this case
advocates for the gay, lesbian and bisexual citizens of Colorado who
are trying to have Amendment Two declared unconstitutional
achieved the strict scrutiny standard not because homosexuality was
deemed a suspect class but because the right of this identifiable

group to participate in the political process was deemed a fundamental one, one that warranted strict scrutiny because the fairness of
the process itself was being challenged. This decision, then, constituted a significant victory for advocates of lesbian, gay and bisexual
people. Whether the reasoning here will have any bearing on the
homophobic amendments being initiated in over a dozen other
states for the November 1994 elections is another matter. *Evans* v.
Romer itself will likely be brought before the more conservative
United States Supreme Court.

The argument presented to the Colorado court in *Evans* v.
Romer, however, did not entirely escape the identity/conduct
distinction so prevalent in earlier challenges. In order to preclude the
argument that *Bowers* burdens the ability of gays, lesbians and
bisexuals to petition for relief from discrimination, the plaintiffs
were forced to distinguish homosexual conduct from homosexual
orientation: 'a person may have a gay, lesbian or bisexual identity
without engaging in gay, lesbian or bisexual conduct' and '[e]ven if
the right to perform certain sexual acts is not fundamental, it does
not follow that individuals of a particular sexual identity may be
subjected to differential treatment with regard to non-sexual
activities . . . based on their sexual orientation'.[83] Thus the analysis
remains tied to whether or not gays, lesbians and bisexuals are an
identifiable group constituted by homosexual identity rather than
homosexual conduct. In an attempt to assert that *Bowers* was
indeed applicable in cases involving homosexual identity, the
opposing side in *Evans* v. *Romer* (the religious Right wing) defined
the phrase 'orientation, conduct, practices, or relationships' in the
amendment solely in terms of conduct, as 'inclinations, acts, and
romantic or passionate attachments', and suggested that homosexuality is a matter of agency, that 'orientation is synonymous with
"preference"'.[84] But the Right wing's contention that homosexuality was a 'preference' rather than an 'orientation' did not
figure in the Colorado Supreme Court's decision: for this type of
equal protection argument to be successful, it is enough that gays,
lesbians and bisexuals constitute 'an identifiable group' – it is not
necessary to prove that we as a group exhibit immutable characteristics. And that crucial move effectively displaces the agency/immut-
ability binarism from its formerly central position in evaluating the

rights claims of gays, lesbians and bisexuals. The preliminary (and still tentative) victory granted to the gay, lesbian and bisexual plaintiffs by the decision in *Evans* v. *Romer* suggests that this type of equal protection approach may bode well for future civil rights struggles by gays, lesbians and bisexuals:[85] it constitutes a signifi-cant departure from the immutability/suspect-class approach, the crux of which is to assert an assigned 'homosexual identity', which allows significant limitations on homosexual conduct, and thus significant limitations on the construction of a homosexual identity.[86]

I want to end this chapter with an example of the second approach, an analysis of a strategy that is much simpler: arguing that discrimination on the basis of sexual orientation is merely irrational, that it serves no legitimate government interest except to give public sanction to private biases. Consider the analysis of the federal district court judge in the case of Keith Meinhold, a sailor discharged from the Navy after he announced on network television that he was gay. The Navy argued that its ban against gays and lesbians was 'rationally related' to the following goals: 'maintaining discipline, good order and morale; fostering mutual trust and confidence among its servicemembers; the need to recruit and retain servicemembers; and maintaining public acceptability of the Navy'. After analysing the Department of Defense's own (previously suppressed) reports that indicate that homosexuality is not, in fact, incompatible with military service, and after examining the effect of allowing gays and lesbians to serve in the armed forces of other NATO countries, the district judge simply concluded that there was no rational basis for the ban:

> Gays and lesbians have served, and continue to serve, the United States military with honor, pride, dignity and loyalty. The Department of Defense's justifications for its policy banning gays and lesbians from military service are based on cultural myths and false stereotypes. These justifications are baseless and very similar to the reasons offered to keep the military racially segregated in the 1940s.[87]

Certainly, the district judge in this case will not have the last word;[88] undoubtedly, this decision will be challenged all the way up to the

Supreme Court where it stands a good chance of being reversed, because of the tradition of judicial deference to the military. But in other areas, where the judiciary is free to apply the Bill of Rights with full force, it seems likely that 'rational basis' challenges to discrimination against gays and lesbians in other areas will begin to be more successful.

Rather than assert that homosexuality is an immutable identity, or that it is constituted by the choice of a coherent, rational subject, it is perhaps more effective to operate under the assumption that homosexuality (and all 'identities', but homosexuality is the object of analysis here) is socially constructed and thus is constructed in and through social practices that in a democratic society are open to revision. Further, while other approaches are mired (some more than others) in the doctrinal mazes of suspect class analysis – mired in an attempt to prove an immutable 'homosexual identity' analogous to racial identities – the rational basis approach is not tied to essentialist arguments about homosexual identity that preclude challenges to limitations placed on the practices through which homosexual identity is produced.

For example, when a civil rights ordinance that included sexual orientation as a protected category was proposed in Tompkins County (where I lived in New York State), some members of the gay, lesbian and bisexual community tried to add 'transexuality' and 'transgender behavior' to the protected categories of homosexual, heterosexual and bisexual. The leaders of the gay, lesbian and bisexual community and some of the legislators who would eventually vote in favour of the ordinance decided against making those additions. Now one cannot be denied housing or fired from one's job in Tompkins County for simply being bisexual, homosexual or heterosexual. But a woman can be fired for not looking feminine enough; likewise, a man can be fired for looking too feminine. Thus the emphasis on an interiorized, authentic gay, lesbian and bisexual identity fails to protect the actual practices through which sexual orientation, as well as gender, is produced.

This 'rational basis' strategy may appear to be much more naive than those discussed above – on its face the rational basis test is the easiest for defendants to meet. And nothing is more closely identified with the epistemological presuppositions of eighteenth-century rights discourse than the notion of 'rationality'. Indeed, the notion that a rational basis test might provide the most viable challenge to discrimination may seem a dubious proposition since both the statute that sanctions the discrimination and the judicial interpretation that evaluates the statute arise out of the same cultural, discursive and historical constructions that give a particular content to what is 'rational' – a closed hermeneutic circle, seemingly. But it may be that the actual contingency of what is construed as 'rational' at any given historical moment makes the rational basis test the most promising strategy. It is not a necessary condition for the courts to sit at an Archimedean point outside of the cultural processes through which identity is produced; instead, the judiciary's very situatedness compels its interpretative acts both to reflect and to participate in the culture's constructions of sexuality, constructions which are never totalizing – the hermeneutic circle is never entirely sealed. The fact that the *Meinhold* judge's view about the rationality of discriminating against gays, lesbians and bisexuals differs so strongly from those of the other courts attests to the dialogic appeal of the rational basis approach. For example, it was the Supreme Court's decision in *Bowers* that reinvigorated a 'new social movement' of gays, lesbians and bisexuals. And that movement generated an oppositional discourse that provided alternative anti-homophobic narratives which in turn made the military's ban on gays, lesbians and bisexuals seem 'irrational' to the judge in the *Meinhold* case. Just as gay, lesbian or bisexual identity is contingent, then, so too is the content of what at any particular time and place is construed as 'rational'. Further, the rational basis approach, construed broadly, compels anti-homophobic activists to step outside of the narrow legal conventions that constrain the kind of arguments we can make and try to infuse the cultural constructions with counter-narratives. The emphasis in traditional rights discourse on a coherent, atomistic subject manifests the fantasy, unsuccessful as it is, to erase politics. In fact it is the very indeterminacy of identity, and the very contingency inherent in the abstract notion of rationality, that produces political subjects, that makes politics possible.[89]

Notes

1   *Padula* v. *Webster*, 822 F.2d 97, 103 (D.C. Cir. 1987).

2   The new US Department of Defense policy guidelines on homosexual conduct in the armed forces, cited in 'Text of Pentagon's new policy guidelines on homosexuals in the military', *New York Times* (20 July 1993).

3   The officer was delivering an arrest warrant to Hardwick and had been directed to Hardwick's bedroom by a visiting friend who was unaware that Hardwick was at home, and had brought a friend with him. The Georgia statute that Hardwick challenged provides that '(a) A person commits the offense of sodomy when he performs or submits to any sexual act involving the sex organs of one person and the mouth or anus of another'; and '(b) A person convicted of the offense shall be punished by imprisonment for not less than one nor more than 20 years'. Before 1968, the statute had defined sodomy as 'the carnal knowledge and connection against the order of nature, by man with man, or in the same unnatural manner with woman'. The statute was changed in response to decisions which held that the original statute did not prohibit lesbian activity or heterosexual cunnilingus. The constitutionality of the gender-neutral statute as applied to heterosexual sodomy was not reviewed. See *Bowers* v. *Hardwick*, 478 US 186, 188 (1986).

4   The district attorney informed Hardwick that he would not pursue the case, although the charges would still be pending until the statute of limitations ran out. For a complete discussion of all the circumstances surrounding the case, see A. S. Leonard, *Sexuality and the Law* (New York and London: Garland, 1993), pp. 153–69.

5   This convention falls under the aegis of 'substantive due process'. In *Palko* v. *Connecticut*, 302 US 319, 325, 326 (1937) it was decided that the rights not elaborated in the Constitution but that do exist are those fundamental liberties that are 'implicit in the concept of ordered liberty'. In *Moore* v. *East Cleveland*, 431 US 494, 503 (1977), Justice Powell describes these unenumerated rights as 'deeply rooted in this Nation's history and tradition'.

6   US CONSTITUTION, amendment IV.

7   *Roe* v. *Wade*, 410 US 113 (1973), *Griswold* v. *Connecticut*, 381 US 481 (1965). Criticisms of *Roe* v. *Wade* and the privacy line of reproductive cases are often based on asserting their similarity to *Lochner* v. *New York*, 198 US 45 (1905), which relied on the notion of substantive due process to strike down state regulations limiting weekly working hours in the baking industry. *Lochner* now epitomizes the substantive due process argument run amok, and serves as the monstrosity of modern constitutional law – to be avoided at all costs. Unfortunately, for gays, lesbians and bisexuals,

the challenge that had been made to the constitutionality of sodomy laws in *Bowers* occurred only after the Supreme Court had been successfully reconstituted by the Reagan administration into a more conservative institution. The conservatives sitting on the court in the 1980s disapproved of the kind of 'judicial activism' associated with the liberal courts of the previous thirty years.

8   *Bowers* v. *Hardwick*, 478 US 186, 188, 192, 194 (1986) (Justice White, plurality opinion).

9   At the time of writing there are laws prohibiting same-sex and opposite-sex oral and/or anal intercourse in sixteen states; six states criminalize same-sex oral or anal intercourse only. States whose sodomy laws cover both same-sex and opposite-sex sodomy and have not been struck down by the highest state courts or repealed by state legislatures include: Alabama, Arizona, Florida, Georgia, Idaho, Louisiana, Massachusetts, Michigan (struck down by a lower court), Minnesota, Mississippi, North Carolina, Oklahoma, Rhode Island, South Carolina, Utah, Virginia. States whose sodomy laws cover only same-sex sodomy laws and have not been struck down or repealed include: Arkansas, Kansas, Maryland, Missouri, Montana, Texas (struck down by a lower court). The actual content of sodomy laws varies widely state by state. For example, Florida's 'unnatural and lascivious act' is defined as the 'commission of any unnatural sex act'; Idaho describes a 'crime against nature' as 'performance of sodomy, fellatio, or any unnatural copulation'; Maryland's 'unnatural or perverted sexual practices' statute defines those practices as 'oral or any unnatural sex act'; Tennessee's law refers only to 'homosexual acts', which are defined as 'engaging in consensual sexual intercourse, cunnilingus, fellatio, or anal intercourse with another person of the same gender'. See N. Hunter, S. Michaelson and T. Stoddard, *The Rights of Lesbians and Gay Men* (Carbondale and Edwardsville: Southern Illinois University Press, 1992), pp. 149–75 and R. Robson, *Lesbian (Out)law: Survival Under the Rule of Law* (Ithaca: Firebrand, 1992), pp. 47–59.

10 For example, in *Eisenstadt* v. *Baird*, 405 US 438 (1972), the court had recognized a right of privacy for unmarried heterosexual couples.

11 See R. Mohr, *Gays/Justice* (New York: Columbia University Press, 1988), pp. 49–62.

12 I use the terms 'gay', 'lesbian' and 'bisexual' to refer to those individuals who identify themselves as gay, lesbian or bisexual. I use the terms 'homosexual' and 'homosexuality' to refer to both female and male homosexuality when the legal and medical discourses use those terms. It is important to point out that there is no one-to-one correspondence between the former and the latter terms, as the

latter terms were coined by the medical discourses of the nineteenth century and are based on behavioural concepts while the former arose out of vastly different historical/discursive contexts. Further, 'lesbian', 'gay' and 'bisexual' are themselves not coterminous with other identities and practices that fall outside of gendered heterosexual norms, such as transgender people and transvestites.

13   Suspect class status has been assigned to the following categories: alienage, see *Graham* v. *Richardson*, 403 US 365, 372 (1971); race, see *Loving* v. *Virginia*, 388 US 1, 11 (1967); national ancestry and ethnic origin, see *Korematsu* v. *United States*, 323 US 214, 216 (1944). Quasi-suspect class status has been assigned to the following categories: gender, see *Mississippi Univ. for Women* v. *Hogan*, 458 US 718, 724 (1982); illegitimacy, see *Lalli* v. *Lalli*, 439 US 259, 265 (1978). The 'suspect class' strategy for gay, lesbian and bisexual rights is clearly outlined in a note published in 1985: 'The constitutional status of sexual orientation: homosexuality as a suspect classification', *Harvard Law Review*, 95 (1985), p. 1285.

14   For a critique of the universalistic Enlightenment notion of equality, and the notion of the transcendental subject that accompanies that Enlightenment narrative, see I. M. Young, *Justice and the Politics of Difference* (Princeton: Princeton University Press, 1990), especially pp. 156–7.

15   See T. Haskell, 'The curious persistence of rights talk on the "age of interpretation" ', in D. Thelen, ed., *The Constitution and American Life* (Ithaca: Cornell University Press, 1988), p. 342. K. McClure argues in a similar vein in 'Pluralism and political identity', in C. Mouffe, ed., *Dimensions of Radical Democracy: Pluralism, Citizenship, Community* (London and New York: Verso, 1992), pp. 108–27.

16   For an example of the communitarian critique of the ontological presuppositions of rights discourse, see M. Sandel, *Liberalism and the Limits of Justice* (Cambridge: Cambridge University Press, 1982). For an example of the postmodern critique, see J. Butler, *Gender Trouble* (New York and London: Routledge, 1990).

17   For a discussion of the language of rights from the communitarian perspective, see C. Taylor, 'Cross-purposes: the liberal–communitarian debate', in N. Rosenblum, ed., *Liberalism and the Moral Life* (Cambridge, MA: Harvard University Press, 1989), pp. 159–82. For a discussion of the importance of rights from a critical race studies perspective, see P. J. Williams, *The Alchemy of Race and Rights* (Cambridge, MA: Harvard University Press, 1991), and K. Crenshaw, 'Race, reform and retrenchment: transformation and legitimation in antidiscrimination law', *Harvard Law Review*, 101 (1988), p. 1331.

18 R. Cover, 'Violence and the word', *Yale Law Journal*, 95 (1986), p. 1601 and R. Cover, 'The Supreme Court, 1982 term-forward: nomos and narrative', *Harvard Law Review*, 97 (1983) p. 7, cited in 'Violence and the word'.

19 *New York Times* CBS poll, conducted 7–11 February, 1993.

20 'Poll finds an even split on homosexuality's cause', *New York Times*, 5 March 1993. The *New York Times* CBS poll's methodology does not address the fact that undoubtedly some of the respondents were self-identified gay, lesbian or bisexual people; instead the poll's methodology implicitly constructs 'the public' as heterosexual.

21 Some genetic scientists have begun (re)inserting themselves into this debate as they try to make causal links between genes and homosexuality, which they construe as almost entirely a biological phenomenon. In the 16 July 1993 issue of *Science*, researchers from the National Cancer Institute reasserted the claim that 'homosexuality' is determined by 'gay genes'. One of the authors of the *Science* article, Dean Hamer, writes, 'All scientists already agree there is little element of choice in sexual orientation'. Cited in 'Genes vs. hormones', *New York Times* (2 August 1993).

22 The Fourteenth Amendment of the United States Constitution is the central venue of anti-discrimination cases: that Amendment was written, along with the Thirteenth and Fifteenth Amendments, to renounce the Supreme Court's decision in *Dred Scott v. Sandford*, 60 US 393 (1857), which held that African Americans were not US citizens. The salient parts of the Fourteenth Amendment are: 'No State shall make or enforce any law which shall abridge the privileges or immunities of citizens of the United States; nor shall any State deprive any person of life, liberty, or property, without due process of law [Due Process Clause]; nor deny to any person within its jurisdiction the equal protection of the laws [Equal Protection Clause]'.

23 This is not a truism, however, for many of those who critically engage with the cultural constructions around race. See K. A. Appiah, *In My Father's House: Africa in the Philosophy of Culture* (New York and Oxford: Oxford University Press, 1992), p. 45.

24 New York state senator Randy Kuhl, cited in 'Gay rights, G.O.P. a national issue in Albany', *New York Times* (6 February 1993).

25 Respondent's Petition for Rehearing at 6, *Bowers v. Hardwick*, 478 US 186 (1986) (No. 85–140).

26 Plaintiff's Answer Brief at 12, *Evans v. Romer*, 854 P.2d 1270 (Colo. 1993) (No. 93SA17).

27 Alberto Melucci has very clearly laid out the emerging influence of 'identity' on the mobilization of social movements. See his 'The new social movements: a theoretical approach', *Social Science Information*, 19, 2 (1980), pp. 199–226.

28   See, for example, J. Butler, *Gender Trouble*; and J. Flax, 'Postmodern and gender relations in feminist theory', in L. Nicholson, ed., *Feminism/Postmodernism* (New York and London: Routledge, 1990), pp. 39–62.

29   See, for example, M. A. Glendon, *Rights Talk* (New York: The Free Press, 1991).

30   The terms 'homosexual identity' and 'gay identity' begin appearing in writings by or about lesbians and gays only in the mid-1970s, according to V. C. Cass, 'Homosexual identity: a concept in need of a definition', *Journal of Homosexuality*, 9 (winter 1983/spring 1984), p. 105.

31   M. Foucault, *The History of Sexuality*, trans. R. Hurley (New York: Vintage, 1990), p. 85.

32   J. D'Emilio, 'Capitalism and gay identity', in A. Snitow, C. Stansell and S. Thompson, eds, *Powers of Desire* (New York: Monthly Review Press, 1983), pp. 100–13.

33   S. Epstein, 'Gay politics, ethnic identity: the limits of social constructionism', *Socialist Review*, 17 (May–August 1987), p. 12.

34   K. A. Appiah, 'Agency and the interests of theory', in J. Arac and B. Johnson, eds, *Consequences of Theory* (Baltimore and London: Johns Hopkins University Press, 1991), p. 74.

35   J. Butler, 'Contingent foundations: feminism and the question of "postmodernism" ', in J. Butler and J. Scott, eds, *Feminists Theorize the Political* (New York and London: Routledge, 1992), pp. 12–13.

36   Butler, *Gender Trouble*, p. 142.

37   See, for example, *High Tech Gays* v. *Defense Indus. Sec. Clearance Office*, 895 F.2d 563, 571 (9th Cir. 1990); *Ben-Shalom* v. *Marsh*, 881 F.2d 454, 464 (7th Cir. 1989), *cert. denied*, 494 US 1004 (1990), *Woodward* v. *United States*, 871 F.2d 1068, 1076, *cert. denied*, 494 US 1002.

38   This strategy was outlined by J. Halley in a 1989 article, 'The politics of the closet: towards equal protection for gay, lesbian and bisexual identity', *UCLA Law Review*, 36 (1989), p. 915.

39   The phrase 'discrete and insular minority' appears in the fount of legal doctrine around suspect class analysis, Justice Stone's famous 'footnote four' of *Carolene Products* v. *United States*, 304 US 144 (1944). See also, *City of Cleburne* v. *Cleburne Living Center, Inc.*, 473 US 432, 440–1 (1985).

40   *Korematsu* v. *United States*, 323 US 214 (1944).

41   Although it has not been difficult to convince the courts that homosexuals have suffered a history of discrimination, strangely enough several appellate courts have argued that homosexuals are not politically powerless, arguing in one case that having two openly gay members out of 435 members in the House of

Representatives constitutes political power (*Ben-Shalom* v. *Marsh*, 881 F.2d 454, 465, 466 (7th Cir. 1989)). This logic puts homosexuals in a quandary, the circularity of which is virtually inescapable: policies that suppress, among other things, the freedom of speech of gays, lesbians and bisexuals, and thus suppress our ability to take part openly in the political process are premised on the legislative decisions to criminalize sodomy upheld by *Bowers*. Those same policies, however, are deemed constitutional by reasoning that gays, lesbians and bisexuals are not politically powerless, that gays lesbians and bisexuals can use legislative channels to seek redress.

42   For an extended discussion of all the variants of suspect class analysis, see L. Tribe, *American Constitutional Law*, 2nd ed. (Mineola: Foundation Press, 1988), pp. 1436–628.

43   *City of Cleburne* v. *Cleburne Living Center, Inc.*, 473 US 432, 440 (1985).

44   *Robinson* v. *California*, 370 US 660, 662, 667 (1962), held that a California statute making it a criminal offence to 'be addicted to the use of narcotics', regardless of whether or not the person had used or possessed narcotics within the state, inflicts cruel and unusual punishment in violation of the Fourteenth Amendment. In *Watkins* v. *United States Army*, 847 F.2d 1329 (9th Cir. 1988), Judge Norris relies on *Robinson* in the panel's majority opinion that found that gay Army sergeant Perry Watkins cannot be barred from re-enlisting because of his status as a homosexual; Judge Rheinhardt counters in his dissent, however, that *Robinson* may be applied only to criminal statutes, not discriminatory regulations.

45   Of course, in some areas, such as universities, the courts have been loath to limit the First Amendment rights of gay, lesbian and bisexual groups. For example, see *Gay Students Organization of the University of New Hampshire* v. *Bonner*, 509 F.2d 652 (1st Cir. 1974). See also *Van Ooteghem* v. *Gray*, 654 F.2d 304 (5th Cir. 1981) (per curium), *cert. denied*, 455 US 909, which held that the gay plaintiff (Van Ooteghem) could not be fired from his county job for exercising his First Amendment rights to speak out for gay rights based on the standard set in *Pickering* v. *Board of Education*, 391 US 563, 568 (1968).

46   See second epigraph.

47   'Policy guidelines on homosexual conduct in the armed forces', cited in the 'Text of Pentagon's new policy guidelines on homosexuals in the military', *New York Times* (20 July 1993).

48   *Ben-Shalom* v. *Secretary of the Army*, 489 F. Supp. 964, 969 (E.D. Wis. 1980).

49   Army regulations AR 140–11, Table 4–2, Rule E, cited in *Ben-Shalom* v. *Marsh*, 881 F.2d 454, 457 (7th Cir. 1989).

50 *Ben-Shalom* v. *Marsh*, 881 F.2d 454 (7th Cir. 1989).

51 *Ben-Shalom* v. *Marsh*, 881 F.2d 454, 462 (7th Cir. 1989), citing *United States* v. *O'Brien*, 391 US 367, 376 (1968), which held that the First Amendment does not protect the symbolic speech of destroying draft registration certificates even though it may have a chilling effect on free speech because the restriction of speech was only incidentally related to the government's legitimate interest in raising armies.

52 *Ben-Shalom* v. *Marsh*, 881 F.2d 454, 462 (7th Cir. 1989).

53 The new policy has already suffered a defeat in the courts, as a US federal Judge, in *Able* v. *United States*, CV 94 0974, granted an injunction barring any actions against six homosexual plaintiffs who are challenging the constitutionality of the policy. By challenging the policy, of course, the plaintiffs had to identify themselves as gay, lesbian or bisexual. Under the new regulations, of course, public coming out speech is classified as 'homosexual conduct'. Cited in 'Federal judge faults military's gays policy', *New York Law Journal* (5 April 1994).

54 *Rowland* v. *Mad River Local School District, Montgomery County*, 730 F.2d 444, 450, 452 (6th Cir. 1984).

55 See, for example, D. Kairys, 'Freedom of speech', in D. Kairys, ed., *The Politics of Law* (New York: Pantheon, 1982), pp. 140–71; L. Tribe, *American Constitutional Law*, 2nd ed, pp. 825–32.

56 In another case involving the Army, a federal appellate court again made a distinction between a lesbian US Army Reserve officer's sexual orientation and her speech about her sexual orientation. In the case of Dusty Pruitt, a captain in the US Army Reserve, a federal appellate court upheld her discharge, denying her First Amendment claim that her coming out in a newspaper interview was protected speech. Pruitt's case, like Ben-Shalom's, was based only on her status as a homosexual. Citing *Ben-Shalom* v. *Marsh*, 881 F.2d 454 (7th Cir. 1989), the Ninth Circuit panel rejected Pruitt's argument that her speech was protected: 'Pruitt argues that her statements about her sexual orientation constituted political speech, touching on a matter of public concern . . . Nevertheless, Pruitt was discharged not for the content of her speech, but for being a homosexual.' (*Pruitt* v. *Cheney*, 963 F.2d 1160, 1162, 1163 (9th Cir. 1991)). The court's opinion could have relied on the test elaborated in *Connick* v. *Meyers*, 461 US 138 (1983), which holds that the First Amendment rights of public employees may be abridged only if the speech in question does not touch on a 'a matter of public concern' and does not interfere with the government's business. But the *Connick* test was effectively elided here when the panel reasoned that the content of Pruitt's speech was irrelevant to the issue at hand

– the 'fact' of Pruitt's homosexuality. The court also relies on the assumption that the object of the Army's regulations is homosexuals as a class, not homosexual conduct. This view seems borne out by the regulations themselves, which allow for retaining soldiers who have engaged in homosexual conduct. According to the opinion: 'The Army discharged Pruitt because she admitted to being homosexual . . . That is it was her homosexuality, and not her speech, that caused Pruitt to be discharged is apparent from the subsection of the regulation under which she was discharged. It provides for separation of a member who "has stated that he/she is a homosexual or bisexual *unless there is a further finding that the member is not a homosexual or bisexual"* ' (emphasis added in the opinion).

57   'Text of Pentagon's new policy guidelines on homosexuals in the military', *New York Times* (20 July 1993).

58   Under the old regulations, the mere commission of homosexual acts is not proof of homosexuality. According to Department of Defense Directives 1332.14 (enlisted service members) and 1332.30 (officers), a member or officer 'has engaged in, or solicited another to engage in a homosexual act or acts unless there are approved further findings that: (a) Such conduct is a departure from the member's usual and customary behavior; (b) Such conduct under all circumstances is unlikely to recur; (c) Such conduct was not accomplished by the use of force, coercion, or intimidation by the member during a period of military service; (d) Under the particular circumstances of the case, the member's continued presence in the Service is consistent with the interest of the Service in proper discipline, good order, and morale; and (e) The member does not desire to engage in or intend to engage in homosexual acts.' The new regulations include the same exemptions from the original DOD directive.

59   Foucault, *The History of Sexuality*, p. 43.

60   For example, it is the practice of sodomy, and not the identity of 'the homosexual' (a term yet to be invented), that John Winthrop, the first governor of the Massachusetts Bay Colony, describes in 1646 in his *History of New England*, 'one Plaine of Guilford being discovered to have used some unclean practices, upon examination and testimony, it was found, that being a married man, he had committed sodomy with two persons in England, and that he had corrupted a great part of the youth of Guilford by masturbations, which he had committed, and provoked others to the like above a hundred times'. Cited in Jonathan Katz, *Gay American History* (New York: Harper & Row, 1976), p. 22.

61   See *Bowers* v. *Hardwick*, 478 US 186, 200, 210 (1986) (J. Blackmun, dissenting). See also *Watkins* v. *US Army*, 847 F.2d 1329 (9th Cir.

1988) (Judge Rheinhardt, dissenting). Rheinhardt argues that *Bowers* precludes the distinction between homosexual identity and homosexual conduct. See also *Pruitt* v. *Cheney*, 963 F.2d 1160, 1166, note 5 (9th Cir. 1991), holding that *Bowers* v. *Hardwick* 'had ruled that *homosexuals* could not rely on a right of privacy to exempt them from criminal laws proscribing sodomy' (emphasis added).

62   Respondent's Petition for Rehearing at 4, *Bowers* v. *Hardwick*, 478 US 186 (1986) (No. 85–140).

63   *Plyer* v. *Doe*, 457 US 202 (1982).

64   J. Halley, 'The politics of the closet: towards equal protection for gay, lesbian and bisexual identity', *UCLA Law Review*, 36 (1989), p. 923.

65   *Bowers* v. *Hardwick*, 478 US 186, 194.

66   See F. Michelman, 'Law's republic', *Yale Law Journal*, 97 (1988), p. 1493.

67   *High Tech Gays* v. *Defense Indust. Sec. Clearance Office*, 895 F.2d 563, 573 (9th Cir. 1990).

68   *Steffan* v. *Cheney*, 780 F.Supp. 1, 7 (D.D.C. 1991). Upon appeal, this district court's decision was reversed by a higher court in *Steffan* v. *Aspin*, 8 F.3d 57 (D.C. Cir. 1993). Unfortunately, however, this latter judgement was vacated when a rehearing *en banc* was granted on 7 January 1994.

69   During the era of slavery and later during the era of the Jim Crow South, the 'one-drop rule' designated any person with any known African black blood as black. See for example: F. J. Davis, *Who Is Black: One Nation's Definition* (University Park, PA: Pennsylvania State University Press, 1991). For other analyses of the historical and discursive construction of race, ethnicity, gender and sexuality see: the essays in D. Goldberg, ed, *Anatomy of Racism* (Minneapolis: University of Minnesota Press, 1990); M. Garber, *Vested Interests: Cross-Dressing and Cultural Anxiety* (New York and London: Routledge, 1990); M. Gatens, *Feminism and Philosophy* (Cambridge: Polity Press, 1991); and Butler, *Gender Trouble*.

70   *Woodward* v. *United States*, 871 F.2d 1068, 1076 (Fed. Cir. 1989), *cert. denied*, 494 US 1003 (1990).

71   For a brief moment it appeared that finally a federal circuit court had granted suspect class status to homosexuals. In *Watkins* v. *Army*, 847 F.2d 1329 (9th Cir. 1988) a Ninth Circuit panel had held that *Bowers* did not preclude the classification of homosexuals as a suspect class. The opinion's author, Judge Norris, found that the Army's regulations discriminated against homosexuals, that homosexuals are, in fact, members of a suspect class, and that heightened review of the Army's regulations does not lead to the conclusion that the regulations are justified. In holding that *Bowers* did not

apply to equal protection claims, Norris asserted that the real object of the regulations was homosexuals, not sodomy. He points out, 'the class burdened by the regulations is defined by the sexual *orientation* of its members, not by their sexual conduct' (emphasis of original). And, as Norris further argued, the implicit target of the regulations is homosexuals who come out, who state their status openly, rather than all homosexuals. 'In short', he writes, 'the regulations do not penalize all statements of sexual desire, or even only statements of sexual desire; they penalize only homosexuals who declare their homosexual orientation.' On rehearing *en banc*, however, the Ninth Circuit decided in Watkins's favour on other grounds (estoppel), without reaching the equal protection issue. 875 F.2d 699 (9th Cir. 1989), *cert.* denied in 111 S.Ct. 384 (1990).

72   K. A. Appiah, *In My Father's House*, p. 45.

73   For example, in *City of Richmond* v. *J. A. Croson*, 488 US 469 (1989), the Supreme Court overturned a city's affirmative action programme for minority-owned businesses because it did not apply only to the actual victims of past discrimination.

74   E. Sedgwick has brilliantly described these epistemic gaps as crisis of definition between the 'minoritizing' and 'universalizing' understandings of homo/hetero definition. See her analysis of the logic of the 'homosexual panic' defence in *Epistemology of the Closet* (Berkeley: University of California Press, 1990), p. 20.

75   *Rowland* v. *Mad River Local School District, Montgomery County*, 730 F.2d 444, 450 (6th Cir. 1984).

76   Obviously, nothing precludes both approaches being used together, as was done by the plaintiffs in *Evans* v. *Romer*.

77   *Rowland* v. *Mad River Local School District, Montgomery County*, 470 US 1004, 1009 (1985) (J. Brennan, dissenting from denial of *cert.*).

78   According to John Ely, 'contrary to the standard characterization of the Constitution as "an enduring but evolving statement of general values," . . . in fact the selection and accommodation of substantive values is left almost entirely to the political process and instead the document is overwhelmingly concerned, on the one hand, with procedural fairness in the resolution of individual disputes (process writ small), and on the other, with what might be capaciously be designated process writ large – with ensuring broad participation in the processes and distributions of government.' *Democracy and Distrust* (Cambridge, and London: Harvard University Press, 1980), p. 87.

79   Cited in *Evans* v. *Romer*, 854 P.2d 1270, 1272 (Colo. 1993).

80   *Evans* v. *Romer*, 854 P.2d 1270, 1285 (Colo. 1993).

81   According to the Colorado Supreme Court, '[t]he value placed on the ability of individuals to participate in the political process has

manifested itself in numerous equal protection cases decided by the Supreme Court over the last thirty years. These include the reapportionment cases, cases concerning minority party rights, cases involving direct restrictions on the exercise of the franchise, and cases involving attempts to limit the ability of certain groups to have desired legislation implemented through the normal political channels.' (Citations omitted.) *Evans* v. *Romer*, 854 P.2d 1270, 1276 (Colo. 1993).

82   *Evans* v. *Romer*, 854 P.2d 1270, 1276 (Colo. 1993).

83   Plaintiffs-Appellees' Answer Brief at 36, *Evans* v. *Romer* (Colo. 1993) (No. 93SA17).

84   Defendants-Appellants' Opening Brief at 12, 13, *Evans* v. *Romer* (Colo. 1993) (No. 93SA17).

85   The decision upheld a lower court's granting of a temporary injunction against the implementation of Amendment Two. (One of the standards that must be met before such an injunction can be granted is whether an existing constitutional right is infringed upon by the statute or constitutional amendment in question.) The fact that the Colorado Supreme Court found that Amendment Two did in fact infringe on an existing fundamental right suggests that they will hold Amendment Two unconstitutional when the actual case is before them.

86   Paradoxically, it is also the departure from the immutability approach that makes the decision's reasoning most vulnerable, and that may cause the decision to unravel when it finally reaches the Supreme Court. Because, as the dissent in this case pointed out, the idea that an 'identifiable group' has a fundamental right to participate equally in the political process may logically lead to a proliferation of 'identifiable groups'. That is, many referendums single out and burden 'identifiable groups': landlords, polluters, farmers, for example. The Supreme Court may decide that the criteria in question cannot be detached from more essentialist notions of immutability, or at least from the particular 'discrete and insular minorities', such as African Americans, delineated in legal precedent. *Evans* v. *Romer*, 854 P.2d 1270, 1299 (Colo. 1993) (Justice Erickson, dissenting).

87   *Meinhold* v. *United States Department of Defense*, 808 F.Supp 1455 (C.D. Cal. 1993). See also *Pruitt* v. *Cheney*, 963 F.2d 1160, 1166–68 (9th Cir. 1991) (declaring that the Army must offer a rational basis for the regulations banning gays and lesbians from serving).

88   The *Meinhold* case continues to work its way through the federal courts. The district court's order permanently enjoining the Department of Defense from discharging or denying enlistment on the

basis of sexual orientation alone was amended by a higher court to apply to Keith Meinhold only, pending the outcome of an appeal at the appellate level, which is now under way. *Meinhold* v. *US Dept. of Defense*, 1993 WL 513209 (C.D. Cal., Sep 30, 1993).

89 Amy Ash, Monica Barrett, Susan Buck-Morss, Zillah Eisenstein, Mary Katzenstein, Isaac Kramnick, Biddy Martin, Shannon Minter, Lisa Moore, Andres Nader and Mark Wojcik have all read or heard drafts of this chapter and provided valuable comments.

Chapter four

Invisible Sexualities: Sexuality, Politics and Influencing Policy-making

Jean Carabine

Introduction

THIS chapter examines the impact of sexuality on the policy-making process at the local political level with particular reference to Section 28 of the Local Government Act (1988; for text see p. 129 below). The material is based on empirical research undertaken in Sheffield over a two-year period between June 1989 and June 1991. A case-study approach using a local government policy-making setting was adopted as a means of exploring specifically the relationship between women's sexuality and policy-making. Information was gathered from a variety of sources including in-depth unstructured interviews with women campaigning around sexuality issues and in-depth semi-structured interviews with policy-makers, reports, council minutes and papers, and media sources. Other campaigns concerned with sexuality were examined in addition to the Section 28 campaign. These covered sexual violence, sexual harassment, domestic violence and policy-makers, and the chapter will draw on some of this material as appropriate.[1]

The aim of this chapter is threefold: first, to examine and discuss the impact of sexuality on local government policy and policy-making through the example of the Section 28 and other campaigns; second, to consider local government responses and attitudes to lesbians in particular, but also to gay men; third, to identify some of the important factors influencing responses at the local government level to Section 28 in particular, and to sexuality issues in general.

Background

Sheffield is a primarily working-class city, once heavily reliant on steel-making and related industries. Working-class politics have been the basis of local politics in Sheffield with a Labourite tradition going back as far as the 1920s. With the exception of two years, 1968–9, the Labour Party has controlled the city since 1926.[2] Parliamentary representation is also predominately Labour, with five out of six constituencies usually returning Labour members. Not only has this shaped policy-making but it is also a significant aspect in the relationship between sexuality and policy-making.

Although Sheffield is predominately Labour, it is subject to, and affected by, national policy and politics, particularly under the Right-orientated Conservative Government[3] which has sought to centralize local government power[4] and influence. In terms of policies relating to sexuality, the research was undertaken at a period which saw not only the introduction of Section 28 but also the increased incidence of HIV and AIDS and with it the popular misconception of the disease as the 'gay plague'. There has also been a reassertion of the importance of the nuclear family, and calls for a return to traditional values from a number of quarters including both the New Right and the Labour Party. Parallel to this the universality and normality of heterosexuality has been emphasized, through for example the concern with 'virgin births', unwanted teenage pregnancies and outcries over the issue of lesbians and gays adopting.

Section 28 – the national context

Section 28, also referred to as Clause 28, was introduced as an amendment to the Local Government Act (1988) and sought to ban the promotion of homosexuality and pretended family relationships by local authorities or the teaching of acceptability of homosexuality in schools. Section 28 came into effect on 24 May 1988.

At a national level, responses, in terms of opposing Section 28, varied. One of the biggest outcries came from the arts lobby, arising from fears about the possible effects of the legislation on the arts, for example, the removal of local authority funding for, and therefore possible censorship in, theatres, arts centres, libraries, galleries and cinemas.[5] It would seem that the arts campaign was more acceptable (media attention tended to focus on this aspect of the opposition) because of the censorship/freedom of speech argument rather than because the media, politicians or public believed in the acceptability of lesbian and gay relationships. The censorship/ freedom of speech argument found resonance with 'ordinary' people (that is, those people who might define themselves as heterosexual) because they feared that Section 28 would threaten to interfere with their civil liberties – evoking memories of pre-1968 state censorship of theatre and publications. 'Generally, the public face of opposition to the Clause has presented a type of political thought broadly falling into the category of liberal humanism.'[6]

Many, irrespective of their party politics, and/or sexuality, supported the campaign against Section 28 under the civil liberties/ equal opportunities flag, the emphasis being on the rights of the individual, equality, tolerance of difference, privacy and freedom of speech. As the Archbishop of York commented, 'the fundamental issue in this clause is civil liberties and the relationship between the individual and the government.'[7]

It could be argued that the effect of this individualistic approach resulted in depoliticizing the issue, and a failure to incorporate any analysis of lesbian and gay oppression. The liberalism of many of the campaigns opposing Section 28 pronounced an equality in the freedom of expressions of sexuality, whilst still upholding the heterosexual system which enshrines the values of the family and traditional notions of morality. In doing so the power and influence of heterosexuality remained unchallenged. Certainly, Section 28 had the effect of publicizing lesbian and gay equality; however, it did not lead either to a challenge to heterosexuality or to a serious redefinition of British society's view of sexuality.

Section 28 – the local context

In Sheffield the emergence of local campaigns against Section 28 mirrored what was happening in many other parts of the country. Once news broke of the proposed legislation a public meeting was organized. This was attended by lesbians, gay men and heterosexuals. Owing to political disagreements – for example, meetings being dominated by Left-wing groups, such as, the Socialist Workers' Party and the Revolutionary Communist Party, as well as fundamental differences in lesbian and gay male politics and ways of working – two groups emerged. These were the Stop the Clause (STC) group – a mixed gay and lesbian and SWP/RCP coalition – and the Women Against the Clause (WAC) group, made up of predominantly lesbian women. It is the campaigning experiences of this latter group which are the focus of this case study.[8]

Women Against Clause 28

The main objective of WAC was to have the offending Section 28 removed from the Local Government Bill through national and local efforts. The campaign aimed to educate people about homosexuality and Section 28; to attract support from other groups and individuals, such as trades unions and heterosexuals; and to publicize the fact that many heterosexual people were opposed to the legislation. WAC was organized on a main group basis with various sub-groups operating on an activity basis. For example, there were sub-groups dealing with lobbying, direct action, publicity, fund-raising, trades unions and organizing a national conference.

Responses to the WAC campaign

Campaigns against Section 28 were successful in Sheffield, and won the support of the Council in opposing the legislation. WAC believed that it was more successful at achieving policy changes and gaining councillors' support than the mixed Stop the Clause campaign, despite the socialist nature of the latter. Mary suggests that this was because

> We were quite professional about it and were willing to compromise where it was worth compromising and it was a way in . . . the only way in that we could see at that time. I thought it was a really legitimate way in to get an emergency motion . . . tabled . . . on the Women's Panel. I don't know how else that could have got in because policy isn't open to members of the public and it wouldn't legitimately have got in on race or disability.

Once a 'legitimate' way had been found the issue could then go to Policy Committee and from there into Council, where there was, according to a number of interviewees, a good debate – 'good' in that councillors were talking about the issues positively and in ways in which they had not debated them before.

The response of councillors to Section 28 appears to have been on three main levels, which incidentally reflected the major responses across the country.[9] Whilst they can be separated for the purposes of clarity, these three responses are interconnected. First, the Clause was an attack on individual civil liberties,[10] particularly artistic expression: 'Oscar Wilde plays on the shelf type of line and not actually looking at the issues – the harder issues of Clause 28' (Sarah). 'They genuinely, in the Labour group, saw it as a civil liberties issue and most of them were genuinely shocked by it – that there would be a proposal to force councils to undermine people's civil liberties. To that extent it galvanized them on the issue' (Jane). Interestingly this seems to imply that the councillors see lesbians and gay men enjoying 'civil liberties' on a par with the rest of the electorate.

The 'harder issues' were the incidence of violent attacks and severe discrimination in housing and child custody cases which lesbians in Sheffield were experiencing. When councillors were made aware of the attacks against lesbians, 'it had a profound effect upon them' (Sarah) and this produced a second response whereby those councillors who were horrified and shocked took a moral stance on the issue. The third response was opposition to the Section as another piece of 'Tory', Conservative Government, legislation. The belief held by many campaigners was that if the Labour Party had introduced the Section it would have prompted an entirely different response from Labour councillors. 'But because it came from the Tories, it was a national government thing, it was another onslaught and they latched on to the civil liberties aspects and they were able to distance their homophobia and look at that' (Sarah).

So the campaign was able to establish formal support early on from the Council which meant that as an issue Section 28 was given a measure of legitimacy: it was on the policy agenda and talked about and 'this was quite crucial really to affecting the council and then it could be legitimately raised at every Women's Panel' (Mary). As commentators said, getting formal recognition meant that lesbianism was legitimately on the agenda as an acceptable policy topic. It could be raised legitimately at every Women's Panel meeting; but was this not marginalizing it to a degree? Section 28 could be said to be firmly and legitimately on the policy agenda only if it were raised at every Policy Committee or Council meeting.

However, the structuring of the Section 28 affair by local councillors and policy-makers as a civil liberties and party political issue meant that the heterosexual power relations could be ignored, thereby leaving the status quo intact, and the hegemonic dominance of heterosexuality unquestioned.

Many interviewees, including women closely involved with policy work within Sheffield City Council, felt that the Council had no politics from which to analyse Section 28, other than class or party politics – the inference being that these were inadequate to deal with sexuality as a political issue. Traditional politics, that is party politics, is unable to encompass an analysis of sexuality which challenges predominant ideologies because of the centrality of the family and heterosexuality as themes in party politics – Conservative and Labour alike. Additionally, this inadequacy is compounded by the privatization of sexuality as a personal and individual matter.[11]

The implication of this privatization of sex, and therefore lesbianism, is that inevitably notions of lesbians as 'other' are reinforced, along with sexualized perceptions of lesbian identity. Thus the tendency of many people, politicians and policy-makers included, is to see lesbianism as being about sex and children at risk, rather than to see lesbians as people who have identities, who may be unemployed or working-class, black as well as white, who have housing problems, are tax payers and are legitimate users of Council services.

Clearly, lesbians and gay men are not seen by policy-makers as the 'ordinary' people of Sheffield and as such have less of a say in determining policy. For issues raised by women to be accepted as legitimate policy topics not only do they have to be thought acceptable to the electorate, but also women have to fit

> into the mythology of the disadvantaged working-class woman who probably aren't black, who definitely [are] not out lesbians. And it is a mythology because you can have a group who are just ... right ... who still don't have any influence because it doesn't fit the picture of acceptable issues that they [the Council] should be saying something about. (Sarah)

Individual women's experiences of campaigning were affected by their status. Women experienced the WAC Section 28 campaign differently depending on whether they were working-class, black, young or older. Many women felt that the campaign presented everyone as being the same, and this led to a reinforcement of popular misconceptions, such as 'all lesbians are white and middle-class', a view held by many councillors. This is exemplified through the experience of black women. Black women experienced racism, not only in their interactions with policy-makers and the policy process but also within the WAC campaign. This racism is also bound up in perceptions of black women's sexuality. Black lesbians are triply invisible: lesbianism is seen by councillors as being white and middle-class; lesbianism is presented by the WAC campaigners as being white and some would argue also middle-class; similarly, the black community also sees lesbianism as about white women.

The appropriateness and acceptability of sexuality as an issue

Sheffield City Council, in common with other authorities, has policy priorities. High on the list are social inequality, poverty and disadvantage. Within these policy parameters there appears to be a hierarchy of disadvantage. 'Race' is relatively high, with disability below it and women's issues next and sexuality somewhere near the bottom. Within this apparent hierarchy of disadvantage lesbians are either ignored or positively excluded. As far as policy-makers are concerned, people fall, or are placed into, discrete categories – the working class, the homeless, the electorate – all of which mutually exclude lesbianism, in a way which does not enable policy-makers to see social inequality issues as affecting lesbians also. This works to exclude other groups of women, as well as specific issues.

> It's [sexual orientation] less of a priority. Members wouldn't think it's a legitimate issue. At any time there might be one or two members who might want to push gay and lesbian issues but they've probably lost ground and they're probably not within the Labour Group Executive. (Senior Officer)

Acceptability plays an important role for Council members in the policy-making process. There is a perception that in the context of sexuality the electorate also has a hierarchy of acceptability. For the electorate it is acceptable for the Council to deal with rape and child sexual violence but not with homosexuality. This hierarchy of acceptability is influenced by ideas about normal sexuality and deserving and undeserving users of Council services. In the context of sexuality, concepts of deserving and undeserving users are influenced by ideas about normality, naturalness, morality and notions of 'guilty' and 'innocent' victims. Survivors of sexual, and to a lesser degree physical, violence are recognized as being 'innocent' victims and, therefore, a legitimate focus of Council services. Homosexuality remains unacceptable because of the constancy of ideas about it being abnormal, perverse, immoral and sick. Anti-lesbian and anti-gay feelings are intensified by myths about homosexuals being child molesters and homosexuality being linked to unacceptable sexual practice and AIDS. For example,

> Child abuse is child abuse but some people connect it with homosexuality, which is stupid, is wrong, is ignorant but that is the only connection. They see both as unacceptable. Though one is a crime as such and one isn't – it's just two consenting adults . . . a lot of people still tie homosexuality up with child sexual abuse. They tend to tie homosexuality up with unacceptable areas of practice. (female councillor, Labour)

This is a powerful association in people's minds, to the extent that councillors who are supportive and work towards acknowledging lesbian and gay relationships in policies often do so through the back door, as this quotation from one councillor illustrates: 'Practice and policy around lesbian and gay parents is quite sound but we don't publicize it . . . so what's happened is that you complicitly take things through as quietly as you can on the back of things. But at least you can be fairly sure of getting things through.' That lesbian and gay issues are dealt with in a secretive manner further reinforces notions about the unacceptability and marginality of lesbians and gay men. Equally, because such policies are unlikely to be widely advertised, how are lesbians and gay men to find out about positive policies or to comment on just how 'sound' they find Council practice?

Additionally, sexuality is a taboo subject, politically and socially, and this is reflected in local politics and policies. Sexuality is what people do at home in private. 'Normal' sexuality does not need to be discussed or require to be dealt with as a matter of policy. It is 'unnatural' sexuality or sexuality 'out of control', needing to be publicly controlled, and so more readily approached and debated by policy-makers. If concerns around sexuality, such as positive approaches to homosexuality or responding to women's demands about sexual and physical violence, are considered the remit of policy, it is often as a result of interest from an individual officer or councillor. Usually though, sexuality is not considered an appropriate policy topic because of perceived prejudice and lack of acceptability.

There has been little debate in Sheffield about sexuality among policy-makers. However, interviewees felt that a positive outcome of Section 28 was that it made it possible for sexuality to be discussed publicly. Ironically, sexuality moved out of the arena of the private and into the public arena of policy and policy-making. At the local level, the shift from the private to the public resulted because councillors were able to frame sexuality within two familiar contexts: first, as a human rights/civil liberties issue and, second, within the framework of party politics.[12]

Issues about sexuality have to be presented in a familiar and identifiable context for councillors and policy-makers. So for issues concerning sexuality to be successful in a policy context they need to be related or even translated to the world with which councillors are familiar. As with women's issues, sexuality has to be closely related to class or the issue has to be redefined or re-presented so that it can be seen in traditional political terms, as with industrial relations. For example, policy on sexual harassment was led by industrial relations staff of the Council, although staff from the Women's Unit were instrumental in getting sexual harassment accepted as a problem. Also of significance in the sexual harassment issue was the dropping of 'sexual' and the decision to refer to it as the harassment of women. The acceptability of 'harassment' as opposed to 'sexual' harassment suggests that, for policy-makers, the women experiencing it and the male perpetrators, sexuality is a forbidden subject.

With 'sexual' removed, harassment becomes a term without definite character, diluted and less threatening. Thereby, harassment becomes something which can happen to everyone. The particular attributes of the harassment – the power aspects – disappear and harassment is no longer something experienced because of 'race', or sex or sexuality. In this way institutionalized racism, sexism and heterosexism remain significantly unchallenged. It is behaviour which is dealt with, rather than attitudes and structural inequalities. Correspondingly, the structuring of Section

28 by councillors and policy-makers as a civil liberties and party political issue meant that heterosexual power relations could be ignored, leaving the status quo intact and the dominance of heterosexuality unchallenged.

The consideration of issues about sexuality may also be affected by class politics in another way. Lesbians and gay men are perceived as being middle-class; therefore, they are not 'needy', do not need Council services, and do not necessarily vote Labour. So lesbian sexuality is invisible to councillors in traditional working-class wards. For councillors to have more understanding of those issues they need to be exposed to them in contexts with which they are familiar. However, although sexuality may be part of everyone's everyday experience it is invisible in social policy. 'Normal' sexuality is so taken for granted that it is not an acknowledged part of councillors' world views. Councillors perceive their electorate as being male working-class redundant steel-workers, not as having any sexuality let alone being lesbian or gay. This, together with the class basis discussed previously and a desire to avoid being associated with the 'loony Left', results in the issue of sexuality rarely being placed on the policy agenda. The myth of the elector as a male redundant steel-worker who is opposed to equal opportunities is a useful device in policy-making. The Council could have used it to validate the introduction of proactive policies which seriously challenge structural inequalities not based on class. Instead, it introduced anti-discriminatory policies, which interviewees saw as having little value beyond the paper they were written on, or as adopting a paternalistic response.

Additionally, policy-makers use the power of the electorate and the fear of electoral backlash selectively. On the one hand, policy-makers argue that they are sometimes influenced by fear of an electoral backlash and, on the other, they assert that there are occasions when principles are paramount, as this quotation from a female Labour councillor illustrates: 'They'll say "you're supposed to be representing me" and I'll say "well I ain't representing you on that basis" and they'll say "I ain't gonna turn out and vote for you." "Well all right, that's absolutely fine by me, therefore, on that basis I don't want your votes".' Many policy-makers seem to take this contradictory stance. On the one hand, they talk about how important the electorate is, and about the fear of an electoral backlash, particularly, in response to lesbian and gay issues. On the other hand, councillors are prepared to risk losing votes. Clearly some principles are more valid and worth standing up for than others. Given Labour's large majority, is the fear of an electoral backlash as real as policy-makers suggest? The 'political is personal' for politicians as well as for feminists, and policy-makers are likely to have their own interests close to heart. It is unlikely that many politicians would wish to risk their personal or political reputations by taking a positive public stance on lesbian issues. Equally, the local is also national in this context: witness the way in which the Greater London Council and Ken Livingstone were attacked on lesbian and gay issues by the tabloid press in the early 1980s.

The invisibility of sexuality

The policy-making process, with its strong ideological input about sexuality and assumptions about women and nature, continues to reinforce a particular model: it replays old scenarios, old assumptions. The problem is the invisibility of sexual dimension in policy and the policy-making process. For example, heterosexuality is taken for granted and runs through all policy.[13] Sexuality as an ideological and power dimension in providing services is ignored, even in issues visibly concerned with sexuality, such as sexual violence.

With sexual harassment, once the 'sexuality' aspect was less visible it became, as we have seen, more manageable. The policy process could deal with it as harassment, as good working conditions, but not as something inextricably linked with male and female power relations. Consequently, sexual harassment is more easily accepted by both male bosses and policy-makers when it is referred to more generally as women being harassed at work because they are women.

In a similar way, once homosexuality was presented as a civil/ human rights issue and as a party political issue it also began to feel 'safer' for lesbians as well as politicians. Child sexual violence had been made visible by dealing with it as an individual and family matter, rather than recognizing it as male sexual abuse of children and as being connected with male power. Issues concerned with sexuality were marginalized, as evidenced by low levels of funding for such projects as the Young Women's Housing Project, Rape Crisis, Women's Aid and lesbian groups.

It is evident from the interviews with the policy-makers that they equate sexuality very narrowly with homosexuality. This is significant because it suggests that sexuality is an invisible aspect in the issues concerned with sexuality, such as child sexual violence and rape. Similarly, the acceptance of the normality and naturalness of heterosexuality results in it being invisible to policy-makers and in policy. Many feminist and womanist campaigns are based on the premise that sexuality and male power are integral in physical and sexual violence. That sexuality as a primary dynamic in physical and sexual violence is invisible to policy-makers suggests that it will be difficult for feminist ideas to impact on the policy-making process and effect change. This reinforces other evidence from the case studies which indicate that policy-makers do not have an analysis of sexuality as a power dynamic in male/female and adult/child relations. Sexuality is also invisible in other ways. Many councillors do not see homosexuality as an issue that requires attention from the Council because they are unaware of the discrimination experienced by lesbians. For example: 'If it's a bigger issue than we are aware of or even an issue. I've never been aware that there's ever been any discrimination on the grounds of sexuality. I'd certainly be horrified and anybody on the Council would be if that was the case' (female councillor, Labour). Another aspect of this is the invisibility of black homosexuality because of racist sexual stereotyping.

The invisibility of sexuality despite the implicit heterosexual nature of social policy prompts a number of important questions.

1 *What can be inferred about the instances when sexuality is considered a legitimate issue for policy?* Let us summarize some of the points made earlier. Sexuality is considered a legitimate issue for policy only when the context is considered acceptable. Acceptable contexts are primarily class-based issues and environments, for example tenants' associations and the District Labour Party, and are determined by the nature of local Labour politics. Additionally, the framework has to be one which allows councillors to respond in an individualistic and paternalistic way, as we have seen with the sexual

harassment and Section 28. Sexuality is accepted as a legitimate issue when its presentation or demands do not challenge the heterosexual status quo and existing power relations. Sexuality is also legitimate as a topic when it is concerned with reasserting the status quo or about statutory responsibility, as with the sexual abuse of children. Outside of these examples sexuality is also accepted on the policy agenda when it evokes a traditional moral response in policy-makers.

2 *Why is sexuality not accepted as a legitimate political issue?* At the local level sexuality is not perceived as being a working-class issue. On a wider level sexuality is seen as a personal rather than a political matter. Women and lesbians are marginalized in society, therefore it is likely that lesbian and feminist politics will be also. Additionally, sexuality is not politically acceptable because of the challenge some sexuality issues pose to prevalent ideas about what is normal and natural in society.

3 *Why is sexuality rarely placed on the political agenda?* Policy-makers believe that sexuality is an inappropriate issue for policy. As the discussion above illustrates, the reasons why sexuality is excluded explicitly from the policy agenda are complex and inter-related. In general, sexuality is implicitly on the policy agenda only as heterosexuality. As heterosexuality it is omnipotent and omnipresent, experienced as natural and normal, and because of this invisible and unquestioned. In this way the local policy agenda promotes heterosexuality and normality. This is achieved in an effortless, taken-for-granted manner. Thus, sexuality is not something either people or policy-makers give much thought to, because it 'just is'.

Campaigners have sought to challenge the commonplace assumptions and complacency of society in general and of policy-makers in particular. If these were left unchallenged it is clear that sexuality would not be an issue for policy. Even when issues of prejudice and discrimination are raised, they still remain invisible because sexuality is not considered a 'real issue' and, therefore, a priority for policy. For this reason even when sexuality gets on to the agenda, as with Section 28, it is not awarded permanent status and is easily forgotten. Policy-makers suggest that sexuality is a temporary visitor to policy because of public opinion. Political fearfulness of an electoral backlash results in policy-makers doing very little or adopting a 'softly softly' approach. Another reason given is simply ignorance of prejudice and discrimination; a case of 'no news is good news'.

However, can these be accepted as valid reasons for the policy response to sexuality? In interviews policy-makers talk about not kowtowing to the electorate, and of the importance of standing up for principles in the face of electorate disapproval. If councillors accept the prevalence of racism, why then can they not accept the existence of anti-lesbian feeling and practice and sexism? Certainly, the Council accepts the need to have policies and practices which remove discrimination. Black people have worked long and hard at getting their voices heard and on to the political agenda. One of the reasons that black issues are listened to is that black, predominantly male, groups have lobbied the Council. They are also accepted by councillors as a deserving minority. Additionally, it may be that black politics can be more readily incorporated into Labour Party politics than sexuality. For example, councillors may not fear an electoral backlash as much as they do the political consequences of 'race riots'.

Sexuality issues, whether sexual or physical violence or homosexuality, are less acceptable because of the challenge they pose to party politics both locally and nationally. Campaigns around these issues pose a threat to traditional and normative values and the omnipotence of heterosexuality and, more significantly, to the power of men over women and children. Thus, for policy-makers, either at a local or a national level, to take on board the demands of womanist or feminist campaigners would signify the need to redetermine the status quo. Evidence from the case studies suggests that policy-makers are reluctant to take on this challenge, preferring instead to deal with campaigners in a piece-meal, individualistic and paternalistic way which maintains prevailing normative values.

Conclusion

Sexuality is considered a legitimate issue for policy when the context is familiar. Acceptable contexts are limited primarily to the class-based issues and environments, and are determined by the nature of local Labour politics. Additionally, the framework has to be one which allows councillors to respond in an individualistic and paternalistic way. Sexuality is accepted as a legitimate issue when its presentation or demands do not challenge the heterosexual status quo and, therefore, patriarchy. Sexuality is also legitimate as a topic when it is concerned with reasserting the status quo or about statutory responsibility. Outside of these examples sexuality is also accepted on the policy agenda when it evokes a moral response in policy-makers.

What then are the possible avenues for effective campaigning around lesbian and gay issues at the local political level? Labour councillors responded on a civil liberties basis to the Section 28 legislation because civil liberties are at the heart of Labourism. The civil liberties response is an important one for campaigners seeking support from politicians. What the research illustrates is that issues concerned with homosexuality, and in particular lesbianism, are difficult for policy-makers to support on an individual and political level. The conceptualization of homosexuality as a civil liberties issue permits politicians the opportunity to support lesbian and gay lifestyles as well as imposing a political and moral obligation on them to oppose anti-homosexual legislation and practice. However, the civil liberties response is valid only in particular acceptable contexts, as with Section 28 (see note 8).

Because councillors, like many other people, are wary of sexuality, particularly male homosexuality and lesbianism, the issues have to be presented in contexts which are familiar to policy-makers. Thus, lesbian and gay issues have to be contextualized within a class framework, for example as an industrial relations issue.

Thirdly, the prevalence of stereotyped images of lesbians and gay men places them in fixed categories in politicians' minds, that is excluding the possibility of lesbians and gay men being in need of Council services or being unemployed, working-class, black or disabled. If campaigners are to effect policy on a wider scale, and if lesbians and gay men are to be accepted as deserving of Council services, then these stereotyped perceptions have to be challenged.

Finally, the research illustrates an interweaving of local Labourist practice with discourses of sexuality revealing the reality of a more complex politics and the interplay of various categories with which Labourist politics is incapable of coming to terms. This is partly because of its reinforcement of fixed categories and hierarchies of need and an inability to recognize the complex interweaving of the social, cultural and material significance of the politics of resistance.[14]

Notes

1   The names of interviewees have been changed to maintain anonymity.

2   P. Lawless, 'Regeneration In Sheffield: from radical intervention to partnership', in D. Judd and M. Parkinson, eds, *Leadership and Urban Regeneration: Cities in North America and Europe* (Beverly Hills CA: Sage, 1990), pp. 133-51.

3   P. Cocker, *Contemporary British Politics and Government* (Sevenoaks: Hodder & Stoughton, 1993).

4   Local government is the 'self-government of Britain's counties, cities and towns' and it accounts for about one tenth of gross domestic product (J. Kingdom, *Local Government and Politics in Britain* (Hemel Hempstead: Philip Allen, 1991, pp. 1, 3)). However, unlike some other countries such as the USA, there is no separation of governmental power. Parliamentary power is paramount, with all constitutional authority being invested in it. Thus local government powers can be revoked or changed at any time by Parliament. Local government is the major provider of public services and is divided into metropolitan and non-metropolitan (or shire) counties which are sub-divided into two main levels – county and district – each of which has different responsibilities for service provision and for different geographical regions. Sheffield, a metropolitan authority, is responsible for the provision of education, social services, housing, technical services, local planning and development, environmental health, leisure and amenities, and other policy areas. Local government is organized into a number of departments representing responsibilities and service provision. All major decisions are made by committees comprising locally elected councillors. The authority is run on a day-to-day basis by paid local government officials known as officers.

5   *Guardian* (23 January 1988).

6   L. Alderson, 'Clause 29', *Trouble and Strife*, 13 (1988), pp. 3–6.

7   *Independent* (2 February 1988).

8   Also of relevance to the local context was the Parkhouse School incident. Prior to the introduction of Section 28 in Sheffield a group of women from the Young Lesbian Group (YLG) was invited by members of staff to speak about lesbianism to a group of students at Parkhouse School. A number of parents were incensed at this, the local media sensationalized it and a public outcry ensued, resulting in the Council suspending its grant aid to the Young Lesbian Group and a request for them to leave GAP – the young women's project of which the Young Lesbian Group was a part. The effect of this was damaging to the Group and was described by one Council officer as 'the most sharp, fierce, homophobic response I've ever seen from them yet' (Sarah). To be fair, some Labour politicians were shocked by the response to the Parkhouse affair, particularly the more 'sophisticated thinkers'. Apparent in the local response to Parkhouse was the idea that young people were in danger of being seduced by lesbians. The idea that homosexuality could be promoted was not new, nor was it a view held exclusively by Conservative Party politicians. Another influential factor affecting the Council response was that of the 'loony Left'. Parkhouse was seen by a number of interviewees as 'a reaction of a post-election Labour Party saying the reason we lost was because of lesbian and gay issues' (Sarah) and the Greater London Council. This is noteworthy also because it highlights the local Council response to Section 28 as being about opposing 'Tory' legislation. In the Parkhouse incident councillors were clearly against homosexuality yet when opposition to homosexuality was introduced as Conservative policy there was seemingly a change of view.

The significance of the Parkhouse School affair to the Section 28 campaign is that is was a catalyst in opening the debate on sexuality within local politics. It was also significant in that many people were involved in campaigning against the Council response to Parkhouse. However, because of this response to the Parkhouse incident, the WAC campaigners were also nervous about raising the issue of Section 28 with the Council.

9   J. Carabine, 'Guardians of civil liberties or mirror of a homophobic society: two newspaper representations of political campaigns against Section 28', M.A. Dissertation, University of Bradford, 1988.

10   This is discussed further, and in relation to councillors' responses to sexuality in general such as sexuality as taboo and as a private and personal issue in J. Carabine, 'Labourism, sexuality and local policy making', in F. Williams, ed., *Social Policy: A Critical Reader* (Cambridge: Polity Press, forthcoming).

11   For further discussion of this see Carabine, 'Labourism'.

12   Carabine, 'Labourism'.
13   See J. Carabine, 'Constructing women: women's sexuality and social policy', *Critical Social Policy*, 34 (1992), pp. 24–37.
14   I would like to thank Diane Richardson, Alan Walker and Fiona Williams for their comments and advice at various stages in the production of this chapter. I would also like to acknowledge the financial support provided by ESRC for the research undertaken during my doctoral study.

Chapter five

(Homo)sexual Citizenship: A Queer Kind of Justice

David T. Evans

Rational debate is not assisted when supporters of the homosexual cause attempt to prove too much. The suggestion that justice requires exact parity of treatment for homosexuality and heterosexuality presupposes that one is comparing like with like. But one is not. The homosexual relationship is fundamentally unlike the heterosexual in being of its nature sterile (and thus necessarily parasitic on the heterosexual) and involving a use of the body for which nature did not design it. These simple facts raise questions . . . suppression [of which] . . . is not in the long-term interests of tolerance and understanding.[1]

Stonewall: the great leap forward?

GREAT claims have been made for the dramatic impact and symbolic significance of the New York Stonewall riots of 1969 ('when gay pride took a quantum leap forward'),[2] for subsequent gay, especially male, politics. Bronski argues that they 'established a homosexual militancy and identity in the public imagination that was startling and deeply threatening . . . [so that] the American press and public could no longer ignore the movement for liberation among lesbians and gay men.'[3] For Bronski these riots were a 'defiant, innately political act' that changed 'the *status quo* between "queers" and "straights" ',[4] and for others 'oppressive Law and Order were from then on increasingly challenged'.[5] The veracity of such claims seems no longer open to doubt, for Stonewall has passed beyond history into folklore: the riots are portrayed as a heroic combustion of justified dissent, the culmination of much concentrated rights campaigning and consciousness-raising especially in territories with high-density gay populations. The freedoms gained were so because of the bravery of those in the political front line of what is implicitly a singular coherent gay community.

Thus has Stonewall been reified as 'the symbolic beginning of the modern struggle for gay liberation'.[7] In truth, however, this is a partial and partially self-deceiving gay history on at least two counts. First, it fails to recognize the prior enabling structural changes in the legal and economic climate of the time, especially the emergent pressures on all populations, including the gay population, towards leisure and lifestyle consumerism. The riots were after all a response to insensitive policing in and around existing early gay commercial venues, the 'freedoms' disputed were specifically those of being at liberty to imbibe and socialize with like others in such premises, to collectively purchase and enact, in at least semi-public spaces, gay status, identity and lifestyle. Second, once past the initial hiatus at least, gay politics has been marked by its lack of militancy, defiance and challenge as most gays and lesbians have become incorporated into what has become a very much expanded commercial culture. If Stonewall signified a 'quantum leap forward' one might now weakly quip that it was a leap into the quantum economics of the Pink Pound or Dollar, into depoliticization; defusion of militancy, defiance and challenge; and a growing willingness to self-policing through the ready acceptance that a gay community exists.

Initially Stonewall did provoke a significant practical as well as symbolic political impetus which was built upon by the various gay liberation groups and manifestos which appeared between 1969 and 1972 in the USA, Britain and elsewhere.[8] Their principles and aims were on the grand scale, concerned with the 'political

significance of sexuality as a system of social control, on the levels
. . . of social structures and belief',[9] as well as the oppressive role of
'bourgeois models of mental health'.[10] As is inevitable in such short-
circuiting rallies to arms, these manifestos were more expressions of
sloganized faith, myths in Sorel's sense, being 'identical with the
convictions of [the] group . . . the expression of . . . convictions in
the language of the movement',[11] rather than analytical starting
points. 'Freedom', '(hetero)sexism', 'patriarchy', 'imperialism',
'oppression',[12] 'capitalism' raised emotions but closed off rather
than opened up debates as indeed did the term 'liberation' itself,
stretched to the tensile limit of meaning: the complete transformation of societies, economic, political institutions and cultures, and of
the gay self within from 'self-oppression'.[13] In those heady days
'Political identity (gay liberation) and personal identification (gay
liberationist) became hopelessly confused',[14] such is the unfocused
mood of passionate beginnings.

This perhaps explains how in liberationist rhetoric revolutionary ambitions so often cohabited with statements of rather more
modest reformist goals within existing structures without any
apparent sense of unease. For example, a 1970 London GLF
pamphlet (*The Principles of the Gay Liberation Front*) included the
following: 'employers should no longer be able to discriminate
against employees on grounds of sexual preference', and: 'the age of
consent for homosexuals should be the same as for heterosexuals'
(modest aims albeit as yet unachieved in Britain),[15] goals more
commonly associated then and subsequently with reformist parties
such as the Campaign for Homosexual Equality (CHE), OutRight
(formerly SMG and SHRG)[16] and now (belying the inspiration of its
chosen name) Stonewall.[17]

Until the mid-1980s and the increasingly routine experience
of AIDS and of governments' and medicine's laggardly and hostile
responses to it, and subsequently in Britain the imposition of Section
28 of the Local Government Act (1988), which banned the
intentional promotion or representation of homosexuality 'as a
pretended family relationship'[18] (for text see p. 129 below), gay and
lesbian politics across the radical-reformist spectrum had been in
progressive decline. There appeared to be an overall lack, which
AIDS and Section 28 have only marginally challenged, of gay

'community' interest in or concern for '(hetero)sexism', 'oppression', 'patriarchy', 'capitalism', 'freedom' or 'liberation'. On the reformist wing, Section 28 has engendered a largely polite, respectful reaction, dominated by the Stonewall spirit of responsible elitist representation ('showbiz' and theatre 'stars' led by such as Sir Ian McKellen and Michael Cashman) and not a spirit of mass mobilization. The re-emergence in the late 1980s of radical combustive, combative politics by such groups as OutRage!, ACT UP and FROCS[19] campaigning on a variety of issues – Section 28 again but also AIDS funding and drug company controls on AIDS knowledge, research and treatments; police harassment; inadequate police protection; sex education and 'outing'[20] – has also been marked by their minority appeal to largely unmoved gay and lesbian populations more inclined to turn out for events such as Gay Lifestyle '93 at Olympia in London[21] or the increasingly apolitical and similarly commercial lifestyle centred on annual Gay Pride rallies.

The overall absence of political consciousness let alone dissent amongst gay and lesbian populations, which on any objective 'rights' count by comparison with the heterosexual norm would appear to have every justification for strong feelings and large-scale action, is intriguing. Whilst the majority would probably support a reduction of the gay male age of consent to the heterosexual equivalent (though it has to be noted that this is not the most important issue for lesbians),[22] it would appear that there is neither a deep nor a broad overall sense of injustice. By the same token it is similarly intriguing that liberationist and especially reformist gay political liturgies have in the post-Stonewall period made so little use of the rhetoric of 'justice' as mobilizer of opinion, shorthand signifier of oppression and/or inequality, or most surprisingly as starting point for political analysis. The adoption, by the American National Gay and Lesbian Task Force for its April 1993 march on Washington of the slogan which has inspired this book, *A Simple Matter of Justice*, is a rare exception, for normally we hear of gay rights and freedoms and perhaps reminisce through the language of 'liberation', but we seldom encounter claims made from or in a paradigm of 'justice'. This is surely surprising, for any gay rights campaigns must presumably commence from a given belief in existing injustices, and 'justice' would appear to provide the necessary mythic concentration required by all such campaigning movements. Perhaps 'justice' is a notion too irretrievably locked into the fetishised legal and political moral order[23] to be rhetorically relevant to radical political groups, but why have reformist parties, respectful of existing legal institutions, also been loath to make claims on its behalf? Perhaps the experience of general 'injustice' is simply too great for sexual minorities to jettison their more active focused concerns with specific civil, political and social rights; or is 'justice' too dense and abstract to serve minority party consensus and mobilization, too opaque to comprehend readily or to challenge its general principles, as the accretion of the question mark in this book's title implies? There is also the distinct possibility suggested by the overall political apathy that most gay men and lesbians believe that being without the full rights of heterosexuals is 'just' because they are not entitled to them.

In order to examine these and other questions concerning the avoidance of 'justice' in gay political rhetoric and action it is necessary first to contextualize post-Stonewall homosexualities in sexual discourse generally as well as within the material parameters in which they have developed.

Sexuality: the will to buy?

The all-enveloping sexualization of advanced societies has been commented on by numerous critics. For Heath we are hooked on the Sexual Fix,[24] for Greer we worship at the altar of Sex Religion,[25] whilst Amis[26] claims that we have witnessed 'the rutting revolution'. Most comprehensively, for Foucault, sexuality, broadened to include the 'bio-political' concerns of bodily health, cosmetic appearance, etc., has become 'the medium through which people seek to define their personalities and . . . to be conscious of themselves'.[27] Foucault's re-elaboration of a theory of power subverts power in the formal juridical sense of negative constraints located in laws and legal institutions, insisting instead that power is an all-pervasive, normative positive presence, as the knowledge/power discourses which imbue language, objects and practices with meaning. We are what we learn, internalize and reproduce as knowledge and the language through which it is understood. We are subjects of the power immanently installed in that knowledge. In a succession of texts – *Madness and Civilisation* (1965), *The Archaeology of Knowledge* (1972), *Discipline and Punish* (1977) and volume 1 of *The History of Sexuality: The Will to Know* (1981)[28] – he charts the growing imperialism of a society seeking to attribute a social status and definition to everything including eventually the unclassifiable, the epitome of the 'personal', 'private', 'mysterious' and naturally unique, that which most resists the cultural: sexuality, *the* most important source of identity for modern subjects, and thus the ultimate means of their complete subjection. We as sexual subjects are constructed out of our obsessive pursuit of ever greater knowledge about our innermost 'essential' sexual selves: ironically so, for sexuality is that aspect of self considered to be the most resistant to explanation through discourse. Thus for Foucault:

> Sexuality . . . is not a domain of nature which power tries to subjugate. . . . It is merely a name which one may give to a historical artefact – rather a hybrid mechanism which links together the stimulation of the body, the intensification of pleasures, incitement to discourse, the formation of knowledges and reinforcements of controls and resistances to it.[29]

It is precisely because sexuality is an historical artefact, defined as a private 'essence' which transcends history and culture and therefore unregulated by juridical power, that it can serve unregulated as 'an especially dense transfer point for relations of (immanent) power'[30] in the modern world. Foucault's elaborate though not entirely unambiguous[31] attempt to develop this 'intricate local understanding of the workings of power'[32] certainly provides a welcome corrective to analyses based solely on objective juridical forms, but his preoccupation with the *completeness* of immanent power in these micrological aspects eradicates human agency and 'blinds him to the perseverance of traditional forms of domination . . . economic, political and cultural'.[33] As interactionist studies demonstrate[34] actors do have choices, and do take decisions as they negotiate with what Gagnon and Simon[35] prefer to call 'cultural scenarios' in the form of intra- and inter-personal sexual scripts as they interact with others in differing contexts. Similarly it is clear that sexual discourses, cultural scenarios and scripts do not occur in a material or power vacuum. On the contrary the sexualization of modern societies has brought with it an increasing array of sexual status groups, gay men and lesbians being the most prominent, which have taken up their places in the complex processes, structures and power relations of capitalism, by partial incorporation into civil, political and social citizenship rights and participation in the consumption markets thus facilitated. If sexuality is 'the medium through which people seek to define their personalities . . . to be conscious of themselves',[36] their search is negotiated within the formal power relations of citizenship and market saturated with sexual rights and commodities; indeed, sexual rights as commodities. As consuming citizens we seek to purchase our fetishized individual unique sexual identities and lifestyles within the increasingly self-imposed confinement of sexual communities.

If our sexual identities are our imperative, the deepest reality with which it is our duty to come to terms, then we must come to terms not only with sexuality as bio-political acts, drives, dysfunctions, 'the Big O',[37] health, pleasure and happiness, but also with sexuality as citizenship status and commodities. If 'sexuality is an especially dense transfer point for relations of *immanent* power'[38] it is especially so through the mechanisms of consumption. If 'Reality as the consumer experiences it is the pursuit of pleasure'[39] as 'on display . . . [we] move through the field of commodities'[40] in 'search of personal and private satisfactions above all else',[41] the latter are increasingly sexual, their construction and realization forged out of material circumstance.

(Homo)sexual citizenship

As I have claimed elsewhere,[42] the progressive movement of gay men and lesbians into partial and specific civil, political and social rights has been facilitated in the post-Wolfenden era by the law's retreat from homosexual liaisons between consenting adults in private, liaisons which however have remained stigmatized as deeply immoral.[43] As a consequence both status groups have become structurally and ideologically contained within the semi-public space which lies between the boundaries of legality and morality which surround the 'moral community'. In this sub-cultural space are sited specifically gay and lesbian associations, friendship networks,[44] institutions and political parties but it is a space increasingly dominated by consumerism and the pursuit of leisure and lifestyle commodities. Status groups are 'communities' with common rights and privileges determined by their relative moral worth and 'stratified according to the principles of their consumption of goods as represented by special styles of life';[45] thus particular constellations of homosexual and lesbian citizenship determine that sexual power-knowledge, whatever its ultimate immanent circulation, is formally juridical and materially valorized. The examination of gay political claims can be comprehended only within and against this framework of existing formal and customary moral as well as economic and legal 'justice'.

The general lack of political consciousness amongst gay and lesbian populations, and the particular lack of 'justice'/'injustice' rhetoric in existing parties and activism, intrigue because it is clear that both status groups 'enjoy' subordinate sexual citizenship owing to their lower moral worth. This suggests various explanations: the possibility of an inarticulate sense of grievance, or one effectively stifled by the likely 'honour' losses of 'out' pursuit of claims. Alternatively the sense of 'injustice' may be relatively slight, indeed there may be little sense of 'injustice', meaning in either of these latter instances acceptance that homosexual claims against hetero-sexual standards are inappropriate because one is not comparing 'like with like'. As Runciman observes:

> Wherever inequalities of class, status or power rise to either a greater or a lesser sense of relative deprivation than the inequalities themselves would appear to warrant there is at once a discrepancy which raises the question what perception of inequalities is 'natural' or 'reasonable' or even 'correct'.[46]

By implication the form and content, as well as low levels, of existing gay and lesbian political consciousness and activism suggest that, at least in part, for most gay men and lesbians, 'like with like' comparisons are not made with heterosexuals, that contextualizing principles of 'justice' in the sense of 'fairness'[47] are not subscribed to; rather the claims which are made employ reduced alternative terms of 'entitlement',[48] on grounds of natural difference, that is inferiority. These by now familiar opposing models of justice are together found in Weber thus:

> In Weber's thought the theory of justice involves a funda-mental antinomy. Men are unequally endowed from the physical, intellectual and moral standpoints. At the outset of human existence there is a lottery. . . . Since inequality exists at the outset, there are two possible orientations: one that would tend to obliterate the natural inequality through social effort (Rawls); and another that would on the contrary tend to reward everyone on the basis of his unequal qualities (Nozick, Friedman and Rand). Weber maintained that between these two antithetical tendencies . . . there is no choice governed by science: every man chooses his God or his devil for himself.[49]

Or, it might be mooted in this instance, there is apparently a severely circumscribed choice governed by the material discourses of homosexual citizenship which formalize an 'entitlement' paradigm of 'justice' which rests on an understanding of essential difference. In order to examine how, it is necessary to return to the persistent moral stigma of homosexuality in the post-Wolfenden era simultan-eously marked by gay and lesbian 'advance' into partial citizenship, a moral stigma which, notwithstanding occasional suggestions of inconsistency and ambiguity, ultimately rests on justifying 'percep-tions of inequalities as "natural", "reasonable" (even) "correct"', and of unequal endowment from 'physical, intellectual and moral standpoints'.

Rawls has identified four socially valued stages in the emergent properties of citizenship rights in their constitutional and institutional forms.[50] The first consists of those primary goods (*social* and *natural*) which any rational person would want 'what-ever his plan of life or social orientation would be'.[51] Social primary goods form the basis of all citizenship and include 'the basic liberties'[52] freedom of thought and liberty of the conscience, indispensable to the protection of determinate conceptions of the good within the limits of justice; freedom of movement and free choice of occupation against a background of diverse opportunities; powers and prerogatives of offices and positions of responsibility which 'give scope to various self-governing and social capacities of the self';[53] and income and wealth defined broadly as 'all purposive means'[54] having an exchange value; and finally the social bases of self-respect. In general: those aspects of basic institutions normally essential 'if citizens are to have a lively sense of their own worth as persons and to be able to develop and exercise their moral power and to advance their aims and ends with self confidence'.[55]

Natural primary goods include health and vigour, intelligence and imagination, qualities which are dependent upon primary social goods,[56] which in 'common sense' and dominant ideological forms are frequently the 'taken-for-granted' cause of natural goods. Rawls locates these primary goods in their specific social contexts as he moves through his other three stages, the second consisting of two 'principles of justice', the first of which is phrased as a right:

(1) Liberties are to be arranged so as to achieve the most extensive justifiable set of equal basic liberties for each and everyone.
(2) Social and economic inequalities are to be arranged so that (a) they are structured by social roles and offices, which are open to all under conditions of 'fair equality of opportunity' and such inequalities in wealth, income and position serve (b) to improve ideally to maximise the life situation of the least advantaged group.[57]

Rawls's third stage is the identification of how (and the extent to which) these two principles of justice are brought to bear on the distribution of primary goods, through any particular society's economic, political and other institutions so that rights and duties are assigned and monitored. Rawls's fourth stage is in many ways the most interesting, for it concerns the 'legitimate expectations' of populations: the extent to which a particular citizenship culture is accepted as given and in which injustices are challenged. Such injustices may be perceived in terms of constitutional rights or State institutional practices (such as the jury system, employment practices, welfare accessibility, etc.). To these four stages Rawls adds the general 'method of effective equilibrium', meaning that in any particular society rights machinery will be mediated by accumulated historical and cultural assessments of what is being done, how, and why, in terms of rationales and so on.

This exposition of universal primary goods institutionalized as extensively as justifiably possible immediately isolates the existing machineries and experiences of citizenship as restrictive on particular subjects' 'self confidence' and 'sense of self worth', 'plan of life', 'scope for self government', realization and expression of 'social capacities of the self' on the basis of their particular (in this instance) sexual disqualifications. Similarly, linking these 'egalitarian' principles of justice to market constraints of wealth and income, as together part of overall 'legitimate expectations', underlines the closeness of the relationship between the two spheres, that citizenship rights are primarily rights of market access and choice.[58] Also a causal relativism is implicitly incorporated, for once such citizenship principles are established, and there is evidence that popular opinion increasingly reflects what has been referred to as 'moral relativism' or 'situational ethics',[59] the history of citizenship rights, whatever the peculiarities of any one society's 'method of reflective equilibrium', becomes increasingly one of battles over the legitimacy of competing claims on the grounds of 'entitlement' rather than 'fairness'. Claims made for 'fairness' may be legally arbitrated only if the law is concerned with *both* criminal and moral decision-making, and 'entitlement' claims are weakened if those making them are disqualified because of their biological inferiority. Post-Wolfenden law has retreated from moral judgements on sexual behaviours, proceeding instead with causal concerns[60] whilst immoral gay and lesbian status has continued to be predominantly justified as 'reasonable' through reference to primary 'natural' difference.

Legal immorality and secondary markets

The post-Wolfenden (1957)[61] reforms which partially legalized citizens into the causalist 'entitlement' marginalized group did not remove from them the stigma of immorality. The Report distinguished between crime and sin as follows: 'it is not the function of the law to interfere in the private lives of citizens, or to seek to enhance any particular pattern of behaviour'.[62] Even so it was still the law's duty to:

> preserve public order and decency, to protect the citizen from what is offensive and injurious, and to provide safeguards against the exploitation and corruption of others. . . . Unless a deliberate attempt is made by society, acting through the agency of the law, to equate the sphere of crime with that of sin, there must remain a realm of private morality and immorality which is not the law's business.[63]

It was argued that there was a need for 'more effective regulation of sexual deviance'[64] for existing legislation encouraged 'disrespect and cynicism'.[65] The recommended shift of legal emphasis was from moral to causal judgements.[66] Rather than appraising behaviours by their moral worth – 'immoral, wrong, wicked'[67] – legal judgements were to be concerned with proven effects: 'if it turns out that more harm is done by forbidding an activity than by allowing it, then Parliament will permit it, even if most of the members consider the activity to be wrong or immoral'.[68] Thus the conjunction of illegality with immorality was severed, and between their boundaries a social, economic and political space created for those newly legalized but still morally reprehensible. More significantly this retreat from private sexual immorality meant that 'fairness' principles of moral justice became formally of secondary importance within a law increasingly concerned with the relativities of causally adjudged 'entitlements'.

It is important to emphasize that this distinction between illegality and immorality was not intended to weaken moral values. Whilst Wolfenden recommended legalization of male homosexual behaviours between consenting adults in private and under further specific limiting conditions, the Report deplored the decline in moral standards, defined homosexuality as 'reprehensible from the point of view of harm to the family'[69] and contemplated the retention of buggery, 'particularly objectionable because it involves coitus and thus simulates more nearly than any other homosexual act the normal act of sexual intercourse', as a separate offence.[70] Above all else, therefore, public manifestations should be severely restricted:

We do not think that it would be expedient at the present time to reduce in any way the penalties attaching to homosexual importuning. It is important that the limited modifications of the law which we propose should not be interpreted as an indication that the law can be indifferent to other forms of homosexual behaviour or as a general licence to adult homosexuals to behave as they please.[71]

Accordingly the policing of this moral boundary through recourse to a variety of usually antique general 'receptacle' laws has, especially in the early post-reform period, been notably increased,[72] but the removal of criminality from certain victimless sexual behaviours made possible the development of causal relativism into the full equation of sexual citizenship, that is with regard to *both* citizen–state and consumer–market relations. 'Discourses hierarchise and distribute the various categories of sexual deviance around the norm of marriage, the family and procreation, which provide the particular "regime of truth".'[73] Rather than all non-monogamous heterosexual behaviours being equally illegal, there has been 'considerable fragmentation of the boundaries of immorality and legitimacy'[74] within this new social space which is 'not the law's business', some more immoral than others. There have developed 'incommensurate and irreconcilable conceptions of the (*sexual*) good',[75] of secondary discreet and 'private' (in the sense of hidden from public view) markets, consumable identities, lifestyles and communities, justified on grounds of natural disqualification and moral threat, but exploitable and commodifiable all the same, by a market which is in this sense justly described as amoral, constraining and constricting:

in present day society [where] consumer conduct (consumer freedom geared to the consumer market) moves steadily into the position of simultaneously the cognitive and moral focus of life, integrative bond of society, and the focus of systematic management . . . [where] individuals are engaged (morally by society, functionally by the social system) first and foremost as consumers rather than producers.[76]

That is, the material construction of homosexualities occurs primarily within the commercial arenas permitted by the partial concessions on citizenship.

Family values: the regime of truth?

Thatcherism's 'Victorian' and Major's 'basic' values have successively served to conceal and reinforce this dislocation between legality and morality and in doing so have targeted various stalking horses, with homosexuality and homosexuals the most favoured – as is nowhere more apparent than with the passing into law of Section 28 of the Local Government Act (1988). At first glance it might appear that this legislation marks a reversal of the law's post-Wolfenden causalist concerns and an attempt to revive the law's moral authority. Nor is it an isolated moralist reaction, as the December 1990 Operation Spanner's successful prosecution of 'consenting adults'' rights to engage in sado-masochistic acts in private has also made clear. However both, especially the former, are most notable for the considerable opposition caused within and without the law precisely because they are at odds with dominant formal and customary practice concerning sexual matters. In particular Section 28 is a legal paradox, a moral reaffirmation that is for most legal critics unenforceable and indeed thus far unenforced. It has certainly worked to inhibit and to impose more stringent self-regulation on numerous individuals and institutions but that is its moral not its legal point. It is precisely because of Section 28's hybrid character that it provides such a fascinating and in many ways oblique codification of the complexities of contemporary moral, legal and material discourses imposed on gay and lesbian populations corralled into the social and economic limbo of 'the gay community'.

By the time Clause 28 became law on 24 May 1988, it was already being authoritatively dismissed as particularly weak legislation; the wording ambiguous, contradictory and sometimes quite meaningless: 'In reality there is little to fear from Section 28 except fear itself. . . . Section 28 is largely redundant. Its most potent effect is as a symbol of the prejudice of the present Parliament',[77] a symbolic affirmation of the immorality of homosexuality which also summarily encompasses other motifs central to New Right philosophy, all with rights implications: threat to the sanctity of the traditional private family;[78] local authority power; the teaching profession and other 'enemy within' elements in the bureaucratized intelligentsia,[79] those most responsible for the 'permissiveness' of the 1960s and the continuing threat of 'permissiveness' in the 1980s; sex education;[80] childhood innocence and suggestibility; illness of plague dimensions, etc. The background to Section 28 thus appears generally to have been the effectiveness of homosexuality as a summary symbol of all threats to 'family values' and, more specifically, the New Right's belief that homosexuality was not being sufficiently inhibited by its 'immorality'.

Overall the New Right's commitment is to nature's values being 'Victorian'. Real, as opposed to pretended, family relationships are at the centre of both, it is claimed by prominent ideologues Gummer, Mount, Scruton, amongst others,[81] and it is the State's responsibility to respect and not to invade this most precious of natural forms: '[We] the defenders of the family . . . assert always [its] privacy and independence . . . its biological individuality . . . its right to live according to its natural instincts.'[82] 'What is the driving force in our society? It is the desire for the individual to do the best for himself and his family. There is no substitute for this elemental human instinct',[83] indeed 'there is no such thing as society, there are individual men and women and their families',[84] who 'have a natural instinct for ownership and possession, and private enterprise provides an incentive, other than force for work . . . . Conservatives value private property and private enterprise primarily as the protectors of the family and of freedom.'[85]

In this defence the family and private property are inextricably intertwined as part of our 'instinctive' natures. Scruton (1984)[86] argues that property is the primary relationship through which man lives socially, morally and economically, that the family is the site of the accumulation and inheritance, not merely of capital wealth but also of key Christian values and attitudes. The family thus stands at the intersection of moral and material spheres: '[it] has its life in the home, and the home needs property for its establishment'.[87] The nation's wealth and well-being are the family's wealth and well-being for 'Let us remember we are a nation, and a nation is an extended family'.[88] 'A nation of free people will only continue to be great if family life continues and the structure of the nation is a family one.'[89]

Set against the natural family, 'unnatural', 'unstable', 'sterile', 'parasitic', 'sick', 'sad', unproductive, hedonistic, predatory homosexuality is a pathological condition manifest in a lifestyle which Scruton[90] calls an 'assault on the self' and on the social order which produces it; thus his concern for the survival of capitalism and the family as its central institution leads to the expected polemic against promiscuity and homosexuality, significantly dealt with together: 'The first [promiscuity] destroys the sacral character of the body, and therefore loosens the connection between desire and love. The second [homosexuality] severs desire from its generative tendency.'[91]

Scruton's opposition to homosexuality is specifically because it encourages a new promiscuity:

> unsubdued by the awesome mystery of another sex, driven always to unite with flesh of his own all-too-familiar kind, the homosexual has no use for hesitation, except that which society imposes. He knows with too great a certainty, too great a familiarity what his partner feels, and has no need for the tiresome strategems of courtesy, courtship and shame. The gateway to desire, which hides its course in mystery, and diverts it to the path of love, has been burst open, and a short path to pleasure revealed.[92]

Prior to Section 28, AIDS had already been ideologically 'captured for the reconstruction of moral imperatives which seek to privilege above all other forms of sexual expression, those that are narrowly focussed on procreative and penetrative vaginal intercourse . . . within the context of exclusive and life-long monogamous relationships'.[93] This was a reconstruction of disease out of 'lifestyle', which, as novelist Christopher Coe has observed, transformed the moral neutrality of Weber's term into one with 'condescension built into it, a xenophobe's word',[94] indicating a disease of 'choice' for promiscuous homosexuals and drug abusers. AIDS has been used to reaffirm the family, through the deserved fate of 'guilty' victims set alongside the corrupted innocence of the duplicitous bisexual male's wife, the child born to infected parents, and the haemophiliac. With specific reference to homosexuality AIDS has been constructed as 'the viral personification of unorthodox deregulative desire',[95] as the triumphant rejection of the promiscuous homosexual; a passionate defence of long-term monogamous heterosexuality.

Section 28: a moral law?

On the specific background to Section 28, proponents' concerns that homosexuality was not being sufficiently contained by its moral stigma have been seconded by some radical gay commentators who view the legislation as the response of people under pressure who 'perceive that people's attitudes are changing, that they are being more tolerant . . . ',[96] who recognize the successful inroads made by gay activism; 'It's tempting to think fascism's just round the corner. But we are being attacked because we are making progress particularly in areas of local government';[97] 'politicians didn't decide to take this issue on, [rather it was] the [gay] community deciding to take on the politicians, and . . . we have chosen to target in particular those we thought would take us . . . Labour Councils'.[98]

For Thatcher, linking the general threat to the specific, 'Young people are crying out for a set of rules and standards to live by. It is up to us to restore them.'[99] At the 1987 Tory Party Conference she noted: 'Children who need to be taught to respect traditional moral values are being taught that they have an inalienable right to be gay.'[100] Elsewhere she expressed the 'real concern that local authorities were targetting some activities on young people in schools and outside, in an apparent endeavour to glamorise homosexuality'.[101] This 'real concern' arose specifically from press reports about the activities of some Labour local councils, notably Haringey in North London, where the policy of 'positive images' of homosexuality intended to respect diversity ('We are trying to help people form a humane approach to what is essentially a human rights issue'),[102] had led to violent clashes between parents and gay rights supporters. But this particular modest affair became the focus for more persistent generalized diagnoses of the moral demise of modern Britain with homosexuality specified as the synonymous agent.

A *Spectator* editorial (14 March 1987) portrayed these concerns with candour:

> The belief that some sexual acts are perverted accords with the emphasis – essential in a civilized society – on the dignity of man. Acts which stray from those for which the human body is designed and which defy the chief purpose of sexual intercourse impair that dignity. Homosexuality is morally . . . a dead end . . . Homosexual acts . . . are beneath human dignity . . . What is needed is a repudiation of homosexuality.[103]

Such a repudiation is both more necessary and more effective if that which is repudiated can be directly associated with a 'mysterious' life and society-threatening disease: AIDS. Geoffrey Dickens MP of the Conservative Family Campaign (committed amongst other objectives to repeal of the 1967 Sexual Offences Act's partial legalization of adult male homosexuality), was reported in May 1987 as saying that:

> Public opinion demands that we do control this killer disease . . . people are quite appalled at the way homosexuality is spreading throughout Britain. . . . Once we introduced legislation in Parliament to make . . . [homosexuality] respectable for over 21 year olds between consenting adults in private, we gave it a sort of currency, a sort of respectability that it was O.K. But it's had a roll on effect on the young . . . not only with teaching and indoctrination in schools, but we've seen set up, gay and lesbian clubs all over the place. . . . They entice and corrupt and bring others into their unnatural net.[104]

Dickens's elision of gays with AIDS with death because unnatural, is by now commonplace rhetoric: 'AIDS is a self-inflicted scourge' to be 'blamed on degenerate conduct' resulting in 'people

. . . swirling around in a cesspit of their own making'.[105] Dickens's concern with the potential of high public profile homosexual lifestyles and culture to 'entice' and 'corrupt' into the 'unnatural' exposes a fundamental contradiction within current dominant ideologies on homosexuality, a contradiction most commonly focused on the threat to those most naturally pure, the young. Paul Johnson, speaking on Radio 4's *Weekend World* in January 1988, demonstrated the contradiction in his warning that

> I have known a great many homosexuals . . . many of them would not stop short at seducing someone under age and that is how many of them acquire their perversion. . . . Male homosexuals feel themselves outside the law . . . they know what they are doing is unnatural. If you break the moral and natural law, you are tempted to break it in other ways. . . . My advice to homosexual leaders is not to ask for equality . . . [but] to keep their heads down.[106]

'Tolerance can only exist when disgust is kept at bay. Flaunting breeds disgust. Flaunting a habit which spreads a fatal disease breeds rage'.[107] It is clear that such fire and brimstone rhetoric was in part responding to some attempts by gay and lesbian claimants to utilize existing rights machineries, as the following observation from David Waddington, then Home Office Minister, makes clear. Reacting to the Labour Campaign for Lesbian and Gay Rights' demand that discrimination on the grounds of sexual orientation should be prevented by law, he stated:

> I cannot imagine anything which is more likely to damage the Equal Opportunities Commission than for it to become identified in the public mind with such crankish notions as that it should be wrong to discriminate against people on the grounds of homosexuality.[108]

Deference and gratefulness for existing rights were what was expected, as had been made clear by Lord Arran, who had helped to guide the 1967 legislation through the House of Lords: 'I ask those who have as it were been in bondage and for whom the prison doors are now open, to show their thanks by comporting themselves quietly and with dignity.'[109]

During early readings of the Local Government Bill there were fears of increased censorship of representations of homosexuality in the arts and media raised by draft wording which, in addition to the provisions finally ratified, also proposed that local authorities should be banned from giving 'financial or other assistance to any person promoting homosexuality'. This last component was removed by the Lords, according to SLD peer Lord Falkland, because the government were fearful that 'a lot of loony groups mainly financed from the United States and mostly born again Christian paramilitary groups would jump in'.[110] The key provisions of Section 28 that became law on 24 May 1988 were as follows:

> (1) A local authority shall not:
> (a) intentionally promote homosexuality or publish material with the intention of promoting homosexuality;
> (b) promote the teaching in any maintained school of the acceptability of homosexuality as a pretended family relationship.
> (2) Nothing in subsection (1) above shall be taken to prohibit the doing of anything for the purpose of treating or preventing the spread of disease.[111]

The weaknesses of the statute as law have been commented on and well detailed elsewhere,[112] but for our purposes here the form as well as content of some of the more telling weaknesses deserves comment. For example Norrie describes the three opening words of paragraph (a) as all potential pitfalls for the eager prosecutor. 'Promote', though widely used in statute formulations, has never been formally judicially interpreted; rather it has been customarily interpreted by the courts in a manner commensurate with everyday usage: i.e. 'to encourage, to develop, or to bring about an increase in'. Doubts over 'promote' lay behind many of the initial concerns about the scope of Section 28 and were recognized by one Environment Minister who, however, did not enlighten with his subsequent attempt at clarification: 'We *think* promote has a *clear* meaning. If one promotes something one is deliberately doing something to give what is promoted more favourable treatment, more favourable status or wider acceptance than other things or than that thing hitherto.'[113]

Legal judgements, however, are spun from finer silk, as Norrie elucidates with telling examples:

> Certain local authority activities clearly are beneficial to lesbians and gays such as giving grants to gay groups, licensing gay venues and stocking libraries with books with gay themes. However none of these things is the intentional promotion of homosexuality. There is a surprising legal authority for this. In the famous Gillick case, the House of Lords held that to provide contraceptives to girls under the age of 16 did not break the law by 'promoting, encouraging, or facilitating unlawful sexual intercourse.' For a local authority to fund gay groups or to license gay venues will undoubtedly make it easier for people to come to terms with themselves, and more likely that they will meet gay people and have gay sex (which *is not* illegal) just as the provision of contraceptives to people under 16 may make it more likely that they will have non-gay sex (which *is* illegal). For a local authority to be caught by paragraph (a) it must provide the grants or issue the licences with the express intention of promoting or facilitating or bringing about an increase in homosexuality, rather than the intention of making life easier for lesbians and gays. It will probably be impossible for a prosecutor to show that the local authority acted with this intention.[114]

Homosexuality: that which cannot be promoted?

What is of particular interest, however, is that following this convincing detail Norrie argues that, because homosexuality is a state of being 'like femaleness and blackness', it is logically impossible to encourage or further the growth of homosexuality. He explains:

> One can only encourage the acceptability of or the teaching about homosexuality, but paragraph (a) does not prohibit any of that. Because it prohibits the promotion of that which cannot be promoted, paragraph (a) prohibits a local authority from doing the impossible.[115]

In that his argument is no doubt in accord with most conventional medical, legal and 'common-sense' judgements, he is correct to conclude that the Section's paragraph (a) is thus unenforceable; but a more tantalizing interpretation of paragraph (a) would be that, albeit in a legal context that is muddied by all kinds of wording problems, for the first time in a British legal statute it has been recognized that homosexuality can be 'promoted' because it is *not* a natural condition but a learnt status dependent upon a range of social, situational and interactional circumstances. Furthermore the wording of paragraph (b) suggests even more forcefully that the social construction of homosexuality is being recognized, for whatever the interpretation given to 'homosexuality' in paragraph (a) it is clear that it can be manifest in a range of ways, whereas paragraph (b) prohibits homosexuality only 'as a pretended family relationship'. Thus the promotion of presumably promiscuous or exaggeratedly effeminate male homosexual behaviour is not prohibited by this Section. That is, to say the least, curious because it undercuts the sub-section (2) which states that 'Nothing in the subsection (1) above shall be taken to prohibit the doing of anything for the purpose of treating or preventing the spread of disease'. It would seem that paragraph (b) is specifically formulated to prohibit because homosexuality is believed to equal promiscuity, learnt, one-to-one, long-term 'pretended family', and thus from the point of view of AIDS transmission, relatively safer forms of homosexuality only.

By contrast Norrie's essentialist critique that homosexuality is a condition pinpoints a prominent peculiarity of Section 28 and the debates it has engendered: it and its proponents acknowledge, albeit in garbled ambiguous terms such as those already encountered from Dickens and Johnson, that homosexuality may be socially determined via seduction in any or all senses of the word, whilst their opponents, including many within radical parties such as FROCS and ACT UP, focus their criticism, as Norrie does here, on emphasizing the irrelevance of the legislation because, 'like blackness and femaleness', homosexuality is a condition. Lord Boyd Carpenter, addressing the Lords during a Clause 28 debate, is amongst the more erudite examples of the former school:

> It is a fact that young males at a certain stage in life – i.e. soon after puberty – in many cases have a homosexual element or tendency in them which the vast majority of them succeed in restraining, to their credit. But if attempts are made deliberately to emphasise that side of their nature and to suggest that the homosexual way of life is just as good as ordinary married life – indeed, perhaps better – it is fairly certain that some of those young people will be led to adopt a homosexual orientation which they would not otherwise have adopted. That is the basic problem.[116]

Indeed it *is*. Section 28, by presenting homosexuality as a relational phenomenon, contradicts the stockpile of cultural representations of homosexuality as 'a psychopathological perversion',[117] a condition hormonal, chromosomal or genetic in origin. If homosexuality is a 'state of being', how can it be promoted or represented as a 'pretended family relationship'? Perhaps it is in recognition of this paradox that 'pretended' is such a required part of the formulation, signifying an attempt, albeit weak, to reconcile the irreconcilable by warning that whilst homosexuality is unnatural, just as the family is natural, it has the capacity to seduce and convert. What it has done, however, is to force those it addresses to defend themselves, as Norrie does, in essentialist terms:

> Clause 28 aims to protect young people from being persuaded to do something they really don't want to do and which goes against all the laws of nature. . . . *Jenny Lives with Eric and Martin*[118] could no more convert a heterosexual into a homosexual than a cabbage patch into an orchard.[119]

Similarly: 'Sexuality is not acquired through teaching, any attempt at proselytising in either direction is both cruel and doomed to failure.'[120] Likewise *School's Out* by the Gay Teachers' Group[121] states that 'Children cannot "catch" homosexuality from openly gay teachers any more than gay pupils "catch" heterosexuality from openly heterosexual teachers.' Well, 'catch' in the germ or viral sense no, but in the sense of 'influenced in the direction of' quite possibly surely. Such essentialism is contradicted by a wealth of social constructionist evidence; psychological (e.g. Freudian theses of innate human bisexuality); sociological (e.g. interactionist accounts of homosexual 'coming out', moral careers and studies of situational homosexualities); and historical evidence on the changing social constructions of all sexual forms including the homosexual. It may be a view that reduces pressure by reassuring the moral community but it is intellectually untenable and crucially delimits the basis upon which radically comprehensive claims for justice might be made: restricting 'entitlements' and effectively ruling out 'fairness' claims altogether.

Section 28 has for some gay commentators had many positive political consequences, such as a strengthening of links, previously seriously strained, between gay male and lesbian 'communities': 'it has given us a common enemy – something worse than each other to fight'.[122] It has exposed and shocked the complacency of many gay males and lesbians who through private relationships and lifestyles have managed to avoid the political implications of being gay; and for a short period anyway it brought sizeable numbers on to the streets to demonstrate and temporarily to unite on a broad front a wide range of particular and not necessarily gay interest groups and individuals such as the Labour Campaign for Lesbian and Gay Rights; the Gay Christian Movement; the National Council for Civil Liberties; the Gay Business Association; the Writers Guild of Great Britain; the Organization for Lesbian and Gay Action (OLGA), etc. It has also been claimed that support for gays amongst the non-gay population has grown: 'For the first time people who have been unprepared to accept that being lesbian and gay is to be oppressed or to get a raw deal, are actually recognising the strength of feeling that exists.'[123] But if the latter is true – and evidence suggests that it is true only in so far as specific isolated legal rights are being recognized – it is on the erroneous grounds that homosexuality is a condition, that gay men and lesbians can't help being what they are, that they are morally, because biologically, distinct and should therefore have the right to be socially and economically distinct, outwith the moral community because of 'physical, intellectual and moral standpoints'.[124] If gay men and lesbians are also convinced that this is so, and the campaigns of various groups to achieve equal age of consent laws have been dominated by essentialist rhetoric, then 'fairness' and 'equality' have been conceded. They may not be completely accepted as ' "reasonable" or "correct" '[125] but only in so far as relative and fragmented rights gains may yet be sought.

Gay politics: a respectful silence?

What I have described is, I believe, the development of a limited (homo)sexual citizenship as a 'just' citizenship on grounds of natural inferiority. The GLF rhetoric of twenty or more years ago signalled the possibility of political challenge with its sweeping but undeveloped attack on the 'political significance of sexuality as a system of social control, on the levels of . . . social structures and belief'.[126] However, the growth of commercial 'community' outlets, and the gradual extension of compromised legal rights encouraging a sense of relative advance within populations remaining concealed from everyday public view within largely self-policed 'communities' set apart from the moral community, charts a willing incorporation into material discourses which proclaim inferior status and 'entitlements' because of natural difference.

This does not mean, however, that the 'unfairness' of existing homosexual citizenship may not be demonstrated following Runciman's largely Rawls-inspired pursuit of a contractual theory of social justice, admittedly rather dense but surely not beyond the wit of popular representation. In addressing status inequalities Runciman draws the distinction between praise and respect, the first a zero-sum concept, the latter not. To praise two people equally is to praise neither unless there are others by comparison with whom the two are being ranked equal first. To respect two people equally, however, is to respect both. Parties to the contract would, he argues, agree on a single maxim: free inequality of praise, no inequality of respect. In a just society inequalities of status would be defensible only where they could be plausibly shown to be inequalities of praise. Any other inequalities of status, in the absence of special justification, would be accounted inequalities of respect, and as such illegitimate. Any group feeling relatively deprived of respect therefore would have a legitimate claim to justice. He gives the following example to illustrate the difference, remembering that in Rawls's justice-as-'fairness' principles we should ask in assessing the merits of rival claims 'what criteria of assessment would have been established by rational persons if we could suppose them to have been required to agree, from a state of primordial equality, on principles by which they would be prepared both to make claims and to concede them', and this agreement, it is supposed, will be made before the parties knew what their relative position would be in the social system within which they would be going to make and concede their respective claims. So here is Runciman's example:

> If we suppose the parties to the contract to be envisaging the possibility that different status may be accorded to them in their eventual society depending on the colour of their skin, it is obvious that they will rule out such a system on principle. I do not know whether I shall have a black skin or a white one, I shall surely be unwilling to agree to any principles whereby either the one or the other will secure for me unequal treatment in the hierarchies of class status and power [sic]. But suppose someone wishes to defend discrimination of this kind as no violation of social justice. It would be absurd for him to try to describe colour prejudice in terms of differential praise. Afrikaaners in South Africa or white Southerners in the United States, can hardly be described as *praising* each other for the colour of their skins. What they accord to each other, and what the parties to the contract would stipulate against, is differential respect.[127]

Thus a just society can accommodate inequalities of status according to differential qualities or talents which attract praise, but when one activity or role is assigned higher status than another irrespective of the praise accorded to the attributes of the person practising it, then the principles of social justice are violated. Runciman then provides another telling example which suggests an application of these principles which by extension are of relevance to the gay male and lesbian case:

> Imagine a society in which physical strength is admired above all other attributes. An anthropologist studying this society observes a number of ways in which higher status is bestowed on the strong; how might we suppose him to be able to distinguish those which could and those which could not be properly described as the bestowal of praise? He might notice that the acquaintance of the strong was curried by the weak, that the strong were often applauded or cheered by the weak on their public appearances, that the strong were awarded medals and decorations for their strength, or that a random sample of parents in this society all said that they would prefer their children to be strong than weak. On the other hand he might notice that when the strong appeared in public all passers-by either bowed or knelt, that the children of the strong were accorded the same deference as the strong themselves, that only the strong initiated conversations or greetings with the weak, not vice versa, or that separate public facilities for washing and eating were provided for the strong and for the weak. In the first case the anthropologist would surely interpret his observations as evidence for inequalities of praise, but in the second for inequalities of respect.[128]

Runciman believes this example demonstrates clearly the difference between the two even though it is difficult to define respect adequately. The analytical strength of such an argument is considerable, but the popularizing of claims according to its principles in the instance of gay and lesbian inequalities is questionable because of the political, material and cultural constraints which are many and powerful. Social justice in these terms appears initially an abstract ideal with little likelihood of broad or broader appeal until there is wider acceptance of constructionist explanations for the causes of gayness and lesbianism enabling 'like with like' comparisons to be drawn. As some critics forcefully claim, there are grounds for believing that various academic disciplines 'have contributed in an unusual interdisciplinary conversation . . . [and that e.g.] social construction theory has become the influential – some charge orthodox – framework in the new sex history'.[129] Also, as I hope has been illustrated above, dominant ideological and political defence of unequal rights is increasingly, though not unambivalently, couched in terms of the potential constructionist 'contamination' threat of positive images of homosexuality and especially on an adolescent population legally entitled to have gay sex at sixteen. What is also most noticeable is that radical as well as reformist claims on the basis of 'entitlement' principles are softened by emphasizing that, for essentialist reasons, no such contamination is possible.

Abstract ideals do make for weak political myths, poor mobilizers of minority consciousness and activism. One cannot realistically envisage a successful promulgation of Rawlsian principles of justice emptying the backrooms of Amsterdam: the New York, Why-Not? and Club X bars of the gay commercial culture worldwide, or likewise the beaches of Sitges, Mykonos and Provincetown. But the debate about the cause of homosexual difference *is* one that engages gay and lesbian opinion at all levels and, as I hope I have convinced, escape from the material constraints of homosexual citizenship, as it currently exists and is developing into a social justice of the kind that Runciman envisages, can only occur with the successful advance of social constructionist arguments and the weakening of those which root our sexual differences in nature. As Runciman observes: 'if [people] accept or are unaware of inequalities which are unjust then they are waiving as it were the right to resent them.'[130] Currently gay men and lesbians do accept inequalities which are unjust because they believe they have lesser entitlements owing to their natural inferiority. Might not resort to 'fairness' principles reveal that in many senses what we currently have is a *queer* kind of justice?

Notes

1   Letter from a J. Harwood Stevenson published in *The Times* (26 January 1994).

2   E. Jackson and S. Persky, eds, *Flaunting It: A Decade of Gay Journalism* (Vancouver: Pink Triangle Books, 1982), p. 1.

3   M. Bronski, *Culture Clash: The Making of Gay Sensibility* (Boston MA: South End Press, 1984), pp. 2–4.

4   Bronski, *Culture Clash*, p. 87.

5   S. Tucker, 'Sex, death and free speech', *Body Politic*, 58, p. 4.

6   E.g. 'San Francisco is a refugee camp for homosexuals. We have fled here from every part of the nation . . . not because it is so great here but because it was so bad there.' C. Wittman, 'A gay manifesto', in K. Jay and A. Young, eds, *Out of the Closets: Voices of Gay Liberation* (New York: Jove HBJ, 1977).

7   J. Gough and M. McNair, *Gay Liberation in the Eighties* (London: Pluto, 1985).

8   Jay and Young, *Out of the Closets*, provide a few. Other sources on late 1960s and early 1970s gay activism in the USA include D. Teal, *The Gay Militants* (New York: Stein & Day, 1971); D. Altman, *Homosexual: Oppression and Liberation* (Sydney: Angus & Robertson, New Century Press, 1972); and G. Tobin and R. Wicker, *The Gay Crusaders* (New York: The Paperback Library, 1972). On the Gay Liberation Front in Britain see J. Weeks, *Coming Out: Homosexual Politics in Britain from the Nineteenth Century to the Present* (London: Quartet, 1977), pp. 185–206; S. Watney, 'The ideology of the GLF', in Gay Left Collective, ed., *Homosexuality, Power and Politics* (London: Allison & Busby, 1980); A. Walter, *Come Together: The Years of Gay Liberation 1970–73* (London: Gay Men's Press, 1980); B. Cant and S. Hemmings, ed., *Radical Records: Thirty Years of Radical Lesbian and Gay History* (London: Routledge, 1988); and B. Mellors, 'Gay liberation', *LSE Magazine* (summer 1990), pp. 31–2.

9   Watney, 'Ideology', p. 64.

10   Watney, 'Ideology', p. 65.

11   G. Sorel, quoted by K. Kumar, *Revolution* (London: Weidenfeld & Nicolson, 1971).

12   S. Rowbotham, *The Women's Movement and Organising for Socialism: Beyond the Fragments* (Newcastle: Newcastle Socialist Centre, 1979), has commented that the idea of oppression is both vague and static, fixing people in their role as victims rather than pointing to the contradictory aspects of relationships which *force* the emergence of new forms of consciousness.

13   A. Hodges and D. Hutter, *With Downcast Gays: Aspects of Homosexual Self-Oppression* (London: Pomegranate, 1974).

14   Watney, 'Ideology', p. 71.

15   For the full text of this pamphlet see D. T. Evans, *Sexual Citizenship: The Material Construction of Sexualities* (London: Routledge, 1993), pp. 114–17.

16   SMG = Scottish Minorities Group; SHRG = Scottish Homosexual Rights Group.

17   The Stonewall Group was formed one year after the passing of Section 28 of the Local Government Act 1988 by a largely media/ arts group to set up an all-party parliamentary working group on lesbian and gay rights and to lobby for legal reforms: lowering the age of homosexual consent to sixteen, abolition of crimes of gross indecency and soliciting; outlawing anti-gay discrimination in the provision of goods and services; legal recognition of same-sex couples; removal of anti-gay laws in the armed services; creation of a new offence of incitement to hatred on grounds of sexual orientation; outlawing discrimination at work, in the provision of hotel facilities, entertainment, education, banking, etc.; ending prosecutions of under sixteen-year-olds engaging in consensual homosexual activities; the creation of a new offence of 'aggravated indecent assault' to cover male rape (at the time of writing to be included in the forthcoming Criminal Justice Act).

18   See the Local Government Act (1988), Section 28, sub-section 3.

19   OutRage is 'a broad based group of lesbians and gay men committed to radical non-violent direct action and disobedience to (i) assert the dignity and pride and human rights of gay men and lesbians; (ii) to fight homophobia, discrimination and violence against lesbians and gay men and (iii) to affirm the rights of lesbians and gay men to sexual freedom, choice and self determination'. ACT UP is a radical and direct action group(s) which specifically targets AIDS-related issues such as government ineptitude in handling and funding research, drug company research programmes, etc. FROCS = Faggots Rooting Out Closeted Sexualities.

20   'Outing' is in the words of B. Marshall, in S. Shepherd and M. Wallis, eds, *Coming On Strong: Gay Politics in Culture* (London: Hyman/Unwin, 1989), 'tabloid witch hunt' tactics adopted by gay activists to expose those reputedly gay in positions of power and authority but who are closeted and abuse their positions of power by supporting homophobic legislation, ideologies, etc.

21   Gay Lifestyle '93 was held at Olympia London on 27 and 28 November 1993. It brought together stands providing information on and/or selling health education, charities, sports clubs, hotels, clubs and pubs, arts and crafts, gifts and shopping, gay businesses, financial services, legal advice, accountants, household services, travel and holidays, print and design, professional firms, and in-

cluded four stage and fashion shows, dance spectacular and review, club stage with competitions, top-name acts and cabaret, string quartet and steel band, seven bars, and five restaurants. Admission was £6.50 in advance, £7.50 on the door.

22 F. Otitoju, in 'Is there such a thing as a gay community?' *Gay Times* (January 1994), pp. 30–2.

23 See discussion of K. Renner, by R. Dahrendorf, *Class and Class Conflict in Industrial Society* (London: Routledge & Kegan Paul, 1959).

24 S. Heath, *The Sexual Fix* (London: Macmillan, 1982).

25 G. Greer, *Sex and Destiny: The Politics of Human Fertility* (London: Secker & Warburg, 1984).

26 M. Amis, 'Making sense of AIDS', *Observer* (23 June 1985), p. 22.

27 M. Foucault and R. Sennett, 'Sexuality and solitude', *Humanities in Review*, 1 (1981), pp. 3–21.

28 M. Foucault, *Madness and Civilisation* (New York: Vintage, 1965); *The Archaeology of Knowledge* (London: Tavistock, 1972); *Discipline and Punish: The Birth of Prison* (London: Allen Lane, 1972); *The History of Sexuality, Volume One: An Introduction* (Harmondsworth: Penguin, 1981).

29 A. H. Hussain, 'Foucault's history of sexuality', *m/f*, 7 (1981), pp. 169–91.

30 S. Bailey, 'A comment on Alec McHoul's reading of Foucault and Garfinkel on the sexual', *Theory, Culture and Society*, 5 (1988), pp. 111–19.

31 See e.g. J. O'Higgins, 'An interview with Michel Foucault', *Salmagundi*, 58–61, (1982/3), pp. 11–24.

32 Marshall, in Shepherd and Wallis, *Coming On Strong*, p. 268.

33 R. Wolin, 'Foucault's aesthetic dimension', *Telos*, 67 (1986), pp. 71–86.

34 See J. H. Gagnon and W. S. Simon, *Sexual Deviance* (London: Harper & Row, 1967); 'Psychosexual development', *Transaction* (March 1969), pp. 9–17; *The Sexual Scene* (Chicago: Aldine, 1970); *Sexual Conduct: The Social Sources of Human Sexuality* (Chicago: Aldine, 1973) and 'Sexual scripts: permanence and change', *Archives of Sexual Behaviour* (April 1986), pp. 97–121; K. Plummer, *Sexual Stigma: An Interactionist Account* (London: Routledge & Kegan Paul, 1975), and *The Making of the Modern Homosexual* (London: Hutchinson, 1981).

35 Gagnon and Simon, *Sexual Deviance*.

36 Foucault and Sennett, 'Sexuality and solitude', p. 18.

37 Heath, *The Sexual Fix*.

38 Bailey, 'A comment'.

39   M. Featherstone, 'Body and consumer culture', *Theory, Culture and Society*, 1, 2 (1983), pp. 8–23 (p.19).

40   Featherstone, 'Body and consumer culture', p. 20.

41   E. Hobsbawm, 'The formal march of labour halted?: observations on the debate', in M. Jacques and F. Mulhern, eds, *Observations on the Debate* (London: New Left Books, 1981).

42   Evans, *Sexual Citizenship*.

43   S. Harding, 'Trends in permissiveness', in R. Jowell, S. Witherspoon and L. Brook, ed., *British Social Attitudes: 5th Report* (Aldershot: SCPR Gower, 1988).

44   Plummer, *Making*.

45   M. Weber, 'Class, status, party', in H. Gerth and C. W. Mills, eds, *From Max Weber* (London: Routledge & Kegan Paul, 1967).

46   W. G. Runciman, *Relative Deprivation and Social Justice: A Study of Social Attitudes to Social Inequality in Twentieth Century England* (London: Routledge & Kegan Paul, 1966), p. 247.

47   J. Rawls, *A Theory of Justice* (Oxford: Oxford University Press, 1972).

48   E.g. A. Rand, *The Virtue of Selfishness* (New York: American Library, 1964), and R. Nozick, *Anarchy, State and Utopia* (New York: Basic Books, 1974).

49   R. Aron, *Main Currents in Sociological Thought*, vol. 2, trans. R. Howard and H. Weaver (Garden City, NY: Doubleday Anchor Books, 1970), p. 254.

50   J. Rawls, 'The basic liberties and their priority', in S. McMurrin, ed., *Liberty, Equality and Law* (Salt Lake City and Cambridge: University of Utah Press/Cambridge University Press, 1987), p. 21.

51   Rawls, 'The basic liberties', p. 31.

52   Rawls, 'The basic liberties', p. 22.

53   Rawls, 'The basic liberties', p. 23.

54   Rawls, 'The basic liberties', p. 22–3.

55   Rawls, 'The basic liberties', p. 22.

56   Rawls, *A Theory of Justice*, pp. 62, 303.

57   Rawls, *A Theory of Justice*, pp. 62, 83, 250, 302–3.

58   T. H. Marshall on A. Marshall, in *Citizenship and Social Class and Other Essays* (Cambridge: Cambridge University Press, 1950), p. 8.

59   S. Harding, D. Philips and M. Fogarty, eds, *Contrasting Values in Western Europe* (London: Macmillan, 1986), p. 227.

60   C. Davies, *Permissive Britain: Sexual Change in the Sixties and Seventies* (London: Pitman, 1975).

61   *The Report of the Committee on Homosexual Offences and Prostitution*, Cmnd 247 (London: HMSO, 1957).

62   *The Wolfenden Report*, p. 10.

63   *The Wolfenden Report*, pp. 9–10, 24.

64   J. Weeks, *Sex, Politics and Society* (London: Longman, 1981).

65   J. D'Emilio, 'Capitalism and the gay identity', in A. Snitow, C. Stansell and S. Thompson, eds, *Desire: The Politics of Sexuality* (London: Virago, 1983).

66   Davies, *Permissive Britain*.

67   Davies, *Permissive Britain*, p. 3.

68   Davies, *Permissive Britain*, p. 3.

69   *The Wolfenden Report*, para. 124.

70   *The Wolfenden Report*, para. 124.

71   *The Wolfenden Report*, para. 124.

72   Weeks, *Coming Out*, and P. Tatchell, *Europe in the Pink* (London: Gay Men's Press, 1992).

73   F. Mort, 'Sexuality, regulation and contestation', in Gay Left Collective, ed., *Homosexuality, Power and Politics* (London: Allison & Busby, 1980).

74   J. Weeks, *Sexuality and its Discontents: Meanings, Myths and Modern Sexualities* (London: Longman, 1985).

75   *The Wolfenden Report*, para. 124.

76   Z. Bauman, 'Sociology and postmodernity', *Sociological Review*, 36 (1988), pp. 790–813 (p. 807).

77   G. Robertson, QC., 'The Section's claws look less sharp now', *The Pink Paper* (9 June 1988).

78   Only an estimated 5 per cent of workers are men with dependent wives and children; only 32 per cent of households are made up of married couples with dependent children; at least 18 per cent of households (excluding pensioners) are substantially or completely dependent upon a woman's earnings or benefits. Ten per cent of the population is homosexual, and substantially more have experienced homosexual sexual encounters and/or relationships. (See H. Land, 'The family wage', *Feminist Review*, 6 (1980), pp. 55–78; K. Phillips, *Policing the Family* (London: Junius, 1988) and S. Allen, 'Gender inequality and class formation', in A. Giddens and G. McKenzie, ed., *Social Class and the Division of Labour* (Cambridge: Cambridge University Press, 1988). Allen might have been correct to observe then that household formations are hidden and unresearched because of the ideological stranglehold that means we don't ask the right questions, but we certainly have sufficient answers now to know that the world being addressed by the present government's ideologues and law-makers is not the world of diversity experienced by the majority of people in Britain. It is a major paradox of Section 28 that through its crude superimposition of ideological motifs we are reminded that this is so. 'One in ten' has

become a familiar, perhaps too familiar, statistic for actual percentages of the population being 'gay' and 'lesbian' which can never be accurately identified. Much depends upon the questions asked, upon criteria employed, circumstances attending information collection, as well as several other factors which lead to under-reportage. Despite the publicity surrounding the most recent comprehensive survey in Britain (K. Wellings, J. Field, A.M. Johnson and J. Wadsworth, 1994) which enabled the media to launch the alternative 'One in Ninety' slogan, accumulated evidence suggests, taking into account all the cross-survey findings and the methodologies behind them, between one in eight and one in ten remains the most accurate estimate.

79 B. Elliott and D. McCrone, 'Class, culture and morality: a sociological analysis of neo-conservatism', *Sociological Review*, 35, 3 (1987), pp. 485–511.

80 Sex education has become an obvious battleground. For example *Gay Times* (December 1986), 7 reported the reprimand by BBC chiefs of a Radio Wales producer whose school programme on AIDS contained 'earthy' and 'coarse' language.

81 J. S. Gummer, *The Permissive Society* (London: Cassell, 1971); F. Mount, *The Subversive Family: An Alternative History of Love and Marriage* (London: Allen & Unwin, 1983); R. Scruton, *The Meaning of Conservatism* (London: Macmillan, 1984); *Sexual Desire: A Philosophical Investigation* (London: Weidenfeld & Nicolson, 1986).

82 Mount, *The Subversive Family*, p. 12.

83 M. Thatcher quoted by B. Campbell, *Iron Ladies: Why Do Women Vote Tory?* (London: Virago, 1987), p. 168.

84 M. Thatcher quoted by D. Keay, 'AIDS education in the year 2000', *Woman's Own* (31 October 1987), p. 10.

85 I. Gilmour, *Inside Right: A Study of Conservatism* (London: Quartet, 1978).

86 Scruton, *The Meaning of Conservatism*.

87 Scruton, *The Meaning of Conservatism*, p. 101.

88 M. Thatcher, quoted by Campbell, *Iron Ladies*, p. 170.

89 M. Thatcher, quoted by Keay, 'AIDS education'.

90 Scruton, *Sexual Desire*.

91 Scruton, *Sexual Desire*, quoted in K. Marshall, *Moral Panics and Victorian Values: Women and the Family in Thatcher's Britain*, 2nd edn (London: Junius, 1986).

92 Scruton, quoted by Phillips, *Policing the Family*.

93 P. Aggleton and H. Homans, ed., *Social Aspects of AIDS* (Lewes: Falmer, 1988), p. 8.

94 C. Coe, *Such Times* (London: Hamish Hamilton, 1993), p. 91.

95 S. Watney, 'AIDS, moral panic theory and homophobia', in Aggleton and Homans, *Social Aspects of AIDS*, p. 60.

96   F. Otitoju, in 'Clause and effect: is there life after Clause 28?', *Marxism Today*, 32 (June 1988), pp. 22–8.

97   J. Parker, quoted by D. Smith, 'Fighting the backlash', *Gay Times* (14 January 1987).

98   Otitoju, 'Clause and effect'.

99   M. Thatcher, quoted by Keay, 'AIDS education'.

100   Reported in *Capital Gay* (October 16 1987).

101   M. Thatcher, quoted by P. Davies, 'Sexuality: a new minefield in schools', *Independent* (26 May 1988).

102   *Gay Times* (May 1988), p. 8.

103   *Spectator* (14 March 1987).

104   G. Dickens, MP, quoted by P. Davies, 'Dickensian dilemmas', *Gay Times* (May 1987), p. 12.

105   J. Anderton, quoted by Smith, 'Fighting the backlash', p. 14.

106   BBC Radio 4 (18 January 1988).

107   *Spectator* (14 March 1987).

108   Waddington, quoted by Davies, 'Dickensian dilemmas', p. 12.

109   Lord Arran quoted by H. M. Hyde, *The Other Love: An Historical and Contemporary Survey of Homosexuality in Britain* (London: Heinemann, 1970), p. 303.

110   *Gay Times* (August 1988), p. 8. Other European countries, including Austria, Finland and Turkey, have legislation restricting the 'promotion' (variously defined) of homosexuality.

111   Local Government Act, op. cit.

112   D. T. Evans, 'Section 28: law, myth and paradox', *Critical Social Policy*, 27 (1989/90), pp. 73–95. K. Norrie, 'How to promote homosexuality', *Gay Scotland* (September 1989), pp. 9–14. Section 28 certainly inhibited various local authorities, schools, etc. from funding, supporting or otherwise enabling gay and lesbian activities, groups, etc., some of a seemingly bizarre character, although not being treated as such by the media: e.g. Hull City Council refused to allow a screening of Genet's *Un chant d'amour*, and Kent County Council excluded Britten's *Death in Venice* from a school festival because it features a man's obsession with a boy. Ironically in January 1994 the British press enjoyed itself immensely at the expense of a primary school headmistress in East London who stopped her pupils from seeing a Covent Garden production of Prokofiev's ballet *Romeo and Juliet* because 'it was entirely about heterosexual love' (*The Times*; 25 January 1994).

113   Lord Caithness, quoted in the *Observer* (21 May 1988).

114   Norrie, 'How to promote homosexuality', p. 10.

115   Norrie, 'How to promote homosexuality', p. 10.

116   Lord Boyd-Carpenter reported Marshall, in *Coming On Strong*.

117 Nicholas Fairbairn's contribution to a Commons debate reportedly included the following: 'Male homosexuality is a perversion of human function . . . it is using the excretory organ and rectum with a reproductive organ' (*The Pink Paper* (17 March 1988)). By comparison, M. Barnes, QC, reported by C. Wolmar, 'Anti-gay law is a non-starter', *Observer* (21 May 1988), argued that the term 'homosexuality' is meaningless by comparison with the term 'homosexual relationship'.

118 *Jenny Lives with Eric and Martin* was the primary school reading text used by amongst others Haringey local authority in London and which received considerable media attention in the early stages of Clause 28's passage through Parliament. For a detailed discussion see D. Cooper, *Sexing the City* (London: Rivers Oram, 1994), pp. 134–7.

119 F. Werge, 'Swinging into action', *The Pink Paper* (18 February 1988), p. 5.

120 I. Boulton, quoted in *Gay Times* (May 1988), p. 11.

121 Gay Teachers' Group, *School's Out* (1980), pp. 3–6.

122 A. Cooper, 'Clause and effect: is there gay life after Clause 28?', *Marxism Today*, 32 (3 June 1988), pp. 22–8.

123 Otitoju, 'Clause and effect'.

124 Aron, *Main Currents*, p. 254.

125 Runciman, *Relative Deprivation*, p. 247.

126 Watney, 'Ideology', p. 64.

127 Runciman, *Relative Deprivation*, pp. 275–6.

128 Runciman, *Relative Deprivation*, pp. 275–6.

129 C. S. Vance, 'Social construction theory: problems in the history of sexuality', in D. Altman, et al., *Which Homosexuality? Essays from the International Scientific Conference on Lesbian and Gay Studies* (London and Amsterdam: Gay Men's Press and Uitgeverij An Dekker Schorer, 1989).

130 Runciman, *Relative Deprivation*, p. 252.

Chapter six

Their Justice: Heterosexism in A Theory of Justice

Angelia R. Wilson

THE introduction to this book began by noting the march on Washington in which three hundred thousand supporters of sexual politics, or the 'gay and lesbian movement', protested discrimination based on sexual orientation. The live television coverage in America broadcast the events of the day, including a panoramic view of the diversity of gay men, lesbians, bisexuals, transsexuals, etc. taking part in the march and rally. And while many individuals, or small groups, carried banners signifying their particular identity or political protest, one banner stood out among the rest. Indeed it became the central prop for the enormous stage upon which celebrities and 'Very Important Gays & Lesbians' announced their support for change. Its words encapsulated the political motivation for the march, if not for the whole American sexual politics movement. The reason for protest, the central message to those in power and to the heterosexual public, was that change in policies relating to sexual orientation was: A Simple Matter of Justice.

This message was carried across the Atlantic and by the June Pride march in London, Stonewall had printed leaflets explaining its work, emblazoned with the call to action: 'A simple matter of justice'. After telling stories of injustice, for example of gay men and lesbians who had been victims of attacks, been harassed as members of the armed services, or been denied the right to settle with their partners in Britain, Angela Mason noted the campaigns undertaken by Stonewall, concluding that 'by supporting Stonewall you help speed up these changes. It is a simple matter of justice and together we can make the difference. Support our work and become a Friend of Stonewall'. In fact this was not the first time the demand for 'justice' had been made by Stonewall. Another leaflet soliciting financial contributions was entitled 'Legal equality and social justice . . . Join the Friends of Stonewall and help us make it happen'. And its mission statement of 'working for equality' is often accompanied by the clarification 'legal equality and social justice'.

Claims for justice, like those for equality, may be simply direct appeals to mainstream western ideals of what should be ensured by the state. Indeed, it is perhaps more strategic to note, as Mason did, the various injustices which have victimized gay men and lesbians; particularly if one is wanting to arouse emotions enough to secure financial support. But in highlighting 'injustice' one implicitly appeals to an overarching notion of justice. If something is seen as unjust, the assumption is that there is a specific criteria of 'just', or justice. The more blatant Americans directly assert this; it is 'A simple matter of *justice*'. In particular I want to examine how this claim might be related to, or interpreted according to, the one theory of justice that has significantly influenced contemporary liberal thought: John Rawls's *A Theory of Justice*. The centrality of this theory, this justice, reflects the kind of interpretation of justice which has captured the attention of political theorists for the past twenty years. The amount of debate it has sparked testifies to its intuitive appeal for liberal theorists, and to its 'intuitive' assumptions attacked by its critics. And so this chapter engages with this theory of justice, and in the familiar words of Alastair MacIntyre, asks 'Whose Justice?'[1]

Family justice

Contemporary liberalism, as it is commonly defended, is essentially about showing equal concern and respect for individuals. Rawls himself prioritizes concepts of equal liberty and self-respect.[2]

However, I will argue here that these concepts are undermined by the 'intuitions' Rawls gleans from 'western democracies'. In an effort to show equal concern and respect, Rawls simply re-establishes the traditional assumptions or historical characterisations of western culture, even those which prove to be oppressive and isolating for individuals who do not represent accepted social roles. Heterosexism is one case in point. Just as feminist theorists have questioned the gender of the liberal individual, gay and lesbian critics must search for their identity within the concept of the individual found in liberalism. And there is one assumption about the liberal individual found particularly in Rawls's work which limits the extent to which gay men and lesbians can identify with his theory of justice. Rawls's theory can be contextualized within, and builds upon, the western democratic culture, influenced by Judeo-Christian norms, which historically idealizes the heterosexual nuclear family. Although the gender-roles within this family structure have been the topic of feminist critiques of Rawls, the assumption of this heterosexual family structure itself actually marginalizes, or completely ignores, the concerns of lesbians and gay men; separating those concerns from a heterosexual justice, or 'family politics'.[3]

In analysing this heterosexual justice, this chapter rests quite heavily on critical examinations by feminist writers, particularly that of Susan Moller Okin in her important text *Justice, Gender and the Family*. She and other feminist critics have produced reams of accusations of 'typical liberal' sexism against Rawls, to which he has indirectly responded.[4] Nevertheless Rawls continues to rely upon the family as a basic social institution. The critique offered here investigates this tie with the heterosexual family structure, suggesting that it reflects 'common-sense' notions of the heterosexual family and as a result limits the extent to which Rawls's theory of social justice can act as a framework for justice for gay men, lesbians or those with a non-heterosexual identity. In particular this chapter will consider the methodology of the original position as described in *A Theory of Justice*. Rawls has 'reinterpreted' his theory since its publication in 1972; however, his more recent formulation of 'political liberalism' fails to address this notion of the heterosexual family as a basic social institution.[5] And since many of the fundamental assumptions that still haunt his work are explicitly articulated in his original theory, I have chosen here to focus primarily on that work.

During this investigation it is important to keep in mind Rawls's understanding of his task. In *A Theory of Justice*, Rawls outlines the fundamental principles of a just society. His methodology, including the original position and conditions governing its parties, is designed to produce principles of justice, based upon shared intuitions about justice, which are agreeable to a range of people with different conceptions of the good. 'Justice as fairness', is proposed by Rawls to be a viable alternative to other philosophical traditions, in particular utilitarianism. His task is not to correct the injustices of our contemporary society.[6] Indeed, such an endeavour would require an in-depth assessment of numerous issues against a pre-determined criteria of justice. Instead Rawls focuses on establishing such criteria: what is justice and how is it best determined? However, it would be naive to think that Rawls himself does not begin with a preconceived notion of what form this justice will finally take. In fact he makes no pretences about this, 'We want to define the original position so that we get the desired solution.'[7] Rawls wishes to create a methodology which will produce principles of justice intuitively acceptable in a contemporary diverse society but he admittedly knows his 'desired solution'.

The way in which Rawls believes principles of justice can best be articulated is by eliminating the peculiarities that set people apart. In creating a hypothetical space in which individuals can consider the best way 'to govern the assignment of rights and duties and to regulate the distribution of social and economic advantages', they must be free from their belief systems that would predetermine, or affect, their notion of justice.[8] So in this 'original position', that hypothetical space, members are placed behind a veil of ignorance which nullifies 'the effects of specific contingencies which put men at odds and tempt them to exploit social and natural circumstances to their own advantage'.[9] 'This ensures', Rawls notes elsewhere, 'that no one is advantaged or disadvantaged in the choice of principles by the outcome of natural chance or the contingency of social circumstances. Since all are similarly situated and no one is able to design principles to favour his particular condition, the principles of justice are the result of a fair agreement or bargain.'[10] Mulhall and

Swift offer these comments about the purpose of the veil of ignorance: 'The intuition being captured here is that which links fairness to ignorance. If I don't know which of the five pieces of cake that I am cutting I am going to end up with, then it makes sense for me to cut the pieces fairly. Similarly, if people don't know who they are going to be, then it will make sense for them to choose fair or just principles to regulate their society.'[11] So the original position is established by Rawls as a space in which individuals are ignorant of their particular contingencies in order to ensure that the principles of justice chosen are fair; thus he claims the result is 'justice as fairness'.

The result, according to Rawls, is two principles of justice: 'Each person is to have an equal right to the most extensive total system of equal basic liberties compatible with a similar system of liberty for all' and 'Social and economic inequalities are to be arranged so that they are both: (a) to the greatest benefit of the least advantaged, consistent with the just savings principle, and (b) attached to offices and positions open to all under conditions of fair equality of opportunity.'[12] The first principle has lexical priority to the second so that, as Mulhall and Swift explain, 'there can be no trade-offs between those liberties and the other forms of advantage that come under the second principle'.[13] Furthermore, within the second principle, the principle of fair equality of opportunity (b) has priority over the just savings principle, or what is labelled the difference principle, (a). Finally, Rawls states that, for reasons of stability, the principles of justice must be agreed upon *unanimously*.[14] These principles of justice are to ensure the fair distribution of what Rawls defines as 'primary goods'. 'The primary social goods, to give them in broad categories, are rights and liberties, opportunities and powers, income and wealth.'[15] Interestingly, he also considers 'a sense of one's own worth' as a primary good and devotes an entire section of *A Theory of Justice* to the importance of self-respect in which he confirms that 'parties in the original position would wish to avoid at almost any cost the social conditions that undermine self-respect'.[16] Below, I will consider the implications of this methodology, and most significantly how this system of justice fails to provide a framework for self-respect, and is instead a 'family', or heterosexual, justice.

As noted above, Rawls is aware of the desired solution, or the principles of justice he wishes this methodology to legitimate. Critics often point out that, if Rawls designed his methodology to reach desired solutions, he is obviously going to incorporate his own conception of justice, which will stem from his own cultural and historical perspective, as well as assumptions which are typically found in liberal theory.[17] And here I want to consider how these assumptions, specifically that of the heterosexual family, affect his sense of justice. I would suggest that, from the perspective of a gay and lesbian critique, the assumptions found in Rawls's work are reflective of heterosexism found in contemporary western democratic culture. The parties of the original position have a specific task: to consider alternative understandings of justice under set conditions and determine which one is most likely to provide the best distribution of primary goods. Two points can be made about the cultural and historical relativity of the resulting justice.

First, Rawls states in 'Kantian constructivism' that his theory is relative to western democratic culture. 'We are not trying to find a conception of justice suitable for all societies . . . [but for] . . . the just form of basic institutions within a democratic society under modern conditions.'[18] Placing his methodology within the democratic system of the modern society *historically* contextualizes the knowledge of the parties in the original position.[19]

Second, in *A Theory of Justice* Rawls acknowledges some of the 'traditional concepts of justice' which are among the alternatives for the parties.[20] Among these are a range of interpretations of utilitarianism as well as perfectionism. Members of the original position also know 'general facts about human society'. 'They understand political affairs and the principles of economic theory; they know the basis of social organization and the laws of human psychology.'[21] They are aware of the realities, the political agenda, outside the original position, but do not know their positioning within that social and political context. So this limited knowledge sets the *political* contextual framework for the alternatives available to the parties.

It is not difficult to connect the alternatives available within this historical and political context with assumptions made about sexual relationships. Carole Pateman specifically notes that the history of the contract theory, appealed to by Rawls, carries with it particular notions of marriage. 'The contractual conception of marriage presupposes the idea of the individual as owner. The marriage contract establishes legitimate access to sexual property in the person.'[22] The family, with its implications about the division of labour, role of women, 'private' justice, and ownership of wife and children, is a strong part of western democratic traditional concepts of justice.[23] Therefore this historical and political context carries with it assumptions about family structure as the model for sexual relationships. The gender division supported by the traditional concept of marriage permeates our culture and brings with it 'natural' assumptions of heterosexuality.

Rawls not only fails to address this cultural heterosexism but builds upon it via the family as an example of a just institution. Early in *A Theory of Justice* he recognizes the fundamental importance of the family, citing as a 'major social institution . . . the monogamous family'.[24] This monogamous family is also a biological one where the man or head of the household is concerned with the 'continuation of his line'.[25] Moreover, the family is the space for moral development.[26] And this development includes acquiring a sense of justice by forming attachments in accordance with the social institution of the family.[27] Rawls blatantly overlooks the difficulties arising from within this social institution. He simply assumes that 'family institutions are just'.[28] By ignoring alternative family structures, and the injustices within the gendered nuclear family, Rawls fails to distance himself from cultural heterosexism. In making such a claim about the family, and using it as an example of a justice institution, Rawls limits the historical and cultural knowledge of the members to that of a particular heterosexual, and heterosexist, context. And it will be argued here that this failure to address heterosexism lessens the effectiveness of Rawls's theory as an appropriate reference for gay and lesbian activists demanding 'justice'.

It is important to note here that feminist critics such as Okin challenge this assumption about the family and the implied 'male' theory of justice.[29] Although their work shows the conflict between traditional notions of justice and the injustices experienced within the family structure, it is not the exact direction chosen for this critique. This distinction between women's struggle and the struggle of gay men and lesbians is exemplified in the debate around the family. Traditional understandings of the division of labour, women's economic dependency and women as primary child-minders limits the extent to which they can determine their own lifestyles. The effects of the traditional family on women has proved overwhelmingly oppressive. While feminists point out the injustices of gender division in the traditional family structure, gay men and lesbians are completely unable to identify with this heterosexual family model. This is not to say that homosexuals are against an idea of family. Indeed at the forefront of legislative debate is gay and lesbian parental rights, for example custody law reform, artificial insemination, recognition of same-sex partnerships. But agreeing with *a* concept of family does not involve accepting *the* traditional family structure inherent in western democratic culture, that is husband, wife and children – with or without the gender-structure. Therefore, a political theory which is in search of the 'shared intuitions' about justice must either explicitly reject this traditional idea of family as a shared intuition or be seen to embrace it. And Rawls leaves little doubt about his affiliation with the traditional heterosexual family structure.

Elizabeth Fox-Genovese in her interesting work *Feminism without Illusions* summarizes that 'cultural representations of sexuality and sexual identity are themselves abstractions from specific social and political relations'.[30] By placing social and historical contextual limits on the parties of the original position, Rawls assumes the institutionalization of the family structure. This not only traps him into a 'traditional mode of thinking that life within the family and relations between the sexes' are beyond the subject of a theory of social justice[31] but also traps him into traditional assumptions about heterosexuality and *proper* structures for sexual relationships. The family is understood in the alternatives available to the parties of the original position as a major social institution. And because of its acceptance in the original position, it determines the structure of family relationships within the resulting well-ordered society. So, as feminists have criticized Rawls for assuming justice *within* the family, I want to investigate his assumption *of* the family.

This chapter then investigates Rawls's assumptions of heterosexuality via the family structure. In order to find firm ground I will ask three rather familiar questions about his methodology: 'Who are the members of the original position?', 'What do they know about their society?' and 'What alternatives are available to them?'[32] After considering each question, the results will show that this assumption of the heterosexual family structure can be quite problematic. It is particularly problematic for those appealing to 'justice' in order to question the injustices experienced by non-heterosexuals. Three alternatives seem to be available for those in the original position. First, given that heterosexuality is the accepted form of sexual relationships, parties might 'play the odds', or gamble that in the resulting society they will find themselves in agreement with the heterosexual family structure. Second, given Rawls's more recent concern for social stability, parties might decide to enforce the heterosexual family structure as ideal, denying that diverse sexual identities should be considered among the basic liberties. Third, given the emphasis of the difference principle, people in a 'well-ordered society' might be able to express different sexual identities, but they would remain subject to the social institution of the family. After considering each question, and Rawls's apparent heterosexism, I will suggest a new direction for examining contemporary liberal political theory as a possible justification for the 'justice' demanded by activists.

Heterosexist members of the original position

First consider the question 'Who are the parties in the original position?' Perhaps the best place to begin is by noting what they do *not* know about themselves. The veil of ignorance places members on equal ground by denying knowledge of 'special contingencies'. These contingencies Rawls initially outlines in *A Theory of Justice*: 'They do not know how the various alternative will affect their own particular case . . . no one knows his place in society . . . nor . . . his conception of the good . . . the parties do not know the particular circumstances of their own society . . . its economic or political situation, or the level of civilisation and culture'.[33] Rawls extends this list in 'Fairness to goodness' to include 'Our social position and class, our *sex* and race should not influence deliberations made from a moral point of view'.[34] It would be fair to say that Rawls's intention is to deny members knowledge about their individual lives which would bias their deliberations in the original position.

However, even though parties in the original position are unaware of these special contingencies, Rawls does give some evidence about who they are. These indications can be identified in two respects. First, the terminology chosen by Rawls in *A Theory of Justice*: references to 'he' and 'father' leave little doubt of the parties' sex. Okin comments on this usage of generic male terms:

> 'Men,' 'mankind,' 'he' and 'his' are interspersed with non-sexist terms of reference such as 'individual' and 'moral person.' Examples of intergenerational concern are worded in terms of 'fathers' and 'sons', and the difference principle is said to correspond to 'the principle of fraternity'. This linguistic usage would perhaps be less significant if it were not for the fact that Rawls is self-consciously a member of a long tradition of moral and political philosophy that has used in its arguments either such supposedly generic masculine terms, or even more inclusive terms of reference . . . only to exclude women from the scope of the conclusions reached.[35]

But even if we grant Rawls linguistic lenience, his second indication returns us again to a male dominated structure.

The imagery chosen by Rawls depicts the traditional patriarchal family structure. As noted above, the monogamous family is regarded as 'a major social institution'.[36] Promoting this image of the family, he delineates the roles within the family structure: 'a good wife and husband'.[37] His just savings principle rests on the assumption of the father setting aside savings for the son. Again Rawls fails to distance himself from cultural assumptions about male heads of family. Deborah Kearns comments that 'he refers to the family as "characterised by a definite hierarchy, in which each member has certain rights and duties". He never questions why this should be so. Family structure does not seem to be an issue.'[38] Surely, it is not a contentious issue for Rawls because he has already assumed a structure, that of the traditional patriarchal family.

Pateman keenly points out this assumption of the patriarchal family structure:

> *Before* ignorance of 'particular facts' is postulated, Rawls has already claimed that parties have 'descendants' (for whom they are concerned), and Rawls states that he will generally view the parties as 'heads of families'. He merely takes it for granted that he can, at one and the same time, postulate disembodied parties devoid of all substantive characteristics, and assume that sexual difference exists, sexual intercourse takes place, children are born and families formed. Rawls' participants in the original contract are, simultaneously, mere reasoning entities, and 'heads of families', or men who represent their wives.[39]

The importance of Pateman's observation is the point at which parties are aware of family ties. The historical and political context set by Rawls carries with it implications about family structure. Simply avoiding gendered language does not combat the cultural understanding of what it means to be a part of a family. Furthermore, adding sex to his list of hidden contingencies does not grant automatic equality for women. This 'add women and stir' approach to political theory simply intensifies the tensions between gender-neutral terminology and rigid gender-structured 'social institutions'. The family structure assumed in the original position gives every indication that members participate in a gendered heterosexual family structure.

Still one might be tempted to extend the veil of ignorance to deny knowledge of sexual orientation. Although Rawls has not explicitly included sexual orientation, Morris Kaplan *does* claim that sexual orientation is included behind the veil of ignorance: 'Although rational agents in Rawls' original position are ignorant of their moral and social particularities, including religious beliefs, gender, social class, sexual orientation, etc. . . .'[40] Kaplan offers no reference to Rawls justifying this assumption. Indeed such an embellishment of Rawls's 'etc.' is quite problematic for a gay critique of Rawls's theory. Not only does Kaplan risk putting words in Rawls's mouth, he does so without reference to Rawls's understanding of family. It simply seems inconsistent with Rawls's theory to claim that, while members are participants, even 'heads' of heterosexual families, they may be unaware of their sexual orientation. Indeed if Rawls had wanted sexual orientation to be unknown, it seems logical that he would have designed his original positions to avoid the assumption of the heterosexual family structure.

Another question might arise concerning knowledge of non-heterosexual sexual desires. After all one may be a head of a heterosexual family and still have desires for same-sex relations. Kaplan argues that we know members will have 'sexual desires and emotional needs'.[41] He continues by implying that this knowledge can be linked to an acceptance of sexual freedoms. Again this argument seems to jump from the realm of the possible to that of the hopeful. If the members are aware that they will have sexual desires, the only structure in which to express such desire is predetermined by Rawls: the heterosexual family. Okin points out that 'since those in the original position are the heads or representatives of families, they are *not in a position to determine questions of justice within the family*'.[42] Adopting this criticism I would argue that because they are participants in a heterosexual relationship, or forced by rules of unanimity to agree with the heterosexual family structure, they are not in a position to determine a structure for meeting sexual desires or emotional needs, or for establishing a justice relevant to non-heterosexuals. Rawls not only assumes justice *within* the family, but wholly endorses the monogamous heterosexual family and in doing so dictates the socially acceptable structure for expressing sexual desires.

Still the possibility remains that a member of the original position may be a participant in the heterosexual family and have non-heterosexual desires. Jane English has noted that 'if only for biological reasons, this [the original position] includes members of at least two generations; typically three or four generations co-exist'.[43] If this is the case, then it is possible that not all members are heads of a heterosexual family. Perhaps some are twenty years old and single. However, because the unanimous adoption of the principles of justice depends upon persons with the same type of moral development, and because the primary place of moral development is the traditional family, we can reason that the single members are products of a heterosexual family. The members of the original position are, therefore, either involved in a heterosexual marriage or are a product of the moral development of a heterosexual marriage. In other words, the parties in the original position are either in a heterosexual marriage, heterosexual and single, or they are not heterosexual but *assume* that the heterosexual marriage/family is the best structure for sexual relationships. While the heterosexual family structure does not rule out the possibility of same-sex desire, it does deny the development of different sexual identities because the family is predetermined by Rawls as the social institution for sexual relations. So in this heterosexist original position, like a heterosexist society, non-heterosexuals are forced to choose principles of justice within a predetermined heterosexist context which denies both the possibility of different sexual identities and a justice applicable to those with different sexual identities.

So what is Rawls's reason for identifying parties as heads of families? The key appears to be the biological link needed for his savings principle.[44] There are at least two implications of Rawls's understanding of this biological link. First, it should be reiterated that the male terminology and imagery of the patriarchal family leave lesbian mothers unable to identify with members of the original position. Second, English notes that the dual link between one generation and the next requires that 'unless every adult and every child belonged to some such family group, these do not figure into the savings principle'.[45] Rawls believes it to be 'more realistic' to assume parents are not uninterested in their children's welfare. Deborah Kearns points out that 'the idea that the family is the place for affection and natural sentiment is institutionalised. Other relationships are presumed to be those of self-interest.'[46] And, similarly, English argues that the assumption of mutual disinterest is just as unrealistic in other cases because people often do care about others. Arguably one case is that of non-biological homosexual parents.

Rawls utilizes the veil of ignorance to deny knowledge of special contingencies in order to avoid biased deliberations in the original position. But his assumption of the heterosexual family structure creates an uneasy tension between accepting this social institution and the possibility of different sexual identities. This tension reflects the conditions of a modern democratic society and remains unanswered by the methodology Rawls employs. Whether or not the members of the original position are heterosexual, they, like Rawls, assume the family as a just social institution and is responsible for moral development. Since Rawls predetermines the just role of the heterosexual family, the members must agree, unanimously, that the heterosexual family is the just structure for sexual relationships. While they may be unaware of their particular contingencies, they are nevertheless heterosexists.

Heterosexist society

The motive behind the methodology of the original position and the veil of ignorance was to arrange basic social institutions in order to assign rights and duties and the appropriate division of social advantages for a well-ordered society.[47] In the well-ordered society, people will have access to the primary goods according to the principles of justice. In a later essay, 'Kantian constructivism in moral theory', Rawls explains that his task was not to articulate an epistemological conception of justice and that 'what justifies a conception of justice is not it being true to an order antecedent and given to us, but its congruence with a deeper understanding of ourselves and our aspirations, and our realization that, given our history and the tradition embedded in our public life, it is the most reasonable doctrine for us'.[48] So, as Mouffe comments, this clarification distinguishes between Rawlsian political liberalism and an epistemological project by interpreting this concept of public justice as a 'practical social task'.[49] In building upon shared intuitions about justice, Rawls is trying to express a sense of fairness that can then act as the basis for social unity. So the members of the original position know the traditions, history, and kinds of aspirations that characterize the modern democracy. And this awareness of social context should lead them to principles of justice which guarantee the basic primary goods, for example liberty and equality, regardless of their position within society. However, while this guarantee may sound like an appealing goal for a theory of justice, the members' knowledge of that social context is overridden by the predetermined belief in the family as a basic social institution.

Therefore in addressing the second question, 'What facts do the parties know about their society?', we already have some idea of their knowledge about society. As noted above, Rawls states in *A Theory of Justice* that 'It is taken for granted, however that they know the general facts about human society. They understand political affairs and principles of economic theory; they know the basis of social organisation and the laws of human psychology.'[50] Although he offers no detailed explanation about these 'general facts', the historical context does provide some indication of the laws operating in the society, particularly the primacy of the nuclear family. He suggests different sex-related roles for the 'wife' and 'husband' or 'daughter' and 'son'.[51] And it is this family which is to be the primary influence for moral development. Rawls explicitly states as the second principle of moral psychology that 'a person's capacity for fellow feeling has been realised by acquiring attachments in accordance with the first law' – the first law beginning with 'family institutions are just'.[52]

What follows from this understanding of moral development is Rawls's apparent intention to continue this heterosexual structure in the well-ordered society. Rawls's affiliation with the heterosexual family structure as *the* primary influence of moral development has serious (dangerous) implications for alternative models of social organization. It is not difficult to accept that the parties would be aware of the uncertainties about the development of sexuality. The aetiology of sexual identity in the form of various psychological, sociological and biological explanations may be available for the parties of the original position. Wolffe offers a particularly interesting critique of Rawls's assumption of knowledge of laws of human psychology in relation to '*understanding*' the homosexual.[53] He argues that the ambiguity surrounding the cause of homosexuality could lead to two possible reactions: either fear leading to rejection or uncertainty leading to restricted acceptance.

These two possibilities will be discussed in more detail below, but here I want to note that while the members may be aware of the diverse explanations of same-sex desire, and that they too might have such desires, they are also 'programmed' to accept the centrality of the heterosexual family. So although they may understand the possibility of same-sex desire, the premises that 'family institutions are just' and that 'the family is *the* place for moral development' require them to agree, unanimously, that the well-ordered society should prioritize the nuclear family as a basic social institution. What they know about their society, is that it is, and will continue to be, heterosexist. This knowledge creates an uneasy tension then between the resulting heterosexism and the methodological purpose of the original position, that is to articulate our shared intuitions about justice in a space free from our particular conceptions of the good life. The options available to the members choosing principles of justice are somewhat limited, and greatly unappealing for those claiming that securing gay and lesbian human rights, or in Rawls's words 'primary goods', are a simple matter of justice.

Heterosexist alternatives

The original question, 'Who are the parties?' led to fairly specific answers about their sexual orientation or about their belief in the heterosexual family as the proper structure for sexual relationships. In addition, the second question, 'What do they know about their society?' also clearly indicated the overriding acceptance of heterosexuality as a social norm which was key to social unity. Parties know that general laws, or academic research, offer no proven coherent causal explanation for homosexuality. But they do know that they affirm the heterosexual family structure. They also know that the monogamous biological heterosexual family determines children's moral development. Given this knowledge, 'What real alternatives are available for determining a just society in which diverse sexual identities may exist?' In this section I will suggest that Rawls leaves us with three alternatives. First, knowing that gay men and lesbians do exist, the parties can play the odds that they will not have same-sex desires and therefore the concerns of gay men and lesbians will not affect them directly. Second, knowing the centrality of the heterosexual family in maintaining social stability, they can choose to enforce this relationship structure as a 'social institution'. Third, knowing the diversity of individual conceptions of the good, and accepting the possibility that they may have same-sex desires, they can interpret justice as fairness to guarantee basic primary goods in accordance with the principles of justice. Each of these I consider in detail below.

First, Rawls insists that the veil of ignorance hides individual contingencies that might otherwise be the source of biased choice. He goes a step further to ensure that members do not even know what the probabilities of the different outcomes might be. By invoking what he refers to as the principle of insufficient reason he assigns equal probabilities to outcomes in such an absence of evidence or information.[54] So the parties have an equal chance of being male or female; from different cultural or racial groups. Rawls admits that there are 'assumptions about society that, if they were sound, would allow the parties to arrive at objective estimates of equal probability'.[55] In addition, to avoid 'guessing games' and to ensure rational assessment of the alternatives for justice, Rawls suggests a 'thicker' veil of ignorance which denies parties knowledge of 'characteristic aversion(s)' to risk.[56] Members of the original position do not have evidence of the likelihood of their special contingencies – including whether or not they are 'riskers'. It is his intention that members do not 'play the odds' when establishing the principles of justice.

Given this lack of knowledge, playing the odds is beyond the capability of the parties – in most cases. However, in the case of sexuality the parties *are* aware of the odds. They know that they are part of a heterosexual family or at least agree to its structure for sexual relationships. In contrast to class, sex or race, the parties are given affection for the heterosexual monogamous family. Playing the odds results in consistently expressing characteristics attributed to them by Rawls, and the cards are stacked in the parties' favour for the 'desired solution', i.e. the heterosexual family as the only just institution for sexual relationships. So, despite Rawls's intentions, members do know that, regardless of their desires, they will agree that the heterosexual family is the proper institution for sexual relationships. In this case the 'odds' are not a gamble, they are a certainty. The well-ordered society that results from the principles of justice will be heterosexist. The question then comes down to how heterosexist the society will be.

With this first 'option' settled, and in the knowledge that the well-ordered society will be based on heterosexism, two options remain. First, the parties in the original position may agree that the heterosexual family should be enforced as a basic social institution. Because they unanimously agree that the social institution of the heterosexual family is the key influence in moral development, they may feel compelled to recognize its importance in the social tradition and in providing social unity. Their task, as Rawls stated in the Tanner lecture, is to 'assess the traditional alternatives in accordance with how well they generate a publicly recognised sense of justice when the basic structure is known to satisfy the corresponding principles. In doing this they view the developed capacity for a sense of justice.'[57] This developed capacity for a sense of justice serves as a criterion to judge the 'stability' of the alternative schemes of justice.

The opening paragraph of 'The idea of an overlapping consensus' shows the importance Rawls places on stability. 'In a constitutional democracy one of its most important aims is present-ing a political conception of justice that can not only provide a shared public basis for the justification of political and social institutions but also helps ensure stability from one generation to the next.'[58] The parties' acceptance of the heterosexual family structure and their directive to ensure stability could lead them to establish the heterosexual family as a part of the 'basic structure' of social and political institutions or *enforced conformity* by either mirroring the sex-roles in the heterosexual family structure or prohibiting non-heterosexual identities and acts altogether.

> It is an important feature of a conception of justice that it should generate its own support. That is, its principles should be such that when they are embodied in the basic structure of society men tend to acquire the corresponding sense of justice. Given the principles of moral learning, men develop a desire to act in accordance with its principles. In this case a conception of justice is stable.[59]

With the heterosexual family as the place of moral development, enforcing it as the social structure for sexual relationships would ensure this continuity and stability.

It might be argued that such a conservative interpretation of the centrality of the family is in opposition to the provision of primary goods intended by Rawls. So the third option available to the parties in the original position could be based upon an interpretation of the basic liberties which would include sexual freedoms, for example freedom to determine sexual orientation. The two principles of justice buttressed by the basic liberties is in fact the most appealing (at least for this critic) interpretation of social justice within the Rawlsian well-ordered society. And Rawls does acknowledge that his concept of 'fair-value' of liberties refers to the actual worth of a liberty to a citizen. The worth of a liberty or its 'usefulness' is determined not by a person's well-being but in relation to the primary goods.[60] The difference principle, therefore, secures the level of liberty for the least advantaged.

> When this [difference] principle is satisfied, however, this lesser worth of liberty is compensated for in this sense: the all-purpose means available to the least advantaged members of society to achieve their ends would be even less were social and economic inequalities, as measured by the index of primary goods, different from what they are. The *basic structure of society* is arranged so that it maximises the primary goods available to the least advantaged.[61]

The outcome of an interpretation of basic liberties that grants freedom to determine one's own sexual identity guarantees the least advantaged, in this case those with non-heterosexual identities, maximum freedoms compared with alternative theories of justice available in western democratic culture. So, those with different sexual identities in a well-ordered society would be guaranteed the maximum level of liberty that is beneficial to them. However, and this is key to understanding the limits of Rawlsian justice, they are allowed only the maximum liberty that can be granted within a predetermined heterosexist society. Rawls's difference principle, which guaranteed maximum freedom, is limited because it is relative to the historical and political limits he places on the original position. It is limited because Rawls himself creates these principles of justice out of his own understanding of the social context, and that understanding is based on the centrality of the heterosexual family.

In addition, Rawls's more recent 'political liberalism' guarantees citizens a 'roughly equal' fair-value of political liberties. The worth of political liberties 'whatever their social or economic position, must be approximately equal, or at least sufficiently equal, in the sense that everyone has a fair opportunity to hold public office and to influence the outcome of political decisions'.[62] Every person *qua* citizen should have the equal opportunity to hold public office and participate in the political system. However, this assurance fails for gay and lesbian citizens in at least two ways.

First, this guaranteed fair-value of political liberties is 'roughly equal' to representation in the original position. Unfortunately, as discussed above, a diversity of sexual identities is impossible to find among heterosexual heads of families. The result is that those whose concerns are not represented in the heterosexist original position are unable to participate in the political system of the well-ordered society. The political liberties of gay and lesbian citizens are 'roughly equal' to their representation in the original position; and, in the words of a recent Stonewall campaign, gay men and lesbians are 'less equal than others'.

Second, the underpinning concern about equal access to the political system is ultimately an issue of power. Norman Daniels rather pointedly comments that an egalitarian political system must address the inequalities of wealth and power.[63] In a similar light, I would add that Rawls's concern for fair opportunity to hold public office or participate in political decisions is weakened, if not completely sabotaged, because he gives priority to the heterosexual family as the basic social institution for developing a sense of justice. The imbalance of power which historically favours the heterosexual majority must be re-addressed to empower gay men, lesbians, bisexuals, transsexuals, etc. seeking equality and justice. In addition, it is difficult to see how the injustices, or inequalities, experienced by gay men and lesbians in Rawls's well-ordered society could be resolved since the power needed for such resolution lies with the heterosexist parties of the original position.

In summary then, the methodology of the original position fails to provide principles of justice which extend to those with non-heterosexual identities. This failure is due to its reliance upon the heterosexual family as a basic social institution, as the place for moral development, and as the source of understanding principles of justice. If the heterosexual family is at the heart of the theory of justice which has informed western political thought and political systems for the last twenty years, it is not surprising that the kind of 'justice' gay men and lesbians experience is tainted by heterosexism. It may be, as the activists have claimed, *A Simple Matter of Justice*. But the dominant interpretation of justice, in theory as well as practice, is not a justice which includes gay men and lesbians. It *is* 'a simple matter of heterosexist justice' that our concerns continue to be overridden by the centrality of the heterosexual family. And while Rawls has reinterpreted his theory in the past few years, it continues to build its political agenda around those issues which can be advocated by the majority, leaving those issues that 'set us at odds with one another' in the private sphere, their advocates unempowered, and gay men and lesbians out of the embrace of a more protective justice.

Self-respect

The main point of the criticism I make here is that, because Rawls assumes the nuclear family, the resulting theory of justice is not reflective of, or sensitive to, the concerns of those with different conceptions of family, and of sexual relationships. This point is akin to that made by other groups who demand that justice should be inclusive of their different needs and applicable regardless of their positioning in society. The tension that arises between the need to respect difference and the need for social unity feeds much of contemporary philosophical debate. And most often the target of the criticisms levelled at liberal political theorists concerns a concept of the individual, or individualism. And so I want to make a few observations about the individual found in Rawls's original position and his concern to protect self-respect. Pateman strikes at the heart of assumptions found in individualism:

The individual as owner is separated from a body that is of one sex or the other. . . . The 'individual' is constructed from a male body so that his identity is always masculine. The individual is also a unitary figure; a being of the other sex can only be a modification of the individual, not a distinctive being, or his unity and masculine identity is endangered.[64]

She does not stand alone; many feminists have challenged traditional liberalism's male 'individual' as representative of all persons. Indeed if one does not find a point of identification with the characters of a theory it is difficult to take its conclusions seriously. Traditional liberalism using the image of the 'male', and in the Rawlsian case heterosexual, individual is often dismissed by those looking for, or being sensitive to, *different* images. This need for different images, or re-imagining, should be the focus of lesbian and gay activism.

Before I conclude this chapter I want briefly to address the concept of respect found in Rawls. As pointed out in the introduction to this chapter, Rawls is well aware of his 'desired solution' before he designs his methodology. 'We want to define the original position so that we get the desired solution.'[65] Rawls's project could be conceived of in this way: In order for society to be free of injustices based on individual contingencies, the methodology must deny or hide knowledge of them. With this, it is easy to see the key role of the veil of ignorance. In the hypothetical original position, parties choosing principles of justice must not be aware of their individual contingencies. 'Somehow we must nullify the affects of special contingencies which put men at odds and tempt them to exploit social and natural circumstances to their own advantage.'[66] The underpinning notion here is that basic institutions should be free from prejudices based on individual contingencies, in order to provide a basis for justice and self-respect.

As mentioned briefly above, Rawls devotes a section of *A Theory of Justice* to explaining why self-respect should be considered a primary good provided by the principles of justice. Self-respect, he defines as having two aspects: 'it includes a person's sense of his own value, his secure conviction that his conception of his good, his plan of life, is worth carrying out. And second, self-respect implies a confidence in one's ability, so far as it is within one's power, to fulfil one's intentions.'[67] Continuing, he adds that 'it is clear then why self-respect is a primary good. Without it nothing may seem worth doing, or if some things have value for us, we lack the will to strive for them.' Later in his article, 'The basic structure as subject', Rawls states that 'an important assumption of my book *A Theory of Justice* is that the basic structure of society is the primary subject of justice'.[68] This basic structure provides the basis for self-respect. 'Self-respect depends upon and is encouraged by certain public features of basic social institutions, how they work together and how people who accept these arrangements are expected to (and normally do) regard and treat one another. These features of basic institutions and . . . ways of conduct are the social basis for self-respect.'[69] From this we can reason that self-respect is regarded by Rawls, and subsequently by the members of the original position, as a primary good which should be ensured for all those within the well-ordered society.

Continuing, Rawls notes the significance of the basic structure; it 'specifies the background conditions against which the actions of individuals, groups and associations take place.'[70] It is this background or social system which often 'shapes the desires and aspirations of its members'. Rawls recognizes that difference, or pluralism, is a fact of contemporary culture, therefore the basic structure should not be biased so as to undermine one's self-respect, which includes one's 'conviction that his conceptions of his good, his plan of life, is worth carrying out'.[71] Joseph Beatty points out the importance Rawls places on this notion of self-respect and self-determination: 'It is precisely because Rawls is aware of the broader socio-cultural dimensions of self-determination that the notion of choice of principles governing our social arrangements looms so large in his thought. Only, then, if free, rational individuals choose the principles which propel their socio-cultural arrangements can they genuinely be said to determine themselves.'[72] But does the Rawlsian framework really show respect for difference, particularly those with different sexual identities?

It is here that the tension between recognizing difference and establishing social unity reaches a critical point. While Rawls wants to ensure self-respect for people with a range of conceptions of the good or life plans, the individual conceived of by Rawls does not represent that diversity. As noted, Kearns has argued that 'Rawls never comments on whether the contracting parties know their sex. He makes the usual misguided assumption that it will not matter.'[73] Now the obvious reaction to such criticism is to state explicitly that sex is hidden behind the veil, which Rawls does in 'Fairness to goodness'. However, is this enough? By answering the criticism about difference or 'contingencies' in this way, Rawls is trapped into constantly revising or 'thickening' the veil in order to take on board previously unconsidered forms of difference. In fact, it not only traps Rawls into such a cycle, but other writers have attempted similar revisions. Both Okin and Iris Marion Young argue that once sex is included behind the veil of ignorance a new interpretation of justice could radically alter the sex roles within the well-ordered society. Previously I noted that Kaplan believes that the veil could hide knowledge of sexual orientation. However, this attempt does not have the same possible impact as that of feminist writers – where sex roles might be radically altered if members of the original position did not know their 'sex' – because the heterosexual family is assumed as *the* social institution for sexual relationships. It is the place where the father, as head of the household, is concerned with the continuation of his line; where the sex-related roles are described as father, mother, son and daughter; where moral development about justice takes place. The difficulty with simply thickening the veil of ignorance is that it does not address these fundamental assumptions of western culture or of the heterosexual family. And 'fixing' the animation of the theory actually raises theoretical inconsistencies. The result is that because a diverse range of sexual identities is not realized within the original position, and subsequently the well-ordered society, the Rawlsian framework cannot provide respect for non-heterosexual identities. In other words, since the heterosexual family is a basic institution, that is part of that basic structure, those not buying into this social norm will not have access to self-respect or be beneficiaries of respect in a socio-political context.

Conclusion

I began by observing the language used by activists, in particular the claim that sexual politics, or the gay and lesbian movement, was about *A Simple Matter of Justice*. The difficulty with employing such phrases is that they can be misinterpreted. My point here is that claims for justice cannot be references to a heterosexual justice which denies, or demonizes, non-heterosexual identities. Indeed, that may very well be the 'justice' we are recipients, or victims, of now. For example, Section 28 of the Local Government Act (1988) states that local governments cannot promote homosexuality or recognize 'pretended' family relationships between partners of the same sex (for text see p. 129). Although the reasons for this legislation echo the beliefs of moral conservatism rather than the tolerance associated with liberalism, the fact that this Act was passed, that it received substantial Parliamentary and public support, does reflect a kind of justice that could be associated with the Rawlsian framework. A Rawlsian liberal could argue that, because homosexuality is no longer a crime, the state is showing tolerance for this 'life plan', or even 'lifestyle'. Furthermore, given the centrality of the nuclear family in British society, the Act simply reflects the beliefs of those who, quite rationally, believe that the state should not be seen to 'promote' any concept of the good, particularly one which could undermine the social 'consensus' about the family. While there may be objectionable premises within this reasoning, for instance that offences like 'gross indecency' actually do continue to criminalize homosexuality, the similarity between Rawlsian justice and the kind of heterosexist justice playout in current American and British social policy is striking. So it is necessary for activists who employ the familiar language of western political discourse to be careful to articulate its meaning. The 'justice' demanded by activists surely goes beyond the heterosexist justice that can be found in the Rawlsian framework.

Fox-Genovese suggests that 'the central problem in the feminist critique of individualism lies in the difficulty of re-imagining the collectivity – society as a whole – in such a way as to take account of women's legitimate needs. There can be no doubt that many, if not most, of our laws and institutions, including our vision of justice, have been constructed on the basis of men's experience.'[74] In the same light, I would add that those laws and institutions, that vision of justice, have been constructed on the basis of heterosexual experience. A justice that assumes 'the heterosexual family' cannot be justice which reflects the experience of diverse sexual identities. And the 're-imagining' referred to by Fox-Genovese must reconsider, or perhaps more radically challenge, this basic assumption of the nuclear family. Lord Devlin argued almost forty years ago that the recommendations of the Wolfenden Report decriminalizing homosexuality would lead to the breakdown of the family, and result in the decline of society.[75] Similarly, the New Right, in the form of the Conservative Campaign for Family Values in Britain, believes that by recognizing gay and lesbian families, even by prohibiting discrimination on the basis of sexual orientation, the social stability of the (heterosexual) family will be threatened. If this heterosexual family is at the root of contemporary 'justice', and it is at least the basic institution of Rawlsian justice, then re-imagining justice must begin with the deconstruction of this assumed family. I am not referring here to a radical utopian theory of society that emerges from an 'essential' gay and lesbian perspective. Instead I would argue that this radical re-imagining challenges those fundamental assumptions within liberal theory that result in our continued marginalization. And, in doing so, we can offer a new image, a new understanding, of what it means to show equal concern and respect.

Deconstruction of this assumed heterosexual family has become the task of lesbian and gay activists. For example, Stonewall has targeted this assumption in a number of its campaigns, particularly in fostering and adoption. An attempt by the child welfare authority to include in its adoption guidelines the phrase that 'gay rights have no place in questions about fostering and adoption' was thwarted by Stonewall activists. Additionally in its recent survey concerning discrimination in the workplace, Stonewall noted several areas where gay and lesbian employees were not given 'equal pay for equal work' because their partners did not receive the same benefits as the spouses of heterosexual employees. But perhaps the most inspiring protest against heterosexism recently was taken by a gay employee of the British Broadcasting Company who filed a formal complaint after being denied 'honeymoon' leave following a commitment ceremony; a company 'perk' readily given to heterosexual 'newly wed' employees. His complaint initially led to a change in policy to be more inclusive of gay and lesbian couples. However, following accusations that the publicly funded BBC was supporting this immoral lifestyle, the policy of linking bonuses to the marriage ceremony came under review. This kind of individual and collective challenge to the assumed heterosexual family must continue if lesbians and gay men, and their families, are to be acknowledged by the legislative system, if they are to be included in a 'just' society.

Notes

1   MacIntyre's communitarian critique of Rawls's theory of justice is not the specific framework for the examination here, nevertheless, the title of that work does depict the need to question any essential notion of justice: *Whose Justice? Which Rationality?* (London: Duckworth, 1988).

2   J. Rawls, *A Theory of Justice* (Oxford: Oxford University Press, 1972), pp. 195–257, 440–6.

3   A few examples of what I refer to here as 'family politics' are the Back to Basics campaign emphasizing conservative morality, recent efforts to blame single mothers for the rise in crime and juvenile delinquency, the Child Support Act requiring fathers to pay child support regardless of the mother's wishes, and of course Section 28 of the Local Government Act (1988) which labelled gay and lesbian families as 'pretended families'.

4   For example, Rawls now includes 'sex' as a contingency hidden behind the veil of ignorance and in his most recent work has avoided gendered language. 'Fairness to Goodness', *Philosophical Review*, 84 (1975), p. 537.

5   For a convincing analysis of Rawls's new political liberalism see C. Mouffe, *The Return of the Political* (London: Verso, 1993).

6   P. Pettit, *Judging Justice* (London: Routledge & Kegan Paul, 1980), p. 151.

7   *Justice*, p. 141.

8   *Justice*, p. 61.

9   *Justice*, p. 136.

10 *Justice*, p. 12.

11 S. Mulhall and A. Swift, *Liberals & Communitarians* (Oxford: Blackwell, 1992), p. 3.

12   *Justice* p. 302.
13   Mulhall and Swift, *Liberals & Communitarians*, p. 8.
14   *Justice*, p. 122.
15   *Justice*, p. 92.
16   *Justice*, p. 440.
17   R. Dworkin notes that 'the critics conclude that the fundamental assumptions of Rawls' theory must, therefore, be the assumptions of classical liberalism, however they define these, and that the original position, which appears to animate the theory, must somehow be an embodiment of these assumptions' ('The original position', in N. Daniels, ed., *Reading Rawls* (Oxford: Basil Blackwell, 1975), p. 52). For an example of these assumptions, particularly the concept of the person as 'chooser', see A. MacIntyre in *Whose Justice? Which Rationality*, M. Sandel, *Liberalism and the Limits of Justice* (Cambridge: Cambridge University Press, 1982), and C. Pateman, *The Sexual Contract* (Oxford: Polity Press, 1988).
18   'Kantian constructivism in moral theory', *Journal of Philosophy*, 77, 9 (1980), p. 518.
19   This clarification was to dispel criticisms that his theory of justice was a universalist, ahistorical notion of justice. It was not his intention, he has argued in 'Kantian constructivism', to provide a comprehensive notion of justice but instead to highlight the intuitions about justice latent in the American democratic culture.
20   *Justice*, p. 122.
21   *Justice*, p. 137.
22   Pateman, *The Sexual Contract*, p. 168. For Pateman's discussion of the history of the marriage contract see pp. 154–88.
23   A. Brittan and M. Maynard, *Sexism, Racism, and Oppression* (Oxford: Blackwell, 1984), pp. 143–52.
24   *Justice*, p. 7.
25   *Justice*, p. 525.
26   *Justice*, pp. 490–6.
27   *Justice*, pp. 490–1. Rawls notes three psychological laws: 'First law: given that family institutions are just, and that the parents love the child and manifestly express their love by caring for his good, then the child, recognizing their evident love of him, comes to love them. Second law: given that a person's capacity for fellow feeling has been realized by acquiring attachments in accordance with the first law, and given that a social arrangement is just and publicly known by all to be just, then this person develops ties of friendly feeling and trust towards others in the association as they with evident intention comply with their duties and obligations, and live up to the ideals of their station. Third law: given that a person's capacity for fellow feeling has been realized by his forming attachments in accordance

with the first two laws, and given that a society's institutions are just and are publicly known by all to be just, then this person acquires the corresponding sense of justice as he recognizes that he and those for whom he cares are the beneficiaries of these arrangements.'

28   *Justice*, p. 490.
29   For examples see S.M. Okin, 'Justice and gender', in M. L. Shanley and C. Pateman, eds, *Feminist Interpretations and Political Theory* (Oxford: Polity Press, 1991), pp. 181–98; S. M. Okin, *Justice, Gender and the Family* (New York: Basic Books, 1989); D. Kearns, 'Theory of justice – and love; Rawls on the family', *Politics (Australasian Political Science Journal)* 18, 2 (1983); Pateman, *The Sexual Contract*, esp. pp 39–49.
30   E. Fox-Genovese, *Feminism without Illusions* (Treble Hill: University of North Carolina Press, 1991), p. 238.
31   Rawls, 'The idea of an overlapping consensus', *Oxford Journal of Legal Studies*, 7, 1 (1987), p. 47.
32   Similar questions are asked by P. Pettit in *Judging Justice*, p. 149; R. M. Hare in N. Daniels, ed., *Reading Rawls*, p. 95; Okin, 'Justice and gender', pp. 181–7.
33   *Justice*, p. 137.
34   'Fairness to goodness', p. 537 (my emphasis).
35   'Justice and gender', p. 45.
36   *Justice*, p. 7.
37   *Justice*, p. 468.
38   D. Kearns, 'Theory of justice', p. 38, quoting from Rawls, *Justice*, p. 467.
39   Pateman, *The Sexual Contract*, p. 43 (my emphasis).
40   M. Kaplan, 'Autonomy, equality, community: the question of lesbian and gay rights', *Praxis International* (1991), p. 208.
41   Kaplan, 'Autonomy, equality, community', p. 208.
42   Okin, 'Justice and gender', p. 185. Okin notes a similar argument made by J. English in 'Justice between generations', where she states: 'By making the parties in the original position heads of families rather than individuals, Rawls makes the family opaque to claims of justice' (*Philosophical Studies*, 31, 2 (1977), p. 95.
43   English, 'Justice between generations', p. 98.
44   English makes a strong argument that the savings principle does not necessitate references to a biological family: 'Justice between generations', pp. 96–103.
45   English, 'Justice between generations', p. 93.
46   Kearns, 'A theory of justice', p. 37.
47   *Justice*, pp. 4–10.
48   Rawls, 'Kantian constructivism', p. 519.
49   Mouffe, *The Return of the Political*.

50 *Justice*, p. 137.
51 *Justice*, p. 468. A discussion of this point can also be found in Kearns, 'A theory of justice', p. 40 and Okin, 'Justice and gender', p. 51.
52 *Justice*, p. 490.
53 R. P. Wolffe, *Understanding Rawls: A Reconstruction and Critique of A Theory of Justice* (Princeton: Princeton University Press, 1977), pp. 119–32, esp. 129–32.
54 *Justice*, p. 168.
55 *Justice*, pp. 169–70.
56 *Justice*, p. 172.
57 Rawls, 'The basic liberties and their priority', in S. MacMurrin, ed., *The Tanner Lectures on Human Values* (Cambridge: Cambridge University Press, 1982), p. 31.
58 Rawls, 'The idea of an overlapping consensus', p. 1.
59 *Justice*, p. 138.
60 Rawls, 'The basic liberties and their priority', p. 40.
61 Rawls, 'The basic liberties and their priority', p. 41 (my emphasis).
62 Rawls, 'The basic liberties and their priority', p. 42.
63 N. Daniels, 'Equal liberty and unequal worth of liberty', in Daniels, *Reading Rawls*, pp. 279–81.
64 Pateman, *The Sexual Contract*, p. 223.
65 *Justice*, p. 141.
66 *Justice*, p. 136.
67 *Justice*, p. 440.
68 Rawls, 'The basic structure as subject', *American Philosophical Quarterly*, 14 (1977), p. 159.
69 Rawls, 'The basic liberties and their priority', p. 33.
70 Rawls, 'The basic structure as subject', p. 159.
71 *Justice*, p. 440.
72 J. Beatty, 'The Rationality of "The original position": a defense', *Ethics* (April 1983), p. 489.
73 Kearns, 'A theory of justice', p. 37.
74 Fox-Genovese, *Feminism without Illusions*, p. 243.
75 Lord P. Devlin, *The Enforcement of Morals* (Oxford: Oxford University Press, 1968).

Chapter seven

A Jurisprudence of One's Own? Ruthann Robson's Lesbian Legal Theory[1]

Didi Herman

Introduction

PEOPLE who feel marginalized, ignored, or just plain unnoticed, often seek the transformation of this experience in the development of new ideas. Frequently, writers choose to construct 'new' theory – both to explain their own social location and to provide strategies for changing the conditions in which they find themselves. Within critical legal theory, the emergence of feminist approaches was one such example of this. And, in the last few years, legal academics have published numerous articles describing the discrimination faced by 'lesbians and gay men' which also advocate arguments and strategies for change.

Yet, despite these developments, the entry of explicitly *lesbian* texts into these debates has remained sorely lacking. By 'lesbian texts' I mean academic writing that prioritizes an analysis of lesbian experience, and insists upon distinguishing this experience from both that of heterosexual women and gay men. Feminist approaches to law have tended to focus upon an implicitly heterosexual 'woman'; most feminist legal theorists do not even begin to take lesbianism seriously. At the same time, 'gay rights' analysis usually strings together the words 'lesbians and gay men' as if there were no differences between them.[2] As a result, many lesbians working within critical legal communities have felt on the outside – our lesbian experience, knowledge and politics rendered superfluous to dominant 'critiques of law', whether mainstream or alternative. There has been some support, then, for the idea that lesbians need to develop legal theory 'by and for' ourselves. Only by writing out of our own experience, and that of other lesbians, can we develop legal analyses and strategies responsive to our needs.[3]

Perhaps the foremost advocate of lesbian legal theory is Ruthann Robson, an American who has published extensively in the area.[4] In this essay, I propose to review Robson's work and, at the same time, highlight some potential difficulties with it. I first wish to perform the task of bringing her writing (and hence the topic of lesbians and the law itself) to the attention of those unfamiliar with it. Second, I hope to engage with Robson's ideas by asking two difficult questions. Do lesbians need *lesbian* legal theory? And, can the complexities of lesbian identities sustain such a project?

Robson's lesbian legal theory

Robson's work covers a range of issues, and her research into the relation between law and lesbianism has been both original and timely. As well as providing much needed historical insight,[5] she has also examined contemporary issues in need of theorization and practical strategizing, such as violence within lesbian relationships.[6] For example, in an article on this latter topic, Robson details the problems encountered by lesbians who seek legal redress for the violence they encounter from lovers. When lesbian abuse cases are before the law, she argues, legal decision-makers are more concerned with the sexual practices of lesbians than the violence between them. In legal proceedings, the few lesbians who have raised 'battered women's syndrome' as a defense to a charge of killing their partner have tended to be laughed out of court and dealt with more harshly than their heterosexual counterparts. Furthermore, lesbians are more likely to be the subjects of *mutual* restraining orders as courts are unable to comprehend the serious-ness of the threat only one party might pose to the other.[7] Robson concludes this piece by arguing that the law must be made to recognize intra-lesbian violence as a phenomenon, and to provide the same remedies to lesbians as are provided to women abused by male partners. At the same time, lesbian relationships must be understood in their specificity, and not reduced to butch/femme hetero-analogies.

Elsewhere, Robson extends her analysis to the area of contractual relations between lesbian couples.[8] She begins by reviewing the increasing number of lesbian and gay legal guides that recommend the formation of contracts between couples. Using feminist theories of contract to show how 'mercantilistic' and patriarchal assumptions underpin the concept, Robson relies on the work of lesbian philosopher Sarah Hoagland to argue that lesbian relationships are about connection and community, not 'bargain' and individualism. Contract, then, imports the 'patriarchal state into lesbian existence'.[9] But Robson also recognizes that contract can perform a useful function for lesbians whose relationships are otherwise denied in public discourse. She therefore argues that it should be used, but used carefully and with knowledge of both its political implications and its limits as a tool for meaningful social change.[10]

Ultimately, Robson's goal is to create 'unique' theory by and for lesbians.[11] It is in an article entitled 'Lesbian jurisprudence?' and her book *Lesbian (Out)Law* that she most explicitly embarks on this project. My subsequent focus will thus be here.

Robson begins her inquiry by asking whether lesbian juris-prudence does and can exist.[12] She does not avoid the hard issues, providing the reader with an initial definition of lesbianism itself: 'a lesbian is one who subscribes to lesbianism as theory; lesbianism as consciousness. . . . Lesbian consciousness, however, needs to be claimed as both an ontological and epistemological reality.'[13] Elsewhere, she has similarly stated that a lesbian 'is a woman who primarily directs her attentions, intimate or otherwise, to other women. Lesbian*ism* is the theoretical grounding for such atten-tions.'[14] For Robson, neither gay male nor feminist approaches adequately take account of lesbian experience. 'Lesbianism as a theory has been and is being developed diversely by lesbians. It is not merely about sexual orientation; thus, it is not coextensive with homosexual theories. It is not merely about applied feminism; thus, it is not coextensive with feminist theory.'[15] The search for a specifically lesbian *jurisprudence* thus follows from this.

Robson views traditional jurisprudence as being 'for men', and feminist jurisprudence as excluding lesbians.[16] Lesbians, she contends, do not wish to be benevolently included within feminist analyses of male/female relations. 'As I conceptualize lesbian jurisprudence, it has a different focus. If lesbians are women-identified women, then measurements are not relative to men; men's measurements are in some sense irrelevant.'[17]

At the same time, Robson argues that 'lesbian jurisprudence' is neither 'a critique of feminist jurisprudence' nor 'paradigmatic'.[18] In other words, lesbian jurisprudence does not attempt to be one theory for everyone. In her view, diverse approaches are suited to different tasks and need not compete with each other for supremacy.[19] *Lesbian* legal theory is for *lesbians*; it is about 'lesbian survival'.

> If a lesbian legal theory is a theory of law that has as its purpose lesbian survival; if it is relentlessly lesbian and puts lesbians rather than law at its centre; if it distinguishes between intralesbian situations and nonlesbian situations; if it is not feminist legal theory and not queer legal theory; if it does not seek to explain the entire enterprise of law, then some of the preliminary work toward developing a lesbian legal theory has begun. Still vague is the content.[20]

In giving 'imaginative content' to lesbian jurisprudence, Robson turns to what she terms 'mythical metaphors and futuristic conceptions'.[21] She draws upon a number of symbolic images, largely represented in the work of North American writers, in order to infuse her lesbian jurisprudence with non-patriarchal ethical content. For example, goddess figures and fictional lesbian utopias, Robson argues, could provide 'role models' for lesbian jurisprudence.[22]

Robson ultimately contends, in her law journal articles, that a 'sovereign' lesbian justice system could develop alongside existing institutions, and that disputes internal to the lesbian community could possibly be resolved there. Likening lesbian communities to First Nations tribes, Robson suggests that

> While 'Lesbian Nation' lacks both the recent history of sovereignty demonstrated by treaties and explicit territories evinced by reservations, some of the same principles of inherent sovereignty might provide an appropriate model. The existence of Native sovereignty stands for the principle – if not always the reality – that there can be more than one jurisprudential system.[23]

Ruthann Robson's work is an important contribution to lesbian scholarship. Her insistence on tackling the 'hard' issues of intra-lesbian violence and the political significance of marriage is laudable, while her social and historical review of the law's treatment of lesbians is an important correction to the largely male-dominated field of gay legal studies. Robson has also made important points in noting both the pitfalls and the real benefits of working with and within law. Further, I am impressed by her commitment to searching for an ethical compatibility between legal practices and underlying political perspectives. Her quest for a lesbian jurisprudence is both bold and innovative. And yet, it is here that my primary difficulty with her work lies.

As I noted above, Robson borrows several images from lesbian literature in an esoteric attempt to suggest what elements she might wish to incorporate within a lesbian jurisprudence.[24] I do not so much wish to discuss the specifics of what a 'lesbian juris-prudence' might look like (although I will briefly return to this); rather, I wish to question the basic assumption behind Robson's project – that what lesbians need is 'lesbian law' – and, further, that such an achievement is indeed possible.

Lesbian standpointism

It is because Robson identifies lesbianism as a 'theory' that she believes it requires its own jurisprudence. It is unclear, however, how she distinguishes between 'consciousness' and 'theory'. Further, her understanding of 'lesbianism as consciousness' would seem to imply that a lesbian subjectivity is, in itself, sufficient grounding for social explanation – in other words, that 'being a lesbian' is enough to give one authoritative insight into the relation between law and lesbianism. Robson underlines this view through her explicit rejection of feminist theory's ability to respond to lesbian concerns and her implicit aligning of feminism with the concerns of heterosexual women.

It seems to me that the underlying assumptions of Robson's approach are those of 'standpoint' epistemology. Various feminist theorists writing within this framework, such as Harding and Harstock, have argued that 'women's' experience can give rise to a better or 'more real' view of gender relations than the experience of men.[25] Similarly, Robson seems to assume, without really problematizing the idea, that out of lesbian experience can emerge 'theory' that is useful and, I think by implication, 'better' for lesbians than theories emerging in different contexts.

Within feminist theory, standpoint epistemology has been the subject of sustained criticism.[26] Various writers have argued that the category 'woman' is not a homogenous one, and that 'real' women are constructed by other sets of social relations in addition to gender. Female identities are, thus, complex, contradictory, and often *un*shared across class and race barriers. One woman's 'reality' may bear little relation to that of another; hence, arguing for the privileged view of 'women' is misguided as there is no unitary, common experience shared by all. As many of these writers have contended, within feminist theory 'women's experience' has often, indeed usually, implicitly meant the experience of white, middle-class, heterosexual women.[27]

Paradoxically, it is Robson's recognition of this last element that leads to her adoption of a similarly problematic 'lesbian standpoint'. At one point, for example, Robson refers to her 'mythical metaphors' as 'our collective past'.[28] While this may simply be a rhetorical turn of phrase, its use highlights the problem to which I refer. The myth of a shared 'collective past' seems a dubious foundation in which to root a contemporary lesbian vision.[29]

Lesbians do not only hold multiple social identities; our communities are also traversed by diverse and often conflicting ideological commitments. Lesbians explain their sexuality in different ways, express primary allegiances which are often not to our 'lesbian sisters', and advocate varying and sometimes antagonistic strategies for change. Robson does acknowledge most of this; however, she seems to minimize the difficulties this acknowledgement raises for her project. For example, my own political views find little expression in the largely religious symbols Robson chooses to select for her 'lesbian jurisprudence' and, as I go on to argue below, the very category of 'lesbian' is a far more contested one than Robson's approach seems to allow for. But to say that imagining is difficult is not to say that it is pointless; my argument is simply that lesbian life is perhaps more complicated than Robson's framework suggests.

Robson does note, in her article on intra-lesbian violence, that a 'lesbian justice system' may, at times, be an inappropriate adjudication forum.[30] In violent situations, Robson grants that lesbians may need the (minimal) protections offered by 'patriarchal law'[31] – such as restraining orders, police intervention, and so on. I agree with this view; yet, it seems to me that there may be many other situations that make a 'sovereign'[32] lesbian justice system unworkable. Inequalities of power are not confined to the display of violence; how would a lesbian justice system deal with employer/ employee relations, racism in lesbian homes and workplaces, and other similar issues? There is nothing inherent in lesbianism that, for example, makes one a good land-'lord'. What about conflicts between heterosexual tenants and exploitative lesbian landlords? Robson perhaps needs to give the reader a fuller picture of what she intends here.

These may be quibbling points. It is, perhaps, all too obvious that an independent lesbian justice system would have enormous problems acquiring any degree of authority. However, my principal difficulty with the idea goes deeper than this. If individual humans are made up of multiple and often contradictory identities, how and why is *one* chosen to form the basis of unity? Why would lesbians want a 'lesbian' justice system and not an 'older people's' or 'Jewish women's' justice system? As a Jewish person, I often feel I share more with other Jews (including straight women and men) than with some lesbians. As a socialist and a feminist, my greatest sense of 'shared values' is usually (not always) with those committed to a similar politics. Lesbians, on the other hand, can be politically conservative, anti-feminist, and/or into wearing Nazi regalia. Lesbian identity, in itself, does not give rise to a shared 'theory' about the world or how to change it, despite some degree of shared experience.

What's a lesbian?

In my view, Robson's work suffers by underplaying an analysis of the external factors that shape the meanings of what it is to 'be' a 'lesbian'. While Robson recognizes the power of law to repress, subvert, and render invisible lesbian experience, she nevertheless appears to assume that, underneath all of this, lies a kind of pure, *un*socially-constructed 'lesbianism'.

In her book, Robson develops the concept of 'domestication' which she uses 'to connote the overlegalization of lesbian life'.[33] More specifically, 'domestication', in Robson's framework, resembles the 'internalized gaze' familiar from Foucauldian texts.[34]

> Domestication also captures the process inherent in colonization and imperialism of the substitution of one way of thinking for another. Domestication occurs when the views of the dominant culture are so internalized that they seem like common sense. Domestication occurs when the barbed wire enclosures are believed to exist for protection rather than restriction.[35]

According to Robson, domestication is an effect of living in 'the dominant culture'.[36] As I discuss further below, Robson uses this concept to argue that lesbians have internalized legal norms, and that this has significant negative effects upon the articulation of lesbian identity. Yet, despite the acknowledgement that consciousness is shaped by external (legal) factors, Robson, at the same time, seems to suggest that lesbianism itself is somehow outside of discourse, that there is some kind of 'natural lesbian' that both produces and *needs* her own theory. Indeed, Robson's imaginings seem premised on the notion that lesbian subjectivity exists in a state of nature, unconstructed by dominant and oppressive social relations.

In an article on privacy, Robson suggests that sexuality 'may be in some ways socially constructed'.[37] What does it mean to say 'may be' or 'in some ways'? Similar ambiguities are evident elsewhere as well. On the one hand, Robson states 'we are born and socialized with reference to the dominant culture';[38] yet, several lines earlier, she argued that 'To have been domesticated, one must have once existed wild: there is the possibility of a feral future. To be feral is to have survived domestication and be transformed into an untamed state. Postdomesticated lesbian existence is one purpose of a lesbian legal theory.'[39] How can human lives ever be 'postdomesticated'? Even if lesbians were to live in Robson's ideal lesbian world surely we would continue to be 'domesticated' by new norms and values. Indeed, many lesbians today are complaining of having been oppressively disciplined by 'old-style radical feminists'. 'Domestication' is not necessarily a function of patriarchy only and it is perhaps Robson's understanding of *power relations* that needs more developing here.

Related to this is Robson's choice to pay scant attention to one of the most divisive debates in lesbian politics today – SM and lesbian pornography.[40] In my view, these issues raise important questions that strike at the heart of any attempt to construct an alternative value-system or even a lesbian 'community' itself. For example, Robson's statement that lesbian relations are not premised on the patriarchal 'contract' seems open to debate. Arguably, consensual SM lesbian relations display several features of the classical exchange or bargain model. Perhaps Robson would argue that such relations were an example of 'domestication' – the internalization of the 'father's rule'. But, if so, this seems, to me, too similar to the largely discredited 'false consciousness' approach; the complexity of the SM debates can easily, I think, withstand such a challenge. In 'Lifting belly', Robson honestly admits a certain confusion in coming to terms with the politics of SM. I only wish that she challenged some of her 'jurisprudential' ideas with these confusions, rather than leaving them to one side.

Yet another strand of lesbian life also does not sit comfortably with Robson's approach – queer politics. Again, the 'queer movement' has shown itself to be a vibrant component of 'lesbian and gay' activism and theory while challenging the very legitimacy (or 'truth') of the categories 'lesbian' and 'gay' themselves. In the opening pages of *Lesbian (Out)Law*, Robson notes the emergence of queer theory and, quite rightly I think, argues that it may, yet again, be a male-dominated movement. Yet the rest of her book goes on as if queer practice and theory did not exist. I would have liked Robson to respond to these challenges more fully. What does 'lesbian jurisprudence' mean in the face of recent shifts in lesbian and gay identities?

Law for lesbians

I want to move on shortly to consider the other half of Robson's project – jurisprudence/legal theory. Before doing so, however, I wish to note a few confusions which qualify my subsequent discussion.

In Robson's work, both 'the state', and 'the law', are collapsed into one and the same. Robson implies that the State is no more than a maker and enforcer of laws, and she seems to equate 'jurisprudence' with 'legal theory' which then is used interchangeably with 'law' and 'the state'. Furthermore, law itself is, to a large extent, reified in her work. *Lesbian (Out)Law*, for example, depicts a 'rule of law' that is coherent, omnipotent, patriarchal, and almost solely destructive in its 'domesticating' force. Despite these difficulties, the basic premise of Robson's work, that lesbians can and should create our own approach to law, can still be usefully discussed.

The development of a 'feminist jurisprudence' has occupied a branch of feminist legal theory for some time. Proponents advocate the need to develop specifically feminist approaches to legal reasoning, judicial interpretation and legal strategy. This work has gone forward largely upon the basis that existing jurisprudence is male, patriarchal, phallocentric and so on. Carol Smart has offered a forceful critique of this project, arguing that 'the quest for a feminist jurisprudence' ultimately reinforces the power of law as discourse.[41]

Instead, she suggests 'de-centring' law, by which she means challenging its authority as truth, and its legitimacy to solve 'social problems'.[42]

Ruthann Robson's work, at first glance, lies clearly within the first approach. As feminist jurisprudence is 'preoccupied with men',[43] lesbian jurisprudence will be 'by and for lesbians'. The idea itself, the need to develop more jurisprudence, is not at all questioned. However, Robson somewhat paradoxically suggests that lesbian jurisprudence might wish to de-emphasize legal solutions to lesbian issues. Citing Carol Smart's work (which she refers to as 'jurisprudential'), Robson argues that law should be 'decentred'.[44] Yet she takes this to mean that law should be made 'not very important'.[45]

I am unsure as to Robson's position here as I understood her to be arguing that some form of law should continue to be very important in lesbians' lives. Yet, if law is to be 'de-centred', why construct an alternative and yet continue to call it 'jurisprudence'? Perhaps my confusion is rooted in Robson's ambiguous use of the terms 'jurisprudence' and 'legal theory', or perhaps Robson is using 'jurisprudence' when she is really talking about an 'ethics' or 'value-system'. Or, perhaps, I have simply failed to understand the distinctions she is making.

I must also confess to a certain confusion in coming to terms with some of Robson's arguments on legal strategizing. In *Lesbian (Out)Law*, Robson makes two claims: first, that, in lesbian and gay rights cases, 'there is nothing wrong' with making immutability arguments to courts;[46] and, second, that such arguments are both 'domesticating' and 'humiliating'.[47] I do not see how these positions can be reconciled, and Robson makes little attempt to do so. She may be usefully touching on the difficult relationship between legal pragmatism and radical politics; however, the issue seems rather undeveloped and the reader is left hanging as a result.

Concluding remarks

Much work in lesbian legal theory rejects the applicability of both gay male and heterosexual feminist analyses to lesbian experience. Writers seek, in different ways, to create a uniquely lesbian approach to the study of law. Much of this is understandable, as neither gay men nor straight feminists sufficiently consider lesbianism in their theory and practice. However, the attempt to correct this, I would argue, has succeeded in obscuring understandings of the relationship between gender and sexuality so importantly made by many of the feminists relied on by lesbian legal theorists – such as Rich, Mackinnon, Frye, and so on.[48]

The work of Adrienne Rich for example, cited by Robson, is firmly rooted in *feminist* theory.[49] Indeed, Rich's conception of the 'lesbian continuum' has been criticized for being insufficiently attentive to the specificity of lesbian experience, and overly concerned with finding common ground for the category 'woman', rather than 'lesbian'.[50] Furthermore, Rich herself has written of her contradictory experiences as a *Jewish* lesbian[51] – one of the many 'complications' of 'lesbian consciousness' both acknowledged and yet marginalized in Robson's work.[52]

Furthermore, Catharine Mackinnon's early work on sexuality was instrumental in exploring the links between heterosexuality and male dominance.[53] Robson's explicit statement that 'male measurements are in some senses irrelevant' to lesbians, and, hence, feminist theorizing on gender unhelpful indicates, in my view, an unfortunate direction for lesbian legal work. Indeed, even within Robson's own framework this seems counter-intuitive. If, as Robson argues (although I disagree), the 'rule of law' equals the 'rule of men', and the 'rule of law' functions to control lesbians, in what 'senses' are men 'irrelevant' to our understanding of law?

The dominant ideology of liberalism in western capitalist societies has been increasingly receptive to lesbian and gay rights claims. However, this has come at a cost. An analysis of the relationship between gender and sexuality, the ways in which enforced heterosexual practice is related to the subordination of women, has rarely entered into public debate. On the contrary, lesbians and gay men have been constructed as a minority in need of protection, an 'other', different and 'less than' the norm, but none the less to be protected within existing liberal human rights frameworks.[54]

Rather than challenging this view, the development of 'lesbian jurisprudence' may reinforce it: first by insisting upon the separation of lesbianism and feminism, second, by positing a homogenous 'lesbian consciousness/theory', and, third, by rejecting an ethic of solidarity with gay men and heterosexual women. Indeed, Robson explicitly refers to lesbianism as a 'minority movement' existing between the 'minority' movements of gay men and women, 'co-extensive' with neither.[55] Rather than exploring the historically contingent production of gender categories and accompanying regulation of sexuality, one would think that Robson views lesbians as a kind of 'third sex', somehow creating our own world outside of dominant social relations.[56]

'Lesbian jurisprudence' thus seems to avoid many of the important questions and, to a large extent, does so on the basis of an underlying faith in the inherent 'difference' of lesbianism. For Robson, out of this different experience emerges theory. However, in my view, personal experience is not in itself sufficient grounding for a theory. The consciousnesses lesbianism gives rise to results from the interaction of a diverse range of discourses and ideologies and, as such, seems a dubious foundation in itself for the construction of systems and theories (leaving aside the question of whether we need more systems and theories in the first place).

In my view, the failure of much work in lesbian (and gay) legal theorizing is a failure to problematize *heterosexuality*. Robson and others focus on the concept of 'lesbian' (as if it was far more than a concept), and fail to acknowledge both how 'the lesbian' is discursively and politically produced and to what (or who) the 'lesbian' is 'other'.[57] By rejecting the analytic relevancy of the category 'men', as well as the utility of feminist theory, these writers are, somewhat ironically, unable to consider lesbians *as women*. In the end, analyses such as Robson's may have the same effects as that of liberal approaches – institutionalized heterosexuality, and its relation to the construction of gender, are left unquestioned.[58]

For Robson, 'lesbian survival is the starting point for developing lesbian legal theory'.[59] For other 'legal lesbians', the deconstruction of gender, the eradication of racism or the transformation of the economy may be as important a starting point. And, despite our starting points, we have little way of knowing what effects, if any, our theorizing will have in the long term. Nevertheless, Robson's work helps to open up an important discussion.

Theorizing the specific relationship between lesbians and law is not an easy task; many of us have tended to avoid the issue for various reasons. And yet lesbian approaches to law put lesbians at the centre of analysis – if we do not do this, no one else is likely to. Robson's work in particular, with its emphasis on strategies for change and the creation of a specifically 'lesbian justice', is of immense value in setting a framework for debate. Her work raises, at least implicitly, many important questions; however, it is not clear how much the wiser we are about them at the end of the day.

Notes

1 This chapter is a review essay reprinted (in slightly different form) from: *Canadian Journal of Women and the Law*, 7: 2 (1994) (Special issue on lesbianism, feminism and law). I thank Susan Boyd, Davina Cooper, Brettel Dawson, and Diana Majury for their comments on that essay, and thank the *Canadian Journal of Women and the Law* for permission to reprint it here.

2 I include my own work to a large extent in this criticism.

3 Examples of lesbian approaches to law can be found in P. A. Cain, 'Feminist jurisprudence: grounding the theories', *Berkeley Women's Law Journal*, 4 (1988–9), p. 191; M. Eaton, 'Theorizing sexual orientation' (LL.M. thesis, Queen's University, Kingston, Ontario, 1991); E. Faulkner, 'Lesbian abuse: the social and legal realities', *Queen's Law Journal*, 16 (1991), p. 261; L. M. Leonard, 'A missing voice in feminist legal theory: the heterosexual presumption', *Women's Rights Law Reporter*, 12 (1990), p. 39.

4 See Ruthann Robson, *Lesbian (Out)Law: Survival Under the Rule of Law* (Ithaca: Firebrand, 1992); 'Lesbian jurisprudence', *Law and Inequality*, 8 (1990), p. 443; 'Lifting belly: privacy, sexuality and lesbianism', *Women's Rights Law Reporter*, 12 (1990), p. 177; 'Lov(h)ers: lesbians as intimate partners and lesbian legal theory', *Temple Law Review*, 63 (1990), p. 511; 'Lesbianism in Anglo-European legal history', *Wisconsin Women's Law Review*, 5 (1990), p. 1; 'Lavender bruises: intra-lesbian violence, law and lesbian legal theory', *Golden Gate Law Review*, 20 (1990), p. 567.

5 See Robson, 'Legal history'.

6 See Robson, 'Lavender bruises'.

7 Robson, 'Lavender bruises', pp. 574–7.

8 See Robson, 'Lov(h)ers'.

9 Robson, 'Lov(h)ers', p. 527.

10   Robson goes on in this piece to consider the argument for lesbian and gay marriage, as well as statutory initiatives that have provided lesbians and gay men with 'domestic partnership' benefits. She considers both feminist and lesbian responses, the former arguing that marriage is an institution oppressive to women and therefore should be abolished not further indulged in, the latter suggesting that legal provision simply means increased state intervention (negative) in the lives of lesbians. Robson finds this latter argument compelling. She also finds that these heterosexual institutions 'colonize' lesbian relationships and force lesbians to model their lives on heterosexual relations. She therefore concludes that the feminist response of marriage abolition may well be more appropriate; see 'Lov(h)ers', pp. 536–541. See also *(Out)Law*, p. 127.

11   Robson, 'Lesbian jurisprudence', pp. 446–7.

12   Robson, 'Lesbian jurisprudence', p. 443.

13   Robson, 'Lesbian jurisprudence', p. 446.

14   Robson, 'Lavender bruises', p. 569.

15   Robson, 'Lesbian jurisprudence', p. 446.

16   Robson, 'Lesbian jurisprudence', pp. 446–9.

17   Robson, 'Lesbian jurisprudence', p. 449.

18   Robson, 'Lesbian jurisprudence', p. 448.

19   Robson, 'Lesbian jurisprudence', p. 451.

20   *Out(Law)*, p. 23.

21   Robson, 'Lesbian jurisprudence', p. 453.

22   Robson, 'Lesbian jurisprudence', pp. 454–61.

23   Robson, 'Lesbian jurisprudence', p. 465.

24   Robson, 'Lesbian jurisprudence', pp. 454–9.

25   S. Harding, *Whose Science? Whose Knowledge?: Thinking From Women's Lives* (Milton Keynes: Open University Press, 1991); N. Harstock, 'The feminist standpoint: developing the ground for a specifically feminist historical materialism', in S. Harding and B. M. Hintikka, eds, *Discovering Reality: Feminist Perspectives on Epistemology, Metaphysics, Methodology, and Philosophy of Science* (Dordrecht: Reidel, 1983).

26   See, for example, J. Flax, 'Postmodernism and gender relations in feminist theory', *Signs*, 12 (1987), p. 621; M. Kline, 'Women's oppression and racism: a critique of the feminist standpoint', in J. Vorst et al., eds, *Race, Class, Gender: Bonds and Barriers* (Toronto: Between the Lines, 1989).

27   See, for example, T. Williams, 'Re-forming "Women's truth": a critique of the report of the Royal Commission on the Status of Women in Canada', *Ottawa Law Review*, 22 (1990), p. 725.

28   Robson, 'Lesbian jurisprudence', p. 443.

29   See also S. Phelan's discussion in *Identity Politics: Lesbian Feminism and the Limits of Community* (Philadelphia: Temple University Press, 1989).

30   Robson, 'Lavender bruises'.

31   Robson equates the 'rule of law' with the 'rule of men'; see *(Out)Law*, p. 11. Forceful critiques of this idea have been made by several writers and, as my focus is with other concerns, I do not intend to duplicate their work here. See, for example, S. Gavigan, 'Women and abortion in Canada: what's law got to do with it?', in H. J. Maroney and M. Luxton, eds, *Feminism and Political Economy* (Toronto: Methuen, 1987); C. Smart, *The Ties That Bind: Law, Marriage and the Reproduction of Patriarchal Relations* (London: Routledge & Kegan Paul, 1984).

32   Robson's use of the concept of 'sovereignty' and her explicit analogy between First Nations and 'Lesbian Nation' is also highly problematic. The analogy seems an inappropriate one for several reasons. Aside from the problems inherent in discovering just what it is that lesbians share in terms of history and culture, there is clearly no land base nor any obvious history of *dispossession*. The concept of a sovereign 'aboriginal justice system' is rooted in the 'real' history and experience of First Nations and the processes of western colonization. It is unclear, to me anyway, how this concept applies to a mythical 'Lesbian Nation' and a modern social identity, and Robson does not develop her analogy further.

33   *(Out)Law*, p. 18.

34   See, for example, S. Bartky, 'Foucault, femininity and the modernization of patriarchal power', in I. Diamond and L. Quinby, eds, *Feminism and Foucault* (Chicago: Northeastern University Press, 1988), p. 61.

35   *(Out)Law*, p. 18.

36   *(Out)Law*, p. 19.

37   Robson, 'Lifting belly', p. 49.

38   *(Out)Law*, p. 19.

39   *(Out)Law*, p. 18.

40   In 'Lifting belly', Robson touches on these issues in the context of the liberal/communitarian debate; however, she does not discuss them further, particularly in terms of how they impact upon her 'lesbian jurisprudential' project.

41   C. Smart, *Feminism and the Power of Law* (London: Routledge, 1989).

42   Smart, *Feminism and the Power of Law*.

43   *(Out)Law*, pp. 21–2.

44   Robson, 'Lesbian jurisprudence', pp. 461–2.

45   Robson, 'Lesbian jurisprudence', pp. 461–2.

46   Immutability arguments contend that humans are 'born into' their
      sexuality, and that it cannot be changed.
47   *(Out)Law*, p. 83.
48   See M. Frye, *The Politics of Reality* (Trumansberg: Crossing Press,
      1983); Catharine Mackinnon, 'Feminism, Marxism, method and
      the state: towards a feminist jurisprudence', *Signs*, 8 (1983), p. 635;
      A. Rich, *Compulsory Heterosexuality and Lesbian Existence* (Lon-
      don: Onlywomen, 1981).
49   See Rich, *Compulsory Heterosexuality*.
50   See, for example, A. Ferguson, J. N. Zita and K. P. Addelson, 'On
      'Compulsory Heterosexuality and Lesbian Existence': defining the
      issues', in N. O. Keohane, B. C. Gelpi and M. Z. Rosaldo, eds,
      Feminist Theory: A Critique of Ideology (Brighton: Harvester,
      1982).
51   See A. Rich, 'Split at the root', in E. T. Beck, ed., *Nice Jewish Girls:
      A Lesbian Anthology* (Trumansberg: Crossing Press, 1982).
52   See also B. Cossman and M. Kline, ' "And if not now, when?":
      feminism and anti-semitism beyond Clara Brett Martin', *Canadian
      Journal of Women and the Law*, 5 (1992), p. 298.
53   See Mackinnon, 'Feminism, Marxism, method'.
54   These ideas are developed in my *Rights of Passage: Struggles For
      Lesbian and Gay Legal Equality* (Toronto: University of Toronto
      Press, 1994).
55   Robson, 'Lifting belly', p. 9.
56   See also, for a development of this approach, M. Wittig, *The
      Straight Mind and Other Essays* (Boston: Beacon, 1992). Robson's
      work seems informed by Wittig's writing, as well as that of several
      other 'lesbian separatists', for example S. L. Hoagland and J.
      Penelope, ed., *For Lesbians Only: A Separatist Anthology* (London:
      Onlywomen, 1988).
57   Thanks to Davina Cooper for articulating this last point.
58   In *Rights of Passage*, I discuss how the Christian Right *does* make
      these connections.
59   *(Out)Law*, p. 19.

Chapter eight

The Space of Justice: Lesbians and Democratic Politics

Shane Phelan

THE task of formulating visions of pro-lesbian society and of its means of achievement has been blocked by the seemingly incompatible aims and perspectives of the two major discourses on lesbianism – lesbian-feminism in its 1970s version, and post-structuralist challenges to lesbian identity – that currently vie for the allegiance of white lesbians. While lesbian-feminism provided a powerful analysis and vision of the future, it was too often perceived and used as a 'party line' from which individuals strayed only at the cost of a loss of membership in lesbian community. Deconstructive treatments of lesbian identity, on the other hand, have been leery of positive formulations. Thinkers such as Judith Butler and Diana Fuss have called for coalition politics, but even the most subtle and original thinkers have failed to flesh out what this coalition politics would mean.

Fuss has noted that politics is the 'aporia in much of our current political theorizing', and she has linked the popularity of the 'politics of x' formula, such as 'the politics of theory' or 'textual politics' to this ambiguity; 'politics' denotes struggle and activism, but so vaguely that it can satisfy a myriad of needs by its invocation.[1] As someone trained as a political theorist, I would go even further.

The term 'politics of *x*' has thrown political theory into a crisis, as we try to untangle the implications of new social movements that do not operate simply on a logic of self-interest or a fight for material goods. Nevertheless, the idea of a wider 'politics' has also served those who resist large-scale institutional politics but who want to discuss power. While this has been an important avenue for new insights, the 'politics of *x*' idea has sometimes led to the refusal to discuss institutional or movement politics, leaving us with the narrowest, popularly US American, vision of 'politics' as the terrain of power, but never of common vision or justice or citizenship. Simply pointing out and condemning oppression or inequality becomes political activism. That one can do this as an isolated academic as well as in concert with others means that this version of politics serves to neglect the force of atomization and isolation in modern US society.

Judith Butler's call in *Gender Trouble* for coalition politics is hedged by cautions that such politics must not 'assume in advance what the content of "women" will be', nor can we predict the 'form of coalition, of an emerging and unpredictable assemblage of positions'.[2] Butler represents perhaps the extreme edge of postmodernist purity in her fastidious refusal to draw lines or name names. While I agree that political agents are constructed through their political action, I do not see the need to abandon completely all categories of identity; recognition of their provisional nature, a key element in both postmodernist and post-structuralist theories, does not necessitate their abandonment but mandates caution and humility in their use. The realities of institutions and US politics require basing common action on the provisional stability of categories of identity, even as we challenge them.

Several issues need to be addressed in order to begin to theorize postmodern lesbian politics. First, we need to discuss our goals critically. We remain within dichotomies of 'assimilation versus transformation', 'reform versus revolution' and the like that can limit our conceptions. It is time for lesbians to confront whether we can and should envision a future, and what that future should be. Following that, we need to examine how to achieve these goals. Specifically, we need to think in more detail about what postmodern alliances and coalitions might look like, and how to maintain them. That will be my purpose in this chapter.

Outlaws and solid citizens

The most striking thing about lesbians is not our difference(s) from heterosexuals or something distinctive about lesbian cultures and communities, but our diversity. There are politically conservative lesbians, anti-feminist lesbians, separatist lesbians (both feminist and non-feminist), Marxist lesbians, radical feminist lesbians, liberal lesbians, apolitical lesbians and others. This was a problem for traditional identity politics because such politics posited an intimate connection between one's sexual orientation or preference[3] and one's political sympathies or 'true interest'. This was best conceived along the lines of standpoint theory. A given lesbian might not currently adopt a 'lesbian' standpoint, seeing things from a 'pro-lesbian' perspective, but the elements of that standpoint are implicit in her life, waiting for consciousness to catch up.

While many lesbians may believe that the daily texture of lesbians' lives in the United States provides the ground for a common vision, the experience of the last twenty-five years indicates that a broad or comprehensive vision is not in fact shared at this point. While white lesbians are notably and consistently more liberal in their voting patterns than are either heterosexual women or men of any sort, they are far from monolithic.[4] Even among feminist lesbians, there are many disputed questions. For example, should lesbians fight for the right to be legally married, with the tax preferences, property understandings and other legal powers that currently accompany marriage in the United States, or should we critique an institution that is inherently patriarchal? Would legal marriage present an improvement for lesbians, or would it signal their assimilation into a heterosexual paradigm? Similar questions arise concerning issues of lesbian motherhood. An even more painful case is that of lesbians in the military. Should we fight for the chance to serve in the military, or be grateful and even proud that we are unwelcome in a destructive and oppressive institution?

Ruthann Robson refers to the two sides in these arguments as 'separatist' and 'assimilationist'. The debate in general, as she puts it, is this:

> Are we sexual outlaws, and perhaps political outlaws as well, who recognize that the law is founded upon the rule of men, upon enforced heterosexuality, and upon violence? Or are we legitimate citizens who have been wrongly excluded from legal recognitions and protections because our private lives are slightly different from some mythical norm?[5]

This is a hard choice. It is also a mistaken one. First, the exclusive choice between being law-abiding and a criminal, between being within (and under, subject to) the law and being an 'outlaw', is not logically given but is socially structured by the current regime of power/knowledge. In this regime, breaking the law 'makes' one into something – a 'criminal', an 'outlaw' – that then, for many, becomes a badge of pride. For others, the encompassing nature of the identity becomes a deterrence to certain sorts of activity – while I wouldn't mind stealing, someone might say, I wouldn't want to 'be a thief'. We already see this in the many men and women who have regular sexual relations with other men and women but refuse the identities of 'gay' or 'lesbian' because they are stigmatized, 'outlaw' identities. Full assimilationists are those who accept the label but refuse stigmatization; they say, 'yes, I am a lesbian, but I'm not a criminal, I'm a law-abiding citizen'.

This dynamic relies on the assumption that 'everyone else' is in fact law-abiding and 'normal'. This is the hegemonic assumption, the assumption that exempts (white, middle-class) heterosexuals from problematization. This assumption assigns difference to the underprivileged side of what is actually a relation of difference. Instead of noting that both sides of an opposition are 'different' from one another, the hegemony works to render the relation invisible and to describe difference as something inherent in one side.

In this (hetero)sexist social ontology, there are two distinct groups: 'Americans' and 'gays and lesbians'. This ontology is shared among Americans of all political stripes. As an example of this, remember Ross Perot's statement in the 1992 presidential campaign that he would not have 'homosexuals and adulterers' in his cabinet because they would be 'controversial' with 'the American people'. It had evidently not occurred to him that heterosexual adultery is the norm among men, or that homosexuals are also among the American people. The strength of feminist and separatist positions has been the ability to question this hegemonic presentation, to challenge the 'normality' of the normal citizen/subject. These analyses have exposed the assumed maleness and heterosexuality of the citizen. Problems re-emerge when we accept the idea that lesbians should not or cannot become citizens. This serves to erase all the (usually, but not always, closeted) lesbians who live 'normal' or 'exemplary' lives.

The second mistake implicit in Robson's choice is the belief that 'legitimate citizens' must not be subject to (or aware of?) social dominance. The guiding assumption of assimilationists is that heterosexuals are not daily coerced and shaped into fit subjects. Because of this assumption, they can see inclusion as enough; if only 'outsiders' are coerced and subjected, then becoming 'insiders' will suffice for freedom. But they are mistaken in this belief. 'Other' populations can be effectively targeted only when the 'core' population is safely domesticated.

In fact, Robson argues, assimilationists and separatists are not necessarily opposed: they are instead the result of legal thought that occludes recognition of differences as other than dichotomous and enduring. 'The law's pronouncement that a person is either law-abiding or a criminal may be a dichotomy that serves the law's interests and does not serve lesbian interests.'[6] This statement presumes in its very structure that lesbians are distinct from 'the society' in which they live. Such positions work for those who experience themselves as true insiders mistakenly disenfranchised, but it does nothing to problematize the inside. And without that problematization of the 'inside', the hegemonic core of social structures, we will continually return to unsatisfying choices.

One of the most important insights of post-structuralist work has been the strong deconstruction of 'society'. While Marx recognized that societies were processes as well as structures, and that the conceptual separation of the individual from society was deceptive, liberal political theory has never made this leap. In Marxism, the problem of society has been that of viewing these systems of processes as a monolithic structure, ruled by 'the economic system'. This formulation still assumes a unity of system in the economy, instead of a plurality of processes and events and positions. Increasingly, these systems, and thus 'society', are giving way to 'the social' as the theoretical space of negotiation of identity and difference. And, with this, the liberal vision of the individual and his or her society finally breaks down. We are 'society', we shifting, incomplete beings. We do indeed live within social formations that possess a certain fixity and provide channels and links and productions of power and meaning, but these formations are not, strictly speaking, separable from us. We are, we speak, those formations.

This insight has been paralleled by the work of writers, especially historians, who have insisted that it is a mistake to distinguish 'gays and lesbians' from 'society'. The question is not, do we 'fit into' 'society' or not, but where and how do we find our places in social formations, and where do we want to be? This is not a question that admits of a singular answer such as 'lesbians fit x' or 'lesbians are y' or even 'lesbians should do/be z'. We cannot simply piggyback on to metanarratives about the progress of freedom and enlightenment that were partial and flawed in their formation without being carried along by their defective assumptions. Lesbian political theory requires a different, more fluid consciousness to move through these dilemmas, exploring our interests and how to further them.

Lesbian interests

Having said the above, the question of what is to be done is not obvious. Robson urges us to centre 'lesbian interests', but it is far from clear what that means. For her it seems to mean the ability of lesbians to choose their circumstances of life. While seemingly concrete in its refusal to privilege certain choices or desires as more lesbian than others, this formulation quickly reveals its inadequacy. In her desire to 'put lesbians at the center', to construct a 'lesbian legal theory', Robson argues that such a theory must centre lesbians over any others. She gives as an example child custody rules. She reminds us that not all lesbians will want custody of their children. If the lesbian does not want custody, then 'lesbian legal theory' should support that decision regardless of the desires of the child or other parents. If a lesbian desires custody, such a theory must 'privilege her position to choose custody'.[7] For Robson, then, lesbian legal theory privileges any given lesbian over any non-lesbian. While this may sound inviting to those of us (most of us!) who have been told in our lives to subordinate our desires and needs to those of others, her alternative is not an improvement.

First, this rule presumes that we know who lesbians are, a presumption belied both by current theory and by political controversies. Are women who occasionally sleep with men lesbians? How often is too often? If a lesbian were to become heterosexual, would Robson recommend that her ex-lover be given child custody? The instability of lesbian identity makes this a much more difficult proposition than it first appears.

Second, Robson's recommendation rests on an impoverished conception of the social landscape. Lesbians become the privileged, whose desires are the command of the law. If I can certify my lesbianism, and I want to abandon my child, then Robson's theory would support that decision. While Robson is not intending a world of all-powerful lesbian choosers, her theory does not sufficiently address the networks of relationships that lesbians emerge and live within.

Robson's proposal in fact has no content beyond particular interests at particular times. It is not a standard that is appropriate to any real humans in relation, much less a full public life. It speaks to lesbians only as consumers of rights, characterized as social or political goods, in a world in which choice is the greatest good. Such a conception of a desired end is unable to articulate with other struggles in any terms other than 'choice', which will not do. At some point, individuals' choices will conflict. If we do not have some sense of how to adjudicate these conflicts beyond the a priori privilege given to one party over another, we will be unable to sustain a common world. Such a 'lesbian legal theory' as Robson proposes guarantees that lesbians will be isolated from others, both in the rigidity of our identities and in the privilege accorded us as consumers of the law.

Behind Robson's recommendation lies a conception of interest that is inimical to building democratic alliances. This conception assumes, first, that identities are easily demarcated, and, second, that interests are attached to identities. A more specific analysis calls into question the simple delineation of identities. If our basis for theory is social practice and structure, rather that rational/ logical categorization, it becomes immediately clear that no one fits within any identity; we are all 'citizens of the lack', as it were, all members of an incompletely filled or stable social space. This lack is what makes politics possible. We all live within multiple valid descriptions of ourselves, choosing from situation to situation which description – which identity – shall come to the fore.

The full political implications of this point emerge only when we look at the second assumption. Its message is that each 'identity' carries with it an identifiable 'interest'. Both interest-group liberalism and Marxism share these two assumptions. They differ in their conception of the goal of politics. For interest-group liberalism the goal of politics is the adjudication through compromise of competing interests. For Marxism, 'politics' is largely secondary, if not distracting; while democratic socialists allow for parliamentary, democratic forms of change, Leninists and many others disavow it. For both orthodox Marxists and liberals, politics is the work of advancing essentially pre- or non-political 'interests'.

Theodore Lowi describes the 'model' of 'interest-group liberalism' as follows:

> (1) Organized interests are homogeneous and easy to define. Any duly elected representative of any interest is taken as an accurate representation of each and every member. (2) Organized interests emerge in every sector of our lives and adequately represent most of those sectors, so that one organized group can be found effectively answering and checking some other organized group as it seeks to prosecute its claims against society. And (3) the role of government is one of insuring access to the most effectively organized, and

of ratifying the agreements and adjustments worked out among the competing leaders.[8]

Thus, interest-group liberalism gives us a description of politics in which the business at hand is that of effecting compromises between, for example, farmers and consumers. To the extent that it surfaces at all, justice is a matter of optimal distribution of goods. Within this model, the purpose of coalitions is to lend support to another's interest in return for their support of yours.

This model works best for interests that are economically defined. The rise of interest-thinking coincides with and reinforces the modern capitalist state, with its primary business of negotiating between competing classes. James Madison underscores this point when he argues that

> the most common and durable source of factions has been the verious [*sic*] and unequal distribution of property. Those who hold and those who are without property have never formed distinct interests in society. . . . The regulation of these various and interfering interests forms the principal task of modern legislation.[9]

The modern category of the 'consumer' has problematized even these identities and interests. A farmer is also a consumer. If interests are attached to identities, as interest-group pluralism suggests, then most of us will find ourselves in positions of internal conflict. When we move beyond economic 'identities' to socio-cultural ones, things get even more confusing.

Interest talk may make sense if all the members of a group share every 'relevant' social characteristic or submerge difference/s among themselves, but this is increasingly unlikely. In modern societies, where overlapping social movements and identities are increasingly present, interest becomes as unstable as identity. It is at least in part this instability of overlapping identities that has given rise to the attacks on identity politics from across the political spectrum. Seeing interest as concretely and stably linked to particular social identities, such commentators have seen in the proliferation of identities a fragmentation of the social world and the impossibility of common action.

Interest and the space of citizenship

If this is all there is to interest, then the post-structuralist critique of identity and the identity politics of new social movements seem to demolish the possibility of interests as the basis of politics. A shift of focus, however, enables us to see those proliferations as the opening to a new citizenship and public life, to a new interest. Without the presumption of stability and predictability of political subjects, the position of 'interest' is opened for re-examination.

Anna Jonasdottir has begun this re-examination. She reminds us that in its root the term 'interest' does not simply refer to the content of people's desires, needs or demands but to the space of politics itself. Its initial construction, from the Latin *inter* (among, between) and *esse* (to be) suggests that interest is also the claim to *publicity* of certain needs or wants; that is, the concept of interest marks those things that are of legitimate public concern, in contrast to those desires and needs that are 'private', my business alone. Thus, claiming something as an interest is both a substantive claim to a good and a formal claim to participation and public recognition.[10] Jonasdottir argues that the formal claim of interest is more 'relevant' than the substantive (content) claim. The formal claim of an interest – say as a lesbian – does not yet commit a lesbian to a particular desire or need. It establishes lesbianism as a relevant political identity from which to proceed. This provides the space to articulate a 'lesbian good' without predetermining what that good will be. It also opens the category of 'lesbian' to negotiation – claiming lesbianism as a relevant identity cannot simply avoid 'common-sense' notions of what such an identity is, but it need not rest with those notions either. The identity itself becomes open to politics.

This is not something unique to lesbianism, or to sexual categories in general. Consider the case of the farmer again. Claiming an interest as a farmer will lead many to conclusions about what that person – the 'farmer' – will want and support. It is not given from the establishment of that interest/identity exactly who will be defined as a farmer, however, nor is it given that the farmer *must* support subsidies or oppose decent wages for migrant workers, or in general think only in the narrowest terms of individual economic advantage. The farmer is also (at least potentially) a *citizen* – not as 'another' identity but as the basis of the claim of interest. The farmer may conclude that the nation cannot afford subsidies, or that decent wages and living conditions are a requirement of justice, without abandoning her 'interest' as a farmer.[11]

In the same way, claiming an interest as a lesbian in this view is a civic act. It embeds the lesbian in her political community/ies, implicating her in responsibilities as well as rights and demands. This point is often missed, both in mainstream political science treatments of interest and in discussions of lesbian politics. Claims made on a community are inseparable from recognition of that community. When lesbians seek to further our interests in US society and law, we are at the same time involving ourselves in the larger affairs of that society. And this is crucial if we are actually to have the option to live 'lesbian-centred' lives. As Michael Walzer points out, within a political community 'the denial of membership is always the first of a long train of abuses',[12] and thus anyone interested in eliminating persecution and oppression must work immediately for recognition of the membership of lesbian citizens. If lesbians are to claim any interest at all, the first interest must be recognition as members of the political community.

If we transform our identity politics from one that assumes an automatic correlation between identity and politics to one based on the spaces of citizenship itself we might, ironically, find more to share both with other lesbians and with non-lesbians. Such a politics will recognize relevant differences in the specific situations of our lives while leaving the political meaning of those differences open to negotiation. This need not be contradictory, though it may sound paradoxical.

We can get at this problem by considering what counts as a lesbian issue. While some might argue that lesbian issues should be only those that concern all lesbians or affect lesbians *qua* lesbians, these break down quickly. Lesbian motherhood is not an issue for all lesbians; many cannot have children, and others are not interested. While lesbophobic violence against lesbians may seem a clear 'lesbian issue', it is irrelevant in less violent cultures or locations in the USA. More basically, any such requirements for lesbian issues presume a stability to lesbian identities that is belied by recent theory as well as by many women's experiences. What is it to act 'as a lesbian' or to have a concern 'in one's capacity as a lesbian'? These essentialisms and reifications have broken down, and with them falls the question of a lesbian issue construed as unique.

Consider the goal of decent housing for all. Surely this is a concern for many lesbians, and is therefore a 'lesbian' issue. It is also a concern for many others, however, and for them it is not configured as 'lesbian'. The difficulty that poor lesbians face in finding decent housing, especially if they try to live openly as lesbians, is both lesbian-specific and reaches beyond lesbians to the problem of decent housing at affordable cost for all. Here we can distinguish the difficulties faced by women marked as lesbians, stigmatized in a heterosexist identitarian society, without attributing to them any essential features or qualities. We can thus establish a limited political agenda without essentializing or over-generalizing.

We could approach this problem in several ways, but I will focus on two here. In this first, lesbian-centred approach, lesbians will work with other lesbians to provide decent housing for lesbians. This will include construction, oversight of landlords and municipalities for maintenance and rate fairness, and work to ensure that lesbians are not discriminated against on the basis of their sexuality. Non-lesbians will be ignored, except in so far as they either control housing or provide something desirable. This is the separatist solution, and there is much to be said for it as an occasional tactic. Working with and for other lesbians is exhilarating and empowering. It cannot be our only position, however.

In the second approach, lesbians will work with everyone concerned to provide decent housing to all citizens. This will look like the first approach in many ways, but there are some differences. First, the non-lesbians will need continual prodding to understand and work for issues of discrimination. Second, the lesbians will have to commit to working with and for people who are not lesbians. In so doing, they will not be able to focus simply on lesbians but will have to work for and talk about the problems faced by the other members and potential members of the group. This does not make decent housing no longer a lesbian issue, however; it simply removes the divide between lesbians and everyone else. Making decent housing a lesbian issue does not remove it from the public agenda, or from that of any other identifiable group. The lesbian concerns may be specific to lesbians, but that does not mean that those concerns cannot be shared and fought for by all.

In this second scenario, the specific problems and desires of lesbians are relevant to the whole group, in so far as it wants to include lesbians as equal members of a democratic organization or polity. This does not mean that the specifics of being lesbian are irrelevant to membership in the group; each is welcome and has an equal voice without regard to sexuality. The equality of membership in the group requires the group to treat all equally, and that means paying attention to the situations and needs of all. It does not mean allowing only those in a given situation to participate in the decision-making, however; that violates equality.[13]

Such a politics allows both for the presentation of something like a 'lesbian interest' and for the recognition that many (if not most) lesbians will not share that interest. In the model described by Lowi, an interest was a 'real' interest only if it was shared by every member of the homogeneously defined group. Thus, if not all lesbians agree on a policy, it must not be a 'lesbian interest'. If we abandon presumptions of homogeneity and identity, however, if we get specific, we can say that non-discrimination in housing is a lesbian interest without thereby excluding others from having that interest or requiring all lesbians to share it.

This has an effect that some may find ironic, even unpalatable. Removing interest from identity forces us to end theoretical imperialism. It makes it impossible for anyone to tell another what their interest 'really is'. It seems, therefore, to pull the ground out from beneath any shared goals. We are forced to recognize non-feminist lesbians as lesbians none the less; outlaws and solid citizens must both relinquish any claims to the truth of lesbianism. It seems to leave us very little to share politically.

This is only half the story, however. If we are left with a less monolithic agenda, the focus on the public nature of lesbian interest invites us into a realm of shared concern extending beyond lesbian communities or groups. Feminist lesbians may be forced to admit that not all lesbians share any version of a feminist agenda, but on the other hand we have a greater opening to work with feminist non-lesbians as well as others with whom we may share a great deal. If the above treatment of interest lowers the substantive goals of lesbians, it raises the procedural/formal ones to the demand for lesbians to be acknowledged as equal citizens, with equal participation and recognition not 'in spite' of our lesbianism but simply regardless of it. Our membership is not qualified or limited by our lesbianism, and thus our concerns, even our concerns as lesbians, are legitimately public ones. Our presence as lesbians is prior to any particular claims we make, and does not require proof of our sameness with heterosexuals. Membership acknowledges our existence, our presence, and it is this which interest-group politics collapses. This is not a liberal abstraction but is the claim of specificity.

Thus, rethinking interest moves us from identity, with the assumptions of homogeneity and privatized consumerist concerns and agendas, to politics as an activity that is valuable in itself. This is not the subsumption or transcendence of 'identity politics' but is a recognition of the fullness of politics that cannot be encapsulated by identity. It is the return of identity politics to its formulation by the Combahee River Collective. They did not say that their only political concerns would arise from their self-interest, which was to be unquestioned and unchallenged; they said that they would no longer accept other people's agendas and models for their politics, that they would look to the specific circumstances of their own lives for their politics. The later problems of identity politics have had less to do with this vision than with its corruption into interest-group liberalism. The homogeneity that appears from the hegemonic position contributed to a vision of masses of women, of lesbians, etc., with a unified interest. The recognition of the diversity of these groups gave rise to descriptions of 'difference', but for many white (and probably many non-white) people this looked like the end of politics, the death of a shared world, because 'differences' appeared as discrete entities, singular atoms on a blank social space, rather than as nodes in social constellations. The refiguration of differences as specificities enables us to return to the strength of identity politics without leading to abandonment of those who do not obviously share our identities.

Getting specific introduces the possibility of thinking of lesbians not as outlaws, nor as solid citizens, but as lesbian citizens.

These lesbian citizens are 'queer' in existing models of citizenship, but this queerness is not itself a virtue. The revolutionary potential of lesbian citizens lies not in separatism, nor in continual elaboration of the law to privilege 'lesbian interests', but in forcing the political and legal systems to stretch and re-form to do justice to our lives. This does indeed demand that legislators and judges should consider lesbian interests, but not as a list of criteria based upon known characteristics. It requires them to learn to frame legislation and adjudication from the standpoint of a lesbian in a given case, to ask what she needs as well as what non-lesbians need. This is not a privileging of lesbians above others; it is, in Martha Minow's words, a process of 'making all the difference', moving to see fields of relations rather than discrete persons labelled as 'different'. If 'difference' is no longer the property of one group but is the mark of a relation of (dis)similarity, then it is not enough to fit 'others' into a previously existing frame, nor can we simply modify the frame to include them. There is no avoiding it; what is needed is not a specific result but a process – that of public deliberation among a group all of whose members are treated as equal participants. While certain particulars, such as civil rights, are a prerequisite for this process, they are not the sum of the goal. The other part is our need for choice if we are truly to reshape institutions and practices. Lesbian citizens will thus be part of the larger project of radical democracy that aims at making all the difference, at eliminating the privilege of hegemonic identity.

Opening the space of citizenship addresses the needs of US lesbians for recognition and self-determination, inclusion and safety. It also provides a means of linking lesbian struggles to other demands for these same things without assuming a priority among those struggles or suggesting a hierarchy of oppressions. It enables lesbians and others to be specific about their own circumstances, to make connections between their circumstances and those of others, and to formulate a common agenda for concrete changes that does not play into zero-sum games of power. The demand for the broadest range of civil rights is not a 'special interest' demand, sought at the expense of the civic good or that of another 'group', but is a demand for equal membership in a democratic polity.

In the end, our goal should be to articulate a lesbian agenda as part of a radical democratic creed shared across sexualities and other differences. In such a future, the interest of lesbians in their lives will be shared by others, and will not need to include reminders that we should not be raped, killed, intimidated, 'cured', or ignored. We will thus be ready for specific citizenships, entry into the multiplicity of public realms that await postmodern citizens.

Interest in the house of difference

Postmodern politics means that as we enter public discourse we do so not as 'lesbians' with a fixed, eternal identity but as lesbians, people occupying provisional subject positions in heterosexual society. As such, we might acknowledge that speaking and being heard does not mean simply drawing on our 'experience' in an unmediated way but means articulating our lives, interpreting and reinterpreting them in ways that link us to others. Coalitions of the future will require us to maintain the subject position of lesbians and our belief in our voices with the growing awareness that our own subjectivity is part of the terrain of possible change. To paraphrase Foucault, 'we must insist on *becoming* [lesbian], rather than persist in defining ourselves as such'.[14] Thus, the problem for coalition politics is not, what do we share? but rather, what *might* we share as we develop our identities through the process of coalition? Coalition cannot be simply the strategic alignment of diverse groups over a single issue, nor can coalition mean finding the real unity behind our apparently diverse struggles. Our politics must be informed by affinity rather than identity, not simply because we are not all alike, but because we each embody multiple, often conflicting, identities and locations.[15]

As an example of the construction of interest and identity as monolithic and natural, we can use the best-selling book on gay politics, *After The Ball* by M. Kirk and H. Madsen. This book was written by two white male Harvard graduates currently working at high-prestige, high-income jobs. They propose a 'marketing strategy' to overcome homophobia in the United States. This strategy includes advertisements that plant the idea that gays and lesbians are 'just like everyone else'. This is not just strategic; they believe that when treated with respect and friendship, we're as happy and psychologically well adjusted as they are. . . . we look, feel, and act just as they do; we're hard-working, conscientious Americans with love lives exactly like their own.[16]

This is a fascinating statement because it follows a hundred pages of castigation of gay male sexual, political and personal behavior. They continually contrast the pathology of gay life to the nice, normal picture of heterosexuality. They manage this dissonance by separating the 'bad gays' from the 'good gays', and claiming that 'good gays' are just like heterosexuals. They experience themselves as just like their straight friends, and so they are embarrassed by the 'deviants'.

There is much to take exception with in this book, and much to think about. Here I want just to focus on a few points. The first is the ease with which these two men subsume lesbians into the category of 'gay'. While they occasionally acknowledge that lesbians do not have the proclivity for casual sex that gay men do (a difference of which they approve) and that we face some problems as women, the bulk of the book makes no distinction between gays and lesbians. This erasure is not simply sexist but reflects their ability to see gayness as a singular distinguishing mark in their lives. Were it not for their 'sexual orientation', they would be just like their (white?) heterosexual friends and fellow Harvard graduates. Thus, 'gayness' appears to them as a discrete identifier, and the 'gay' they are discussing emerges as male, white, and middle- (or upper-) class. They seek simply to end anti-gay prejudice, to get equal rights, such as formal marriages, with heterosexuals, and eventually just to fit in with every other white affluent citizen. They have no problem with any other structures of oppression in the United States, and so they urge 'gays' not to distract themselves from the fight for gays by 'admixture with superfluous issues that might further upset or distract ordinary Americans'.[17] Included in the list of 'superfluous' or 'utterly extraneous' causes are racial justice, feminism, environmentalism and others. They disdain the Rainbow Coalition concept as a distraction.

What is a lesbian to make of this? What is a Chicana (or Black, or Asian, or Native American, or poor, or . . .) lesbian to think? Kirk and Madsen are telling us that feminism is not simply not equivalent to lesbianism but that it is dangerous to the cause of gay rights. Discussions of race or class are divisive.

Imagine the response of Audre Lorde. In *Zami: A New Spelling of My Name*, Lorde describes her position as a black lesbian among lesbians in Greenwich Village:

> Being women together was not enough. We were different. Being gay-girls together was not enough. We were different. Being Black together was not enough. We were different. Being Black dykes together was not enough. We were different. . . . It was a while before we came to realize that our place was the very house of difference rather than any one particular difference.[18]

Within the 'house of difference', Kirk and Madsen's advice is inadequate. And not only black lesbians dwell in that house; the differences were differences among that progressively more narrowly defined group, inseparable from the individuality of its members. From this perspective, Kirk and Madsen's prescription is both politically naive and theoretically incoherent. It rests on the idea of gayness as a discrete identifier, in the manner of interest-group liberalism, and reduces that identifier to the person we have sex with. It then colonizes all those who have or would like to have sex with members of the same sex (or gender? who knows?) as 'gays', and tells them to address that in isolation from the rest of their lives. While their aim is to 'keep the message focused', the effect is to isolate white bourgeois gay men from any potential allies other than straight white men. Just as the phrase 'as a woman' has been discredited in feminism as 'the Trojan horse of feminist ethnocentrism',[19] we cannot rest with 'as a gay' or 'as a lesbian'; we need to produce public spaces to discuss what these words can mean, and we need to recognize their insufficiency in fully capturing the nature of our sexualities.

Kirk and Madsen provide us with an example of how a simple white identity politics can fail. While they have many good suggestions for media campaigns to convince heterosexuals that we are 'just like them', they fail to provide any reason for the majority of lesbians or queers of colour to work with them. Theirs is a pre-

Stonewall, pre-feminism politics. (While they state that 'the gay revolution has failed', that post-Stonewall gay activism has been a 'disaster', the legal and social advances of lesbians and gays in the last two decades, when compared to the advances under homophile organizations, are staggering.)

The narrowness of this prescription rests on the assumption of a clear 'gay interest'. As we saw earlier, this is a problematic notion. Even if we could/can posit a discrete 'gay interest', however, there is no entailment between such an interest and the rejection of coalition. One could assume such an interest and still advocate coalition politics. The motivation of such a politics would be a *quid pro quo* understanding: I'll protect you from 'them' if you protect me. I'll support racial or class advances if you support feminism and lesbian rights.

Such models collapse in the face of specific thinking about our lives. 'Overlapping' memberships in various social groups may cause some people to hold 'several agendas' for change at once: black lesbians will have an agenda on the basis of race, on gender and on sexuality. Thus, for some, coalitions will be the only way to do justice to their concerns, their 'interests'. Even so, this argument still remains in the realm of essentialist thinking about social groups. It conceives of 'blacks' and 'lesbians' as distinct and uniform groups; the anomaly of black lesbians is precisely that they do not fit the modal version of either group. From an essentialist viewpoint, black lesbians become 'bridges' between groups that are otherwise coherent. But none of these groupings is 'natural'. *All* are the result of particular historical discourses about race, sexuality and gender. The coherence and unity of the category of 'blacks', 'whites', 'lesbians', etc. is a politico-historical event, not a logical or a natural one.[20]

Once we see that social formations and memberships are not naturally given but are invented or imagined, we can see the bonds between us. These bonds are not ones of mutual affection or concern, not ones of nature, but are the creation of systems of discursive power and hegemony that tell us who we are and where we fit. This recognition in turn forces us to rethink common action. If common action is not (or not exclusively) jostling for one's (pre-given) interest against others who would deny it, what is it? If our group memberships are provisional because those groups are provisional entities/concepts, how do we know whom to work with?

Lesbians are involved in every struggle, sometimes on sides I would not choose. Before it is an identity, lesbianism is a characteristic of many diverse people. Audre Lorde's powerful response to the charge that black lesbians don't support black struggle is a documentation of her presence, a black lesbian presence, in all the struggles that supposedly did not involve gender or sexuality.[21] Lesbians active in anti-racist work, in work against violence against women or US imperialism or AIDS or for economic justice all remain lesbian, as do their Republican, anti-feminist or militarist sisters. All belie a monolithic politics of unitary subjectivity.

This is not news. However, this has historically been explained or prescribed on the basis of oppressions that share the same root and the same oppressor – white straight bourgeois men versus everybody else – and the false consciousness of those who deny the connections. Such arguments do not prepare us for the inevitable contradictions and conflicts among and within members of these various groups. A postmodernist coalitional politics can avoid this by recognizing that such conflicts are inevitable, and that they are not cause for despair but grounds for continued rearticulation, new narratives of political structures and change. As a more modest politics, it reduces the invitation to despair and burnout that is such a chronic problem among the various opponents of the established order(s). In this project, the issue is not whom to work with, but how to work with them; or, it is both. If politics is a matter of negotiating identities and discourses as much as distribution of goods, then we cannot assume that the people we work with will remain the same (or that we will, for that matter).

Queer – a coalitional identity?

'Queer' politics is often presented as this articulation of a coalitional identity. Queer theory and politics are products of the 1980s. This new identity has several sources. First, the feminist sex wars exhausted many lesbians and led them to seek new locations. Second, the rising demands of bisexuals for inclusion in gay and lesbian communities and organization invited a new analysis of the relationship between politics and sexuality. Third, AIDS introduced new patterns of relationship between men and women and provided a basis for alliances. Lastly, the ascendancy of post-structuralism provided a theoretical terrain for a queer theory in the academy.

'Queers' are on a path that follows a geography different from that of their older sisters and brothers, a postmodern landscape sculpted by performance art, by punk rock and its descendants, by Madonna and multiculturalism, and by Reagan and Bush. They are unafraid of camp, or of 'roles' that do not mean what they once did but do not mean nothing. They have a sense of humour unlike that of 'gays' or 'lesbians'. The 1993 march on Washington exemplified much of this: while the march was organized along 'political' lines, issues of justice and equity and inclusion and dignity, the marchers were much more diverse and hilarious. 'We're here, we're gay, can Bill come out and play?' in front of the White House has a very different tone from 'hey hey ho ho, homophobia's got to go!' I was raised on anger, but I was delighted in DC.

In a deeper way, though, 'queers' have not transcended any of the challenges facing 'lesbians' or 'gays'. There are several angles to this. First, who is queer? To many, 'queer' is simply a new label for 'lesbian and gay'. Among these, there is a split between those who use 'queer' simply as a convenient shorthand and those who imply a nationalist politics. This usage provides nothing new, and recycles much that is better left to decompose. While the shorthand usage is a matter of claiming a word that was used against us, the nationalist version of 'queer' reanimates the problems of lesbian-feminism in its cultural feminist versions without resolving them.

For others, 'queer' moves beyond lesbian and gay to encompass bisexuals, transgendered people and other sexual minorities. This is the move towards a coalitional identity. In Lisa Duggan's words, this usage points toward a 'new community' that is 'unified only by a shared dissent from the dominant organization of sex and gender'.[22] 'Dissent from the dominant organization of sex and gender' does not, however, guarantee a feminist position. The feminist heritage of 'lesbians' is crucial if queers are to avoid the pitfalls of 'gay' (white male) politics. While Queer Nation chapters worked consciously at being non-sexist and non-racist, and casti-gated gay men for their sexism and racism, the later battles within chapters demonstrated that nirvana had not yet been achieved. Both of these understandings of queer, the reclaiming and the new identity, must be challenged to deny the colonization of lesbians and people of colour that occurs within 'gay' politics.

The tension between nationalism and its most thoroughgoing deconstruction lies latent in queerdom. Self-described queers include both those who see queerness as a cross-cultural and transhistorical 'natural' identity or position and those who use 'queer' to designate a liminal position within the contingent sexual and gender frontiers of contemporary capitalist societies. This is not a tension to be resolved by the ceding of one side to the other, but will remain a field of contestation. As a lesbian feminist, however, I can only fear nationalism. To the extent that queers become nationalist, they will ignore or lose patience with those among them who do not fit their idea of the nation. This is a dynamic in nationalism that will always limit its political usefulness. The only fruitful nationalism I can imagine is one that has at its heart the idea of the non-nation – the nation of non-identity, formed not by any shared attribute but by a conscious weaving of threads between tattered fabrics. And at that point, why speak of nations? Alliances are not nations, and need not be to be strong.

'Queer' does not guarantee a better alliance politics than 'gay' or 'lesbian' have. The larger notion of queer as encompassing all sexual minorities does not eliminate this problem but reinscribes it in the heart of the queer. The alliance with (heterosexual or homosexual) sadomasochists, fetishists, paedophiles that is adumbrated in this usage does not enlarge the field of alliance but simply shifts the privilege within it. When others are faced with a 'nation' that they do not recognize or desire, they will simply leave. The hegemonic inscription of the queer as *the* sexual minority will then amount to an exclusionary colonization of those who refuse their membership.

Character and coalition

In the end, identity politics will always be either a nationalist politics or a 'practical politics of the open end'.[23] Doing a better identity politics does not mean finding the best definition of our identities so as to eliminate problems of membership and goals, but means continual shuffling between the need for categories and the recognition of their incompleteness. No one can decide simply on the basis of identity whom any of us will be able to work with. Simple versions of identity politics, in which we know who and what we are and we know who is trustworthy by their identifications, are inadequate. The contingency and multiplicity of agendas furthers this indeterminacy. Because lesbians, gays and queers differ in their political aims among themselves as well as between groups, the ground for common action cannot be 'identity' but must be shared commitments; it must be sympathy and affinity rather than identity. Sympathy and affinity need not be total to be real and effective. They do, however, require a self-consciousness about one's actions and allegiances that is often taken for granted in identity politics. If identity is not sufficient ground for trust or political agreement, but abstract principles in the manner of liberalism or Marxism are not sufficient either, then we need to get specific with one another about what we value and what we will do to realize that value.

Getting specific helps us to locate our allies at particular points, for particular struggles. Paying close attention to our particular social locations forces us to go beyond simple counting of the categories. Our lives are not lived as chunks; though we can certainly specify in some instances structural conditions and inequalities that produce results, most of the time we just live, all of our elements jostling together. Our identities are those jostling, shifting elements. Our politics must account for this. I may work with gay men because we are both targets of a larger hegemonic culture. When I do such work, I do not experience the euphoria of community. I am often downright disgusted. But it is necessary none the less, because heterosexism and homophobia structure my existence inescapably. When I work with women of other racial and/or ethnic identifications, I do so not out of 'compassion' for them, or to assuage my guilt. I do so, first, because injustice is not segmentable, but spreads beyond garden borders laid down for it. I do so, second, because I value them in spite of my own racism. That value is not just the value of 'difference', of the sort we see on the 'ethnic days' in cities where groups gather to dance and sing and eat before returning to being Anglo. I value specific different voices because they intersect with my own, creating a world. There are other different voices that I do not value and do my best not to support: Nazis, white supremacists, anti-feminists, corporate polluters, George Bush. And then there are people in neither camp; those who, while racist, sexist, classist and heterosexist, share concerns and try to overcome their pasts and presents.

The question to ask about 'allies', then, is not whether they are 'really' allies, but how to *make* them allies. While identity politics has sometimes been framed in terms of identity checklists, a larger identity politics will ask instead about character. Identity politics, as a politics arising out of the specific oppressions faced by each of us, need not result in a politics shared only by others sharing those oppressions – indeed, it cannot, for that sharing will always be tested as we dwell together in the house of difference. The questions to ask are not whether we share a given position but whether we share a commitment to improve it, and whether we can commit to the pain of embarrassment and confrontation as we disagree. The question is whether we can *decide* to be allies, and whether we have the strength to follow through on that decision. Unless these questions are addressed, no theory and no identity will provide a satisfactory result. With positive answers to them, we can forge the bonds between specificities to create a fence against oppression. These very local links can provide the ground for the strength needed to address structures that currently appear insurmountable.

Thus the relevance to political theory both of ethics and of a certain aesthetics of the self. Ethics, treated not as simple rules but as guidelines and starting points for choice; aesthetics, as the conscious fashioning of character, are both required if politics is to change and produce anything of lasting value. If we fail to address questions of character, formulations of identity will never produce the changes we (any of us) seek. Character is not a static entity on which we will be judged by some distant god; character is one name for the processes of the self. Those processes are inseparable from the processes of politics.

Where will this character come from? From practice. Those looking for allies must begin by volunteering to become allies, developing a commitment to challenge racism in ourselves and in others. Middle-class and wealthy lesbians must work to learn about and support working-class and poor people's lives and struggles. Men who want to be allies must become knowledgeable and become willing to learn from women. And so on. Alliances are not a matter of harmony and univocity. The distinction between coalitions and alliances is not one of unity or even of durability (though I think there are reasons to expect greater durability from alliances), but of motive and purpose. Recognition of the publicity, the *inter esse* of interest, requires the self-extension of each person toward others. Awareness of others must be developed into a conscious commitment to the welfare of others, both in general and in each person we meet. This is a form of love. It is a love of the world, a love of democracy, a love of others as inseparably part of the community within which we live. As an activity based on conscious commitment rather than a feeling, love can be chosen and it can be refused. Love need not entail self-negation, but it does require a willingness to 'go under', to suffer the small deaths of humility and pain and self-examination. And as love does not come from others unless we offer it to them, so allies will develop as we ally ourselves with their causes. As we increasingly open our eyes and hearts, we will help to create those fences against oppression by modelling decency. Without decency and love, bringing us towards one another without requiring sameness, our rhetorical and heartfelt commitments to others will continually be frustrated in the face of ineluctable difference.

The awareness of the incompleteness of any narrative, of the instability of identities and of social topologies, is the opening from modern arrogance to such humility. It requires not only theoretical elegance and acuity but profound interrogation and transformation of oneself. While not all arrogance is modern, surely the postmodern, 'that which denies itself the solace of good forms, the consensus of a taste which would make it possible to share collectively the nostalgia for the unattainable',[24] that which confronts the abyss of responsibility and choice, is inconsistent with arrogance of any sort. Faced with such an awareness, bereft of models that justify theoretical imperialism on anyone's part, we are forced to confront one another, to build a ground together instead of finding one and inviting others to sit on it.

Lesbians should not refuse the specificity and reality of lesbian experiences, nor should we reify it into an identity and history so stable that no one can speak to it besides other lesbians who agree on that particular description of their existence. Our politics, disappointingly enough, must consist of continued patient and impatient struggle with ourselves and those 'within' and 'without' our 'communities' who seek to fix us (in the many senses of that term). We can afford neither simple assimilation into main-stream politics nor total withdrawal in search of the authentic community – or we must demand the right to both. We have to stand where we are, acknowledging the contradictions and forging the links between ourselves and other marginal citizens of the world, resisting the temptation to cloak crucial differences with the cloak of universality while also refusing to reify those differences into hardened identities that cannot be crossed. The promise of getting specific is the promise of theorizing, which is to say discussing and working on, the possibility of such a politics.[25]

Notes

1   D. Fuss, *Essentially Speaking* (New York: Routledge, 1989), p. 105.
2   J. Butler, *Gender Trouble* (New York and London: Routledge, 1990), p. 14.
3   There is great ideological disparity even in these words. The 'preference' language is liberal, implying a purely private desire along the lines of consumer choice. The 'orientation' discourse is denser, aiming at suggesting an enduring, probably innate, facet of one's identity. I include both terms here because both have been used in lesbian identity politics, and the oscillation from one to the other continues even as 'orientation' becomes the legal term of choice.
4   Murray Edelman, 'The gay vote, 1990: preliminary findings', paper presented at the annual meeting of the American Political Science Association, August–September 1991, Washington DC. Approval ratings of George Bush were most striking: when asked 'Do you approve or disapprove of the way George Bush is handling his job as President?' the total ratio was 57 approve/40 disapprove, the ratio for 'all women' was 54/42, that for gay men was 45/53, and that for lesbians was 32/60. When asked whether they considered them-selves liberal, moderate, or conservative, the total was 18/46/33; gay men 47/41/9; lesbians 48/38/13. I have no explanation for the

greater percentage of lesbian conservatives than gay male conservatives, but I do not know the margin of error in this sample; it does not strike me as a terribly great difference.

5   R. Robson, *Lesbian (Out)law: Survival Under the Rule of Law* (Ithaca: Firebrand, 1992), p. 19. It should be noted that the division between outlaw and solid citizen here is not the same as the 'good girl/bad girl' split of the 1980s 'sex wars'. There, many of those who would be 'outlaws' in Robson's sense because of their feminist agenda were 'good girls' in their critique and/or rejection of sadomasochism and butch/fem. For a review of those debates, see S. Phelan, *Identity Politics: Lesbian Feminism and the Limits of Community* (Philadelphia: Temple University Press, 1989), ch. 6; C. Vance, 'Pleasure and danger: toward a politics of sexuality', in *Pleasure and Danger: Exploring Female Sexuality*, C. Vance, ed. (Boston: Routledge and Kegan Paul, 1984), pp. 1–28.

6   Robson, *Lesbian Outlaw*, p. 19.

7   Ibid., p. 134.

8   T. Lowi, *The End of Liberalism: The Second Republic of the United States*, 2nd ed. (New York: Norton, 1979), p. 51.

9   J. Madison, 'No. 10', in *The Federalist Papers*, intro. Clinton Rossiter (New York: New American Library, 1961), p. 79.

10 A. G. Jonasdottir, 'On the concept of interest, women's interests, and the limitations of interest theory', in B. Jones and A. G. Jonasdottir, eds, *The Political Interests of Gender* (London and Newbury Park: Sage, 1988), pp. 39–40. See also I. Balbus, 'The concept of interest in pluralist and Marxian analysis', *Politics and Society*, 1/2 (1971), pp. 151–77; W. E. Connolly, 'On "interests" in politics', *Politics and Society*, 2/4 (1972), pp. 459–77; I. Diamond and N. Hartsock, 'Beyond interests in politics: a comment on Virginia Sapiro's "When are interests interesting? The problem of political representation of women" ', *American Political Science Review*, 75/3 (1983), pp. 717–23.

11 If the farmer does make such a decision, all hell will break loose in American politics. For the behaviour of the national and state governments makes clear that they expect their citizens to construe their interest as narrowly as possible.

12 M. Walzer, *Spheres of Justice: A Defense of Pluralism and Equality* (New York: Basic Books, 1983), p. 62.

13 Anne Phillips makes this point about women's participation when she says that 'the crucial requirement is for women's political presence: which is not to say that only women can speak on "women's" issues, that women must speak only as a sex'. A. Phillips, *Engendering Democracy* (University Park, PA: Pennsylvania State University Press, 1991), p. 167.

14   M. Foucault, 'Friendship as a way of life', in *Foucault Live* (New York: Semiotexte, 1989).

15   D. Haraway, 'A manifesto for cyborgs', in L. Nicholson, ed., *Feminism/Postmodernism* (New York and London: Routledge, 1990), p. 197.

16   M. Kirk and H. Madsen, *After the Ball: How America Will Conquer its Fear & Hatred of Gays in the 90's* (New York: Doubleday, 1989), p. 379.

17   Kirk and Madsen, *After the Ball*, p. 180.

18   A. Lorde, *Zami: A New Spelling of My Name (A Biomythography)* (Freedom, CA: Crossing, 1982), p. 226.

19   E. V. Spelman, *Inessential Woman: Problems of Exclusion in Feminist Thought* (Boston: Beacon, 1988), p. 13.

20   For a discussion of social formations as historically specific and 'imagined', see B. Anderson, *Imagined Communities: Reflections on the Origins and Spread of Nationalism* (London: Verso, 1983). The most impressive example of personal recognition and exploration of these bonds by a white person remains Minnie Bruce Pratt's essay 'Identity: blood skin heart', in M. B. Pratt, B. Smith and E. Bulkin, *Yours in Struggle: Three Feminist Perspectives on Anti-Semitism and Racism* (Brooklyn, NY: Long Haul Press, 1984). Rather than discuss that work here, I recommend every reader of this book to drop everything and read it!

21   A. Lorde, 'I am your sister: black women organizing across sexualities', in *A Burst of Light* (Ithaca: Firebrand, 1988).

22   L. Duggan, 'Making it perfectly queer', *Socialist Review*, 22/1 (January–March 1992), p. 20.

23   See G. C. Spivak, 'The practical politics of the open end', in *The Post-Colonial Critic: Interviews, Strategies, Dialogues* (New York and London: Routledge, 1990).

24   J. F. Lyotard, *The Postmodern Condition: A Report on Knowledge* (Manchester and Minneapolis: Manchester University Press/University of Minnesota Press, 1984), p. 81.

25   This essay is derived from two chapters in Shane Phelan's book *Getting Specific: Postmodern Lesbian Politics*, University of Minnesota Press (1994). Copyright 1994 by the Regents of the University of Minnesota. Published by the University of Minnesota Press.

Index

Also available from the Cassell Sexual Politics List:

Coming Out of the Blue: British Police Officers Talk about their Lives in 'The Job' as Lesbians, Gays and Bisexuals
Marc E. Burke

'Marc Burke's path-breaking study helps give a voice to the previously hidden pains and dilemmas of lesbian, gay and bisexual police. It will become required reading for all those who wish to understand this controversial issue of the 1990s.' Ken Plummer, University of Essex

Safety in Numbers: Safer Sex and Gay Men
Edward King

'In the proliferation of writing about AIDS, *Safety in Numbers* stands out for its careful analysis of one of the most important areas of all – the need to develop and support effective prevention programmes for those most at risk. This book will play an important part in helping to save lives and combat homophobia.' Dennis Altman, La Trobe University, Australia

Speaking of Sex: The Limits of Language
Antony Grey

'. . . beautifully written in his usual easy and felicitous style. The plea for sex respect should convince anyone; but it was his chapter on love I found especially moving.'
Francis Bennion, author of *The Sex Code: Morals for Moderns*

Broadcasting It: An Encyclopedia of Homosexuality on Film, Radio and TV 1923–1993
Keith Howes

'Its range, rigour and thoroughness are breathtaking. More impressive still, it's a great read – fun, insightful and surprising.'
Richard Dyer, University of Warwick

Male Impersonators: Men Performing Masculinity
Mark Simpson

'Discussions of masculinity have hitherto been characterized by a timid tone of pious apology – here at last is the antidote to that all-too-sombre debate. Sharp, astute and decidedly spunky, Simpson's essays are guaranteed to amuse, provoke and illuminate.' Andy Medhurst, University of Sussex

From the AIDS Awareness series:

How can you write a poem when you're dying of AIDS?
(ed.) John Harold

'This is a moving anthology. So many pieces mention people going away, leaving a room, parting, missing one another, but there's also much about renewal and reunion, in dreams or reality, and about hope and love; it's very inspiring.' Antony Sher

Positive Lives: Responses to HIV – A Photodocumentary
(eds) Stephen Mayes and Lyndall Stein (Terrence Higgins Trust)

'An exciting demonstration of how powerfully photography can communicate one of the most critical global challenges of our age.' Richard Branson

From the Women on Women series:

Daring to Dissent: Lesbian Culture from Margin to Mainstream
(ed.) Liz Gibbs

'Radical, readable and feisty, this new collection of essays from very different dykes gives us all the courage to insist on our difference and the energy to dissent.' Patricia Duncker, University of Wales, Aberystwyth

Challenging Conceptions: Planning a Family by Self-Insemination
Lisa Saffron

'This pioneering book will be invaluable for lesbians contemplating motherhood.' Angela Mason, Executive Director, Stonewall

Portraits to the Wall: Historic Lesbian Lives Unveiled
Rose Collis

'In this all-too-slender volume, Collis has captured the danger and exuberance of some dozen historic lesbian lives. The book is well researched and accessible, journalistic and witty.' Fiona Cooper, novelist